THE GERMAN RUSSIAN WAR 1941—1945

THE

GERMAN RUSSIAN WAR

1941 — 1945

BY

GÉNÉRAL A. GUILLAUME

OF THE FRENCH ARMY

WITH A PREFACE BY

GÉNÉRAL DE LATTRE DE TASSIGNY

WITH SIXTY-THREE SKETCH MAPS

LONDON : THE WAR OFFICE

1956

Author's Note

SO FAR, no comprehensive work has been published, even in the U.S.S.R., about the operations which took place between 1941 and 1945 on the Germano-Soviet front. It must be agreed that a methodical analysis and collation of the belligerents' documents will require several years. Without waiting for such a time, we wish to bring our contribution to this research and to bring within reach of French readers the sum total of the works published during and since the war by Soviet military writers and by the History Service of the Red Army.

This documentation still reveals many gaps : for instance the first phase of the war, preceding the battle of Moscow, does not appear anywhere. On the other hand, the U.S.S.R., which does not rule out the possibility of a third world war, maintains a strict silence over certain essential data concerning the last war. More particularly, there is nothing permitting identification of the Soviet units engaged in the various battles, or knowledge of their precise strength. We have therefore had to avail ourselves of various sources of information, German, French and Allied. But as regards the operations from the Battle of Moscow, 1941, until the Battle of Berlin, 1945, Soviet sources alone have been used.

The bibliography will be found at the end of this book. Imperfect as it is, our survey permits us nevertheless to determine the character and gauge the unprecedented magnitude of the struggle which steeped that immense front in blood, and the stages of which are marked by four dates : 1941, failure of the Barbarossa plan before Leningrad and Moscow ; 1942, advance to the Volga and the Caucasus, threat to the Caspian Sea and the Stalingrad disaster reversing the fortunes ; 1943, the failure of the attack on Kursk, the Red counter-offensive on Orel and Kharkov, the crossing of the Dnieper ; 1944, the year of the Allied landing in the West, in the course of ten battles the Soviet Army secures a yielding of the front, frees territory, gets rid of Finland and drives the Germans from Poland and the Balkans. Following these four stages we have in 1945 the combined effort with the Western Allies, the settling of East Prussia, the conquest of Budapest, the invasion of Austria, the forced crossing of the Oder, the bombardment of Berlin which, encircled and subjugated, capitulated and collapsed.

A. GUILLAUME.

1949.

Preface

GENERAL GUILLAUME, who, immediately after victory, was appointed Chief of our Military Mission in the U.S.S.R., has brought back from his visit to Moscow a book of capital interest in which he displays his remarkable capacity for work, his military knowledge and his already well-known talent as a writer.

If we were to believe his unassuming statements, his book would be just a piece of documentation, the methodical exposition of all pieces of research work on the operations of the Germano-Russian war printed in Soviet publications, and nothing more.

Basically it is that, and on that ground alone, it deserves all our attention, for it is the first time that we have at our disposal reliable and verified information on one of the most essential aspects of the Second World War. But the comments with which General Guillaume supplies each of his chapters are clever original syntheses which throw a remarkable light upon the great stages of the fantastic struggle in the course of which, for nearly four years, the Wehrmacht and the Red Army were at grips with each other.

Whilst remaining concise and scrupulously objective these comments give a sound explanation of the Soviet's victory. The failure of the Blitzkrieg at Moscow in 1941, the disastrous ending of Hitler's big offensive thrusts at Stalingrad in 1942, the decisive wearing down battles of the Summer of 1943. All these successive phases, which are too superficially known, become defined and explained by logical and judiciously analysed motives.

Similarly the use of the Foch strategy is fully brought to light with the masterly application made by Soviet Command. As soon as its artillery succeeded in definitely breaking the German armoured forces, it had enough men and material to keep the initiative and impose its superiority over the enemy.

Then came the uninterrupted series of dazzling victories which shook the whole Eastern front at the same time as the British, American and French Armies overran the 'European fortress' in the west and in their turn entered Germany, with General Guillaume at the head of our 1st Army. Zhukov was in Berlin and Nazism collapsed.

From now on General Guillaume's book will have to serve as a reference for all those who will wish to write a history of the last war. It will also become a classic for those officers and specialists who will look into this glorious gigantic experience for lessons for the future.

For such is the irreplaceable value of history. General Guillaume, old African soldier, incomparable leader of the Algerian Contingent, magnificent chief of the 3rd Algerian Infantry Division, is far too dynamic a man of action to look to the past for absolute and everlasting rules. But he realizes the wealth this past brings to whoever understands its main lines. He has put all his heart into showing these, and not only his heart but also his rare knowledge of warfare as well as his slavophile's erudition. That is why his book is a credit both to French historical science and to our military literature.

J. DE LATTRE.

PART I—THE FAILURE OF THE BLITZKRIEG (1941-1942)

PART II—THE UPSETTING OF THE EQUILIBRIUM (1943)

PART III—THE WITHDRAWAL (1944)

PART IV—THE COLLAPSE (1945)

PART ONE

The Failure of the Blitzkrieg (1941-1942)

1941

THE BARBAROSSA PLAN AND THE INVASION OF THE U.S.S.R.

(Sketches No. 1 and No. 2)

HITLER'S MAIN IDEAS are known to us : settle in a few weeks the U.S.S.R.'s accounts in the same way as he did for Poland and France and through this victory do away with any risk of a war on two fronts, which was the constant fear of the German Command.

Everything seemed in favour of such a victory. The invasion of the Balkans in the Spring of 1941 covered the right flank of his armies and ensured the co-operation of the Rumanian and Hungarian divisions. Moreover, from the Black Sea to the White Sea he held a very wide base for his manoeuvre, The Russian plains afforded the ' Blitzkrieg ' the most favourable ground for the deployment of armour and aircraft. Before the beginning of winter the German Army would have reached its objective, the Archangel-Astrakhan line beyond Leningrad, Moscow and the Ukraine ; Moscow, the very heart of the U.S.S.R. and capital of world Communism, a road, rail and river junction east of which, in 1941, no railway, no road joined North and South Russia ; Leningrad, the key to the Baltic with Kronstadt, the Soviet North Fleet port—the railroad to Murmansk would be cut at the same time ; finally the Ukraine and the Donetz basin, the richest agricultural regions. The chief industrial centres being lost to Russia, Germany would be able to pursue, in the best conditions possible, her struggle against the Western Powers if these refused to bow in the presence of this new triumph.

It may have been necessary to maintain a few mobile forces on the Volga in order to keep watch over the vast spaces of the east but no serious threat would rise any more from that quarter. Besides, Hitler believed that the Soviet masses would readily accept a defeat which would free them from the Communist yoke and that the mixed peoples of the Union—Ukrainians, Tartars and others—would be glad to escape Russian protection, as new Quislings proved even more ready than in the west to facilitate the exploitation of conquered territories.

Finally, the Caucasus, once reached, would form a start line symmetrical to Egypt, Rommel's objective, to destroy for ever British supremacy in eastern countries.

Within this general framework the Barbarossa plan for 1941 fixed the missions of the German and Allied Armies under Field Marshal von Brauchitsch as follows :—

1. The Central Army Group, commanded by von Bock, coming from the Lublin-Suvalki line was to annihilate the Soviet forces of White Russia and march straight on to Moscow via Minsk and Orcha. It comprised five armies, two of which were armoured : IInd, von Weichs—IVth, von Kluge—IXth, von Strauss—IInd Armoured, Guderian—IIIrd Armoured, von Hoth.

2. The North Army Group, under von Leeb, coming out between the Baltic and Suvalki would destroy the Soviet forces in the Baltic States, march towards Lake Peipus and take Leningrad jointly with the Finnish Army of Field Marshal Mannerheim. The latter, reinforced with a few

German divisions was, moreover, to cut off communications with Murmansk. This North Army Group comprised three armies, one of which was armoured: XVIth, von Busch—XVIIIth, von Kurchler—IVth Armoured, Hoepner.

3. The South Army Group, commanded by von Rundstedt, coming out between the Carpathians and Lublin would march towards Kiev. It consisted of three armies, one of which was armoured : XVIIth, von Stulpnagel—VIth, von Reichanau—Ist Armoured, von Kleist. Its action would be covered in the South by that of Field Marshal Antonescu's Rumanian Army and the XIth German Army, von Schubert, coming out of Moldavia.

This deployment clearly expressed the intention of the German Command to sweep down on Moscow with its main forces, and at the same time its wish to reach all its objectives at one stroke, from the Black Sea to the White Sea. It indicated its certainty *a priori* to destroy in a few battles the whole Red Army as it did the Polish Army in 1939 and the French Army in 1940, with deep thrusts by powerful armoured groups, breaking up the Soviet's dispositions, surrounding and then eliminating the segments and consistently pushing forward towards the vital centres of the country.

On the Soviet side the Red Army organized before 1939 the ' Stalin Line ' resting on the Narva, the Dnieper and the Dneister. But as the French Army had in 1940 accepted battle in the Ardennes and the Belgian plain beyond the Maginot Line, so in 1941, the Soviet Armies, in order to remain in the Baltic States and the territories wrenched from Poland, received the German impact west of the Stalin Line, whose fortifications no longer delayed the enemy's advance.

Balancing the German dispositions, the Soviet forces formed three large masses : in the centre, opposite von Bock, Timoshenko ; in the north, facing von Leeb, Voroshilov ; in the south, Budenny facing von Rundstedt.

The operations which had been scheduled for May, when the state of the ground would permit a speedy advance for tanks, were delayed for six weeks by the Balkans campaign and began without any declaration of war on 22nd June 1941, the anniversary of the entry into Russia of Napoleon's army in 1812. The Soviet frontier was crossed over its whole length.

The successes achieved in July and August seemed at first to have justified the optimism of Hitler's Command (Sketch No. 2).

In the centre von Bock pushed the flanks of the IXth Army and the IIIrd Armoured Army towards the north, about fifteen divisions, six of which were armoured ; towards the south the IInd and IVth Armies with the IInd Armoured Army, that is nearly forty divisions, eight of which were armoured. In a pincer movement towards Minsk he took the chief forces of White Russia and claimed 323,000 prisoners, 1,800 guns and 3,000 tanks either captured or destroyed. Without waiting for these forces to be liquidated, von Bock charged upon Moscow and crossed the Beresina and the Stalin Line. But the Red Army held him up for several weeks before Smolensk, and whereas on 10th August he was able to claim again the capture of 210,000 prisoners, 3,200 tanks and 3,210 guns, his divisions no longer found empty space in front of them. In order to reach the capital they would have to fight again. Weeks went by and victories cost more and more.

In the north, von Leeb pushed the XVIth and half the IVth Armoured Army (fifteen divisions, three of which were armoured) in the direction of Kovno, Dvinsk and south of Lake Peipus. The XVIIIth Army and the rest of the IVth Armoured marched upon Riga. By the 15th August he had crossed the Dvina and advanced towards Leningrad, but he had captured only 35,000 men and 650 guns. He was stopped for several weeks before the organized positions of the Louga and it was only in September that he drew near to Leningrad where resistance became stubborn once more. The Finns reached the Svir beyond Lake Ladoga and took Schlusselburg, but all efforts to encircle Leningrad failed.

In the south the successes went beyond all dreams. Rundstedt's left flank, VIth Army and Ist Armoured—twenty divisions, a third of which were armoured—marched on Jitomir and Kiev and pushed the Russian Armies of Galicia south-eastwards, partly achieving the encircling attempt with the IXth Army coming from Jassy. At the end of July the Dnieper was reached. Hitler then removed Guderian's IInd Army from the centre and placed it at Rundstedt's disposal. After three days' fighting towards Uman the Germans claimed on 12th August twenty-five divisions destroyed and 150,000 prisoners ; the XVIIIth Army and the Ist Armoured marched on Poltava, the VIth crossed the Dnieper on each side of Kiev, the IInd reinforced by the IInd Armoured Army, coming from Orcha, extended from north to south along the east bank of the Dnieper and completed the encircling of Budenny's forces towards Kiev. On 27th September the Germans claimed 665,000 prisoners, 3,718 guns captured and 886 tanks destroyed and von Rundstedt marched towards the Donetz, the XIth Army, under command of von Manstein, invaded the Crimea. Stalino fell 20th October, Kharkov 24th, Kursk 2nd November. The XIth Army besieged Sebastopol. On the Soviet side, Budenny gave up his post to Timoshenko who was in turn replaced by Zhukov. After a siege of two months Odessa fell into the hands of the Rumanians and the Germans. Its garrison, travelling by sea, went to reinforce that of Sebastopol.

The Battle of Moscow

(2nd October 1941—20th January 1942)

1. PRELIMINARIES OF BATTLE

There is no arguing about the early successes of the Barbarossa plan. It foresaw, however, that ' only a speedy and unexpected collapse of the Russian resistance could lead to a simultaneous advance on both Leningrad and Moscow '. Now, far from collapsing, and in spite of the losses received, the resistance of the Red Army was increasing, and slowing down the German advance in the chief strategic directions. Moreover, the Battle of Smolensk had decimated the Hitlerite units : let us mention the 20th Armoured Division which lost half its equipment, the 19th Armoured Division which, having lost all its weapons, remained as an infantry division, the 7th Armoured Division which by the end of August had no tanks left and less than 40 per cent of its men. It only came back in mid-November to fight in Moscow.

On the other hand the battle of Smolensk gained eight weeks for the Soviet Command which was concerned with the grave problem of delaying the German advance whilst avoiding the destruction of its own forces, until the large second echelon units would come into the line.

Thus, from this double point of view, the situation did not fulfil the requirements of the Barbarossa plan. Overestimating its early successes, the German Command, without however interrupting the effort upon

Leningrad and Rostov, launched the battle for Moscow at the beginning of October, having for this purpose returned the IInd Armoured Army to the Central Group.

2. THE GERMAN OFFENSIVE UPON MOSCOW
(Sketch No. 3)

It opened in a solemn atmosphere. On 2nd October Hitler addressed the troops on the Eastern Front, ' Finally ', says his Order of the Day, ' the preliminary conditions are fulfilled which will deal the powerful final blow and lead to the annihilation of the enemy before winter comes. All preparations humanly possible have been made. Today the last and greatest battle of the year is about to begin '.

A few hours later on 3rd October, opening the ' Winter Aid ' campaign he said to the Germans, ' 48 hours ago new operations on a gigantic scale began. They will help to annihilate the enemy in the east. He is already defeated and never again will he be able to reconstitute his forces . . .' [1]

The plan aimed at breaking down the Soviet front north and south of Moscow by means of powerful groups of tanks meeting east of the encircled town. Thirty-five divisions of infantry and tanks took part in the operation and practically all armoured forces with the exception of von Kleist's army engaged in the south.

On the Soviet side, the defence was given to Army General G. K. Zhukov, commanding the western front. His orders were to hold Moscow against the Germans, to cause them losses and to spare his own forces in view of a new offensive. Being outnumbered he was to rely on wearing down the enemy and to hold on until a concentration of large new units tipped the scales in his favour. Stalin, who remained in Moscow, would give his personal support to the High Command during the whole battle.

The struggle assumed a fierce character from the beginning. In the face of the enemy's superior resources, the Soviet troops yielded ground. On the battlefield of the Moscova, where on 6th September, 1812, the fate of the capital had been at stake, within sight of Bagration's famous ' spearheads ' and the Raievski redoubt, a Russian infantry division, clinging to a makeshift anti-tank obstacle, held in check for four days the attack of two SS divisions, one of which was armoured ; these latter lost 100 tanks and 10,000 men. Then, being threatened with encirclement, the Russians withdrew towards Mojaisk. Similar battles took place towards Tula on the southern axis and Kalinin on the northern. The Soviet communique of the 15th stated— ' The situation has deteriorated. The German fascist forces have succeeded in one sector in breaking through our defences. Our troops . . . oppose with heroic resistance and inflict heavy losses upon the enemy, but have had to fall back in this sector '.

Nowhere, however, was there any deep break-through, the Russians clung to prepared and organized positions. In Moscow and the neighbouring zone there had been a state of siege since the 19th October. Upon an appeal by Cherbakov, the local Party Leader, the capital was turned into an entrenched camp. The Rostokine district alone, renamed the Cherbakov district since, sent over 100,000 workers. An engineer's report stated definitely that

---

[1]The offensive upon Moscow which began on 2nd October met with great success at first. 600,000 Russians, encircled near Kazma, were captured owing to a pincer movement of the Panzers. Beyond this the advance was slowed down by the mud and checked by the arrival of Soviet reserves.

thousands of housewives and students, whole families, insisted on contributing to the defence of their native city. Even those who had never handled a shovel or a pickaxe worked at a rate of 120 per cent to 130 per cent of the average, staying two or three consecutive weeks away from home. Factories evacuated their most precious machines towards the Urals and met the most urgent needs of the troops with those that were left. In addition the Party organized battalions of workers, the nucleus of four divisions. A very efficient fighter force and A.A. defence kept all except the odd aircraft away from Moscow.

On 7th November the annual Red Army Parade was held in Red Square. The night before, Stalin addressed the city of Moscow above the roar of A.A. guns—' There is no doubt that after four months of war, Germany, whose reserves are dwindling, is weaker than the Soviet Union whose reserves are only now being deployed in all their magnitude '. On the day itself Stalin addressed the troops and the partisans—' The whole world is watching you. It looks upon you as the only force capable of destroying the army of the German plunderers. The peoples of Europe, fallen under the German yoke, see in you their liberators. A great mission has fallen upon you. Be worthy of that mission '. From Red Square, tanks, artillery, mortars and infantry were leaving directly for the front. On each vehicle was written the watchword ' Death to the German invaders '.

By October the Germans had taken Kalinin and Mojaisk and with huge resources reached the line Lake of Moscow, Volokolamsk, Naro-Fominsk, Taroussa, and in the south the outskirts of Tula. But at the beginning of November the Russian resistance had already checked their advance.

On 16th November a new offensive was launched with new forces, fifty-one divisions, of which thirteen were armoured, thirty-three infantry and five motorized and which were supported by 3,000 guns and 500 aircraft. The German Information Bureau stated ' Moscow will remain the essential objective of the German command even if Stalin should attempt to shift the centre of gravity of operations to some other point. The offensive has progressed so far forward that through a good pair of field-glasses it is possible to see inside the city '.

The plan remained the same as for October (Sketch No. 4). Von Bock engaged his armour and motorized units heavily on the flanks. In the north, Hoth and Hoepner, with the IIIrd and VIth Armoured Groups were to occupy Kline, Solnetchnogorsk, Regatchevo, Yakhroma, Dmitrov and push on to Zagorsk with seven armoured divisions, two motorized divisions and three infantry divisions. In the south, Guderian was to take Tula, Kachira, Riazan and Kolomna with the IInd Armoured Army, i.e. four armoured divisions, two motorized divisions, one infantry division. Having reached these objectives, the north and south flanks were to join up and, attacking the Soviet rear, occupy Moscow, while in the centre the IVth Army, with two armoured divisions, five infantry divisions and the 43rd Army Corps were to hold the Soviet forces. Thus did the German Command believe that the conditions would be realized to deal the blow, before winter came, which would decide the fate of Moscow and the conclusion of the war. In his Order of the Day to the soldiers on the Eastern Front, Hitler stated, ' Considering the importance of the events in preparation, and especially the coming of winter which the equipment of our troops is insufficiently provided for, I order you to finish at all costs and in the shortest possible time with the capital Moscow '.

5

As to the Soviet Command, it could only claim to wear down the enemy by means of active defence while new divisions were being created and equipment was being piled up. The first army echelon intended for the counter-offensive was just due to complete its preparation and armament during the second fortnight in November.

The battle was waged from the 16th of November to the 5th December in all three sectors at once.

In the north, the Germans marching upon Kline had three times as many tanks, twice as much artillery and air power as the Russians. The latter fell back on the right to the Kline-Istra line. Certain units showed considerable heroism. Witness the already legendary death of twenty-eight soldiers of the 316th Infantry Division, known today as the 8th Division of General Panfilov's Guards. Under command of Sergeant Dobrobadine, this detachment made up of Russians, Ukrainians, Kazaks, Dirghizes were established in a short trench near the Doubosekovo Station, bore without weakening the repeated attacks of fifty tanks supported by infantry. Only one man put his hands up before a German tank—his comrades shot him dead. After four hours' fighting eighteen tanks had been destroyed by means of anti-tank rifles or set fire to by means of incendiary bottles, then the last attack was launched. The political instructor of the company, Vassili Klotchkov, then said these words which are now history, ' For all of us the time to die is probably at hand. Russia is large but there is nowhere to fall back, Moscow is behind us . . .' Its ammunition being exhausted the detachment perished except for two or three wounded, but it had held out long enough for reinforcements to arrive and break the enemy's attack. In the same way General Dovator's Cossacks, ambushed and destroyed tanks in the forests by means of grenades and incendiary bottles.

After a fierce struggle against the Hoth group the Soviet troops left Kline which was surrounded by five or six divisions, then beyond the Leningrad road. They followed up towards Solnetchnogorsk on one side and Rogatchev, Dmitrov and the Moscova-Volga canal on the other. Further south the Hoepner group came up against General Rokossovski's troops on the Istra positions, which it could neither take nor get round. When the Hoth divisions reached Solnetchnogorsk, Rokossovsky was outflanked but escaped encirclement and withdrew on to the Krioukovo, Dedovski line where he dug in. On the 28th the Hoth group reached the canal towards Yakhroma and sent across the undamaged bridge a battalion supported by tanks, which was destroyed by a Soviet counter-attack and the bridge recaptured. Everywhere, on the canal as well as further south on the Krasnaia Poliana, Krioukovo line, the Soviet resistance made itself felt. German armour gained only six to ten kilometres a day—a speed which did not fit in well with the German forecast. Between the 1st and 5th December it became clear that the efforts to outflank Moscow from the north had failed.

The situation was no different in the centre where the Soviet armies covering Moscow faced the IVth German Army, fifteen divisions strong, two of which were armoured, and with a dense road system in its favour. These armies, established on the Fomkino, Apaltchina, Miakichevo, River Nara line, were subjected to a later attack than those on the flanks. On the right, the Vth Army (General Goverov) took part in the battle of Istra with Rokossovsky's troops as early as 19th November, falling back later towards Zvenigorod, the approaches to which it covered strongly. In order to take it from behind the Germans tried to break through in front of Miakichovo, but the plan was discovered in time and routed by the artillery and air force.

On 1st December the decisive game was played. Testing the Russian defences towards the Mojaisk road and the Minsk road, the Germans aimed at outflanking these two roads from the north and from the south in order to arrive in the immediate vicinity of the capital. Two infantry regiments and some sixty tanks broke through the Nara near Novaia and attacked Kubinka from the south while the 267th Infantry Division approached it from the north. Almost at the same time a mixed group of tanks and motorized infantry reached Iuchkovo in an endeavour to reach Golitsino, threatened from the north by the 252nd, 87th and 78th Infantry Divisions advancing east of Zvenigorod. This double pincer movement cut deeply into the Soviet defences, especially towards Golitsino. Moscow was exposed to long range gunfire. Further south, a group breaking through the Nara in the Atepsevo, Sliznovo sector pushed on towards the north-east.

The situation became critical. The German attack threatened to disrupt the front, to jeopardize the cohesion of the Soviet units and to divert the reserves intended for a counter-offensive. As early as 3rd December, however, vigorous counter-attacks stopped the enemy's advance. In the Iuchkovo, Burtsevo area the Germans left 2,000 dead, the Soviet troops captured 27 tanks, 36 guns, 40 machine-guns. On the 5th, the battle came to an end in favour of the Russians, the Germans were on the defensive and dug themselves in.

In the southern sector the IInd Armoured Army under Guderian was to have taken Tula, then pressed through Ouzlovaia, Stalinogorsk, Venev and Kachira to outflank Moscow from the east while the 43rd and 53rd Army Corps, attacking Alexino, were to reach the Tula-Moscow road. This army, which had a crushing superiority in equipment, had four times as many tanks as the Soviet forces.

Its frontal attack upon Tula via the south suburbs having failed between 30th October and 6th November, as well as a first attempt at outflanking from the east on the 10th, Guderian regrouped his army. He concentrated on a narrow front three armoured divisions and two infantry divisions, the ' Gross Deutschland ' regiment and a strong air force, and launched a new offensive. On the 18th he took Stalinogorsk ; on the 24th, after twelve days' fighting, Venev, then he divided his forces and threw them partly in the direction of Riazan and partly towards Kachira. Having reached Piatnitsa, seven kilometres from Kachira, he left two covering divisions to face the resistance encountered and swept towards the west in four columns with almost the whole of the 3rd and 4th Armoured Divisions, making for the Tula-Moscow road. Simultaneously the 43rd Army Corps attacked this road facing east. After gaining during the first day, the 31st Infantry Division lost ground the next day to the Siazov formation. But Guderian's tanks were still advancing, twenty entered Kostrovo, thirty Reviakino and forty Rudnevo. One armoured column reached the Tula gates by way of the Venev road, and on 3rd December tanks advancing west reached the Moscow road. The ring round Tula was going to close at any moment. On the 4th there was only a five to six kilometre passage left near Kostrovo. The Germans were within reach of their goal.

In fact they were on the brink of disaster. Thrusting deeply to the north and north-east they had stretched their communications and supply lines to the point of danger and exposed their flanks in order to threaten the enemy's, and near Kachira the very thin pincer ran the risk of being cut through.

Since October Tula had been the pivot of the resistance south of Moscow. Its inhabitants took part in the defence, built fortifications and formed battalions of volunteers, vying with the people of the capital in heroism. Tula gave the Soviet Command the time needed to bring up by the end of November the reserves of tanks and infantry held further south.

Between the 1st and 5th December the second German offensive against Moscow was being checked. A number of divisions had lost 50 per cent of their men in ceaseless fighting. According to Soviet reports, after a twenty days' attack the Germans had 55,000 dead and 777 tanks, over 500 vehicles, 178 guns, 119 mortars and 224 machine guns destroyed or lost. From the Lake of Moscow to Tula and Venev, a three hundred and fifty kilometre front, they were gasping for breath. The grand plan had failed. The reserves were exhausted and the double outflanking movements had created two ' pockets ' from which they found it difficult to extricate themselves.

On the other hand the Red Army was feeling the benefit of fresh strategic reserves built up inside the country. They came from the Volga, the Kuban, the Urals and Siberia. Soviet Command had, since 20th October, seen through the enemy's plan and was preparing a counter-stroke. On 1st December General Zhukov's front was reinforced by three fresh armies which deployed, two on his right flank and one on his left. The ratio of forces was now reversed and the decisive turn anticipated by Soviet Command and eagerly awaited by the whole country had now come.

3. THE RED ARMY'S COUNTER-OFFENSIVE BEFORE MOSCOW

(Sketch No. 5)

On 1st December two Russian assault groups were massed on the right of their Moscow front, one of them facing towards Yakhroma, Kline, and other Krasnai Poliana, Solnetchnogorsk. On the left, between Riazan and Riajsk, General Golikov's troops were being concentrated. The 1st Guards Cavalry Corps was being pushed towards Kachira. The Soviet plan was to crush the German forces which attempted to outflank Moscow north and south, by encircling them, then to switch over to the offensive. The plan was launched on 6th December on Stalin's orders.

In the north, General Leliuchenko's troops overthrew the 1st Tank Division and the 14th and 15th Motorized Divisions, occupied Rogatchevo and encircled Kline. General Kusnetsov expelled the Germans from Yakhroma, chased the 6th and 7th Tank Divisions and the 23rd Infantry Division and reached a point south-west of Kline. Further south General Sandapov hustled the 2nd Armoured and the 106th Infantry Division out of their positions, occupied Solnetchnogorsk on 12th December and freed Krasnaia Poliana, the German key position fifty-eight kilometres from Moscow.

In the direction of Istra, Rokossovsky's army broke down the resistance of the 5th, 10th and 11th Armoured Divisions, one SS division and the 35th Infantry Division after seven days' hard fighting. General Reviakine's and General Kukline's units broke the counter-attacks of the 35th Infantry Division and the 5th Armoured Division sometimes at the point of the bayonet. The Germans gave up Kriukovo. In spite of tank and infantry ambushes intended to delay them, the Soviet troops advanced, reducing points of resistance and bombarding, from the air and with artillery, the roads choc-full of convoys where as many as six hundred vehicles piled up.

On 11th December General Beloborodov captured the ruined city of Istra. Clinging for a moment to the west bank of the Istra, threatened with encirclement from both north and south while an infantry division broke through the river, the Germans fled madly westward.

On the 14th a Soviet unit cut off the Kline-Vissokovski road and Kline fell during the night of the 14th/15th after a fierce battle. Leaving behind their tanks, guns, arms and vehicles, closely pursued and always outflanked in the north, the debris of German units were unable to resist from intermediate positions. Not until the 20th were they able to restore their position in front of the Soviet right, on a line prepared in front of the Lama, while the Russian left reached the Rouza.

Within a fortnight the German forces which attempted to outflank Moscow from the north were either destroyed or thrown back to their start line.

In the centre, General Govorov's armies, having been ordered to hold the enemy forces, did even better than to prevent any diversion to the north and south sectors ; on the 5th, 6th and 7th December they threw back the Germans who, east of Zvenigorod, were trying to break through towards Golitsino. Then on the 11th without any artillery preparation they dislodged the Germans from their positions on the north bank of the Moscova, broke down the resistance of the 78th, 87th, 252nd and 267th Infantry Divisions and took the Koliubakino and Lokotnia area.

In the south the Soviet Command intended to encircle and destroy Guderian's divisions which had advanced recklessly. Partial counter-attacks preceded its main offensive. On 3rd December, General Boldin's troops deployed towards Laptevo and attacked the German forces north of Tula at Reviakino, defeating the 3rd and 4th Armoured Divisions and the SS 'Gross Deutschland' Regiment and driving back and encircling the 196th Infantry Division. Creeping by night through the woods as far as the village of Kolodeznaia, the Petrukhov group surrounded the village and exterminated in the dark the 5th 'Gross Deutschland' Battalion. The same night, another group supported by artillery destroyed the 3rd Battalion. Harassed by day and night by mobile assault units, the armoured divisions disintegrated, leaving tanks, cars and motor-cycles.

Whilst being attacked south, north and west by General Boldin, the German units were also attacked from the east by General Belov's 1st Guards Cavalry Corps. As early as 25th November the latter had held the enemy forces which had broken through at Venev, blocked the attacks against Kachira and with his sub-machine gunners taken Pianitsa, a main centre of resistance, by night and the next day had hurled an armoured detachment into Bara-banovo in the enemy's rear.

On the heels of the Germans, the Soviet troops occupied Mordaves, Venev, Stalinogorsk, defeated the 17th Armoured, the 29th Motorized Division and the 167th Infantry Division, killed 1,500 men and captured over 60 guns, 80 tanks and 2,000 vehicles. Being marvellously well informed by agents who collected their information by day and night in the midst of foul weather conditions and under the enemy's fire, it can be said that the Red Army fought with its eyes open. Its scouts crossed the lines, attacking headquarters and dispatch-riders, by day its mobile artillery supported the mounted infantry which, after thorough preparation swept into villages and shot the panic-stricken Germans at point-blank range. By night it was the turn of sub-machine gunners to carry out raids even into houses.

On 6th December, following these preliminaries, General Golikov's assault troops deployed and took the offensive with all the forces of the southern sector and General Rotminstrov's tanks coming from Kazan. Thus they completed from the east the encirclement of Guderian, already held tight in the north by the Belov Corps. German attempts at diversion failed, as for instance, night attacks conducted against Boldin's troops by the 521st Regiment of the 296th Infantry Division. ' On the 6th at 22.00 hrs the 521st formed in companies and battalions and preceded by 80 to 100 sub-machine gunners approached the town by way of Maslovo . . . When it was two or three hundred metres away our searchlights were switched on and halted it, our heavy machine guns opened a raging fire mowing down whole rows of drunken fascists. The regiment fled towards Maslovo in order to reform. We had anticipated that and our heavy guns pounded the village, covering our sub-machine gunners who outflanked it and captured it at dawn. The remains of the 521st scattered leaving behind arms and ammunition. . . . Confusion spread. On the 7th we tapped a radio line on which panic-stricken 3rd Armoured were asking for orders. Guderian replied " Burn the vehicles and fall back towards the south-west " '. Near Laptevo they burnt 200 lorries ; at Reviakino they left 16 tanks either damaged or burnt. Elsewhere they drew red stars on their turrets in order to cover their flight. But all roads were cut off.

In vain did the Germans try to halt on the Upper Don or the Chatt. After two days their resistance broke down. On the 13th Golikov occupied Mikhailov and Epifane and pushed on to Bogoroditsk whilst Belov's cavalry had taken Stalinogorsk as early as the 11th. Bogoroditsk was taken on the 15th and on the 19th the Plava, north of Plavsk was reached.

In their turn the defenders of Tula swept towards the south and west, reaching the Upa and capturing the lines on the other side of the river, whilst on the 17th General Zakharkine occupied Alexine pushing beyond the Oka some remains of German units. The Soviet plan for the south had now been realized by the crushing defeat of Guderian.

This Russian counter-offensive cost von Bock losses which the Soviet estimate gave as over 70,000 dead left outside Moscow ; this together with the wounded and casualties from the cold gave a total of nearly 250,000 for the period 6th to 25th December only. The Red Army captured 1,000 tanks, 1,500 guns, 500 mortars, 1,600 machine guns and 1,200 vehicles.

After a short respite Zhukov started a new offensive at the beginning of 1942. On 10th January, on the right, his troops launched an attack on the Rouza and the Lama, breaking through west of Volokolamsk, reached Chakhovskaia on the 17th and arrived on the 20th north of Gjaisk. In the centre, where Naro-Fominsk had fallen on 26th December, armoured units captured Maloiareslavetz on 2nd January and on the 3rd Borovsk, where the encircled garrison was annihilated. They outflanked Medine on the 13th, took Miatsevo on the 20th and on the 24th, after having beaten off all counter-attacks, reached the German lines south-east of Viazma. At Medine the Germans left 2,000 dead.

Zhukov's north flank captured Dorokhovo on the 14th. Mojaisk, attacked frontally and outflanked by Rouza, fell on the 20th. On the south flank, Boldin took Kaluga on 30th December. Golikov and Belov's cavalry came from the Plava and marched upon Kozelsk. Sukhinitchi was reached. Further north, after occupying Metschevsk and Mossalsk, the Soviet forces reached the Viazma-Briansk railway on 2nd January.

From the beginning of January the extreme cold and the deep snow had appreciably impeded the progress of the Russian troops. However, being well equipped, they continued to advance. The Germans were without winter clothing, decimated by the cold, ceaselessly attacked by twice as strong an air force and still being tracked in the woods by Siberian sharpshooters who crept through the gaps. ' Being perfectly equipped against the cold,' says the Borsenzeitung, ' these Siberians are perfectly comfortable in winter. The frost stops our machine-guns and our vehicles. Then the terrible Russian hand to hand fighting takes place . . .' Without using the main roads, General Dovator's Cossacks covered as much as thirty kilometres a day through snow-covered paths and took the Germans by surprise. This same General Dovator was killed by a burst of machine gun fire but his Cossacks kept his motto : ' Life is short, glory is long-lived '.

The Germans, numb with cold and on the alert night and day, had a real terror of the Siberians and the Cossacks. This terror was increased by the ceaseless action of the partisans, in hot pursuit of small detachments, harassing convoys and destroying bridges. The Germans paid them back savagely. They erected gallows in each village and thousands of partisans and hostages perished, more than two thousand of the latter in the districts of Istra, Rouza, Volokolamsk and Lotochinsk alone. Whole villages were set ablaze. The Soviet forces glorified the memory of a young woman, Zoia Kosmodemiansk of Petrichevo, suburb of Vereisk. Affiliated to the partisans, she was arrested and tortured and died on the gallows without having spoken.

These atrocities stimulated the Soviet soldiers to commit similar acts in revenge. This accounts for the small number of prisoners taken as compared with the heavy German losses.

Ovarove, the only remaining occupied locality in the Moscow area, fell on 22nd January. The Germans had retreated over 400 km. The battle of Moscow was over.

Comments

The Battle of Moscow, a battle of attrition of four months' duration, followed a three months' campaign in the course of which the opponents had worn each other down in hard fighting. On a front of 350 kilometres long (London-Plymouth) and 300 kilometres deep there were a series of battles. After the two German offensives in October and November came the Soviet counter offensive in December and January. Each opponent in turn scored important tactical successes, encircling and destroying considerable forces but never attaining a strategic break-through. It is true that in January the cold and snow prevented the Soviet Command from exploiting its victory.

For two months the Germans persisted in their encircling manoeuvres while from the early days, on either side of Moscow, the tanks were hurled in, eliminating all element of surprise. The Soviet troops were thus able to defend themselves on successive lines and bring fresh troops whose intervention reversed the situation.

The German defeat before Moscow cannot be separated from this picture of tanks being hurled in on both sides of the capital and being slaughtered wholesale by the Russian anti-tank artillery. Out of twenty-four armoured divisions available in 1941 the German Command used thirteen round Moscow.

The ground, having few irregularities would, it seemed, be favourable to the movement of armour. Quite the reverse was true. The Moscow area constituted a huge forest with very few clearings, which were the only cultivated and inhabited spots. West of the capital, with the exception of the Moskova battlefield (which Kutuzov selected in 1812 on account of its unrestricted view and fields of fire) only one clearing worthy of the name was to be found over a stretch of a hundred and twenty kilometres, that of Mojaisk.

On this wooded and more often than not marshy ground the early rains rendered movement singularly difficult off the beaten track. Three roads converged towards the capital, running at different places along lakes and marshes. East of Mojaisk the Minsk road ran between the Nara ponds in the south and the tributaries of the Moscova in the north. Between Istra and Solnetchnogorsk the Istra lake blocked the thirty kilometres which separated the Volokolamsk road from the Leningrad road which in turn was bordered on the north by Lake Sinej. These bottlenecks, situated between lakes and marshes, lent themselves admirably to well camouflaged anti-tank blocks on the outskirts of the woods. Apart from these three main axes, the Hoth and Hoepner groups, aimed at outflanking Moscow from the north towards Dmitrov and Yakhroma, and found only bad earth tracks which the rain turned into quagmires. Similarly there was no metalled road between the Leningrad road and the Moscova-Volga canal or between Solnetchnogorsk and the Lake of Moscow.

If, in spite of their losses, armoured vehicles broke through a barrage and reached a clearing, they came upon a new anti-tank ditch on the opposite side covered with new *abattis*. They fell under the fire of anti-tank units all possessing brand new equipment which opened fire at short range. Thus the 289th was engaged first at Volokolamsk and then at Solnetchnogorsk and destroyed 186 tanks. It was acclaimed as ' First Anti-tank Artillery Regiment of the Guard '. For its part the 296th destroyed 22 tanks on 22nd November.

South of Moscow, beyond the Oka, forests appear only as odd green spots among extensive cultivation ; marshes were few and this accounted for the quick advance of Guderian as far as the outskirts of Kachira. It seemed here that the stubborn defence of Tula hypnotized and paralysed the German Command.

When they used nine armoured divisions west and north of Moscow the Germans did not seem to realize the difficulties which awaited them. Being stopped by the efficiency of a new anti-tank weapon they had not enough infantry to get round the anti-tank blocks by way of the woods. In any case they would have found these gaps strongly held by a large Soviet infantry and cavalry force, guided and aided by the partisans.

On the road axes armour and lorries piled up and got jammed, providing targets for the Soviet long range artillery and the Stormovik fighter aircraft which, flying at low altitude, attacked motorized columns or preferably tanks, of which they destroyed 400 between 1st and 11th November. This was the first time that the Soviet fighter force, with its Yaks, equalled or surpassed the Messerschmidts. Night bombing added its moral effect to the material effect.

Being compelled by the nature of the ground to run into anti-tank traps manned by an excellent artillery, lacking the necessary infantry to outflank them and harassed by an air force which had the mastery in the air, the German armoured divisions to which Hitler owed his triumphs in Poland,

France and the East, suffered heavy losses each day. They became gradually exhausted in the face of renewed resistance, always stronger than before. Attack, a hundred times renewed, was stopped a hundred times. Each bound, however short, cost more tanks and more men.

Such were the real causes of the German defeat before Moscow. Rather than acknowledge them the Germans resorted to a fairy tale. They claimed that the battle was won, not by the Red Army, but by the terrible ' Russian winter '. But the action opened several weeks before the severe cold. In his Order of the Day of 2nd October Hitler exhorted his armies to gain victory before the winter.[1] For the second offensive only, that of 16th November, the weather conditions made the struggle more difficult. But if the frost caused the troops to suffer cruelly, it hardened the marshes and made the movement of tanks off the roads possible. The German soldiers owed it to Hitler's insane stubbornness that they were caught in summer outfits in temperatures of $-20°$ and $-30°$ Centigrade, but when the winter battle began was not the fight before Moscow definitely lost ? In spite of the danger which, until 6th December, hung over the capital, the Soviet Command had the situation well in hand. The October and early November battle had proved that German armour was not invincible. ' The devil is not as black as he is painted ' said Stalin in his proclamation of 7th November.

In fact, Hitler's obstinacy against his Army staff was due to his pride which refused to acknowledge defeat, his first defeat. His generals begged him to suspend the offensive and take it up again in the spring after restoring communications, converting the Soviet railway tracks to normal gauge and reconstituting the units. His answer was a new order to attack. When the defeat of Moscow failed he sacrificed his chiefs who were guilty of not having carried through the plans his genius inspired! Brauchitsch was discharged on 23rd December in the midst of a battle, von Bock was replaced by von Kluge who in his turn was replaced by Heinrichi at the head of the IVth Army. Guderian, after a stormy interview with Hitler at the GHQ in East Prussia, made way for Schmidt.

Fifteen hundred tanks were destroyed before Moscow. More severe still were the losses in personnel. They affected the Armoured Corps especially, a weapon of war and of conquest wrought by Hitler himself and which gathered the elite of the Hitler Youth. Together with Guderian's units the victors of the Battles of Poland and France died before Moscow. The tanks could be replaced, but the crews never.

From a strategic point of view the Moscow defeat marked the complete collapse of the ' Barbarossa ' plan. After being bled white, the German army, having reconstituted and regrouped its forces, would be able to take the initiative again in the operations of 1942, but it would no longer be able to act simultaneously in several important strategic directions. The Soviet defence would consequently be made easier. Moreover, while pushing deeply into the U.S.S.R. the Germans were getting further away from their bases, lengthening their communication lines in a hostile atmosphere and exposing their lines of communication to grave dangers. The action of the partisans already forecast in peace-time, was beginning to reveal itself and not without causing the High Command great anxiety.

In spite of its losses the Red Army arose all the greater for its ordeal. With its anti-tank artillery and its ' Stormoviks ' it felt now capable of destroying the steel monsters which nothing had stopped hitherto. The

---

[1] The first snowfalls of mid-October were followed by a period of thaw.

remorseless slaughter of the German units encircled in the Moscow forests strengthened the feeling of superiority among the Soviet infantry and cavalry which even the later setbacks of 1942 were powerless to dim and which still existed as strongly at the time of the Stalingrad battle.

This army had forgotten the disasters of the early months of the war and had regained confidence in its leaders, its weapons and in itself. During those four weary months of hand to hand fighting the Red soldiers had shown an endurance, a steadfastness and a spirit of sacrifice which compels admiration. The expressions of gratitude which reached them, not only from their own country but from the whole world, glorified their pride and stimulated their courage. From a more general point of view the myth of the invincibility of the German army had been exploded by the Moscow victory. It was also apparent to both the German troops and people who were losing their blind faith in the Fuhrer's star. It appeared so in the eyes of the Red soldiers and of the peoples of the U.S.S.R. who reaped from this victory the right to hope again. Finally, it appeared so in the eyes of the Allies, particularly of the peoples of Europe who had been temporarily enslaved and who regained new courage.

Such appear to be, both militarily and politically, the consequences of the German defeat. In the course of the Second World War, the victory of the Red Army at Moscow in December 1941 had no less importance than the victory of the French Army on the Marne in September 1914 had in the course of the First World War.

The Battle of Moscow opened another type of war on a world-wide scale, the war of attrition. The era of Hitler's sensational coups was over. German resistance, strained to the utmost since the beginning of hostilities, was not able to hold out indefinitely against the united forces of the whole world.

For the French the Red Army's victory at Moscow had a very special significance. During the most painful hour of their history, immediately after the greatest disaster that had ever befallen their army, a voice arose from the other side of the Channel, calling to them that the Motherland was not dead but had merely lost a battle and that new forces were rising throughout the world. It urged the French, wherever they were, to go on fighting so that France should be represented in the final victory. Months went by. Impressed by Germany's strength and bent under her yoke, there were many who, without giving up hope, were wondering where salvation would come from.

But now Hitler had chosen a new victim. On 22nd June 1941 he hurled his armies against the U.S.S.R. Anxiously France and all the oppressed watched the gigantic duel. German communiques were already claiming the defeat of the Red Army. Would Leningrad and Moscow share the fate of Paris ? Suddenly, as the German guns were getting ready to fire upon Moscow, already doomed to destruction, while the fall of the city, two-thirds encircled, was expected at any moment, the grip loosened. Forsaking their prey the German armoured forces withdrew hurriedly, the Soviet troops on their heels inflicted upon them enormous losses. The Russian winter made the German retreat more tragic and more costly. In this war, in which the fate of so many nations was at stake, the Wehrmacht met for the first time with a heavy defeat. The withdrawal became more marked. Moscow was now clearly freed. The German Army was no longer invincible—De Gaulle was right. Hope sprung again everywhere ; everywhere there was a wish for action. While a few heroic Frenchman went on fighting beside the

14

British in North Africa, weapons and men were being hidden. The hope to fight again had become a certainty. In France the resistance movements were being organized.

The Moscow victory was more than a Russian victory. True it had been gained by the Red Army with its own weapons, but to the French it was their first return victory.

In 1942 the Red Army underwent new ordeals over which it triumphed with the same heroism, but Stalingrad cannot make us forget Moscow. At Moscow, Hitler met with his first defeat. At Moscow his dream of world domination collapsed before the magnificent resistance of the Soviet Army.

THE DEFENCE OF LENINGRAD

(Sketch No. 6)

The battle of Leningrad began in July 1941 when the Northern Group of Armies, having crossed the Baltic States, arrived from the Narva and attacked the Luga Line.[1]

During their withdrawal the Soviet forces slowed the German advance down and inflicted considerable losses on the enemy. The Soviet Command continued to send reserves and newly formed units to Leningrad. The resistance kept on increasing.

Since the beginning of hostilities the mass-mobilized workers of Leningrad had been building deep defences. Within a few weeks a line rose along the Luga. Positions were set up near Leningrad and the city itself set into a state of defence. Labourers, clerks, scholars, all answered readily the call for volunteers : 70 per cent of the inhabitants enrolled as local defence units. Between the 30th June and the 10th July ten infantry divisions, seventeen machine gun battalions, seven anti-tank regiments, twelve infantry battalions, in all 135,000 men, were raised. Fighting had been going on on the Luga since 7th July. It took the Germans until the middle of August—over a month—to break through towards Kinguissep and Novgorod.

By the middle of September, after losing 170,000 men, the Germans reached the southern and south-western suburbs of Leningrad. They reached the south bank of the Gulf of Finland in the Petrodvorets (Peterhof) region and Lake Ladoga in the Petrokrepost (Schlusselburg) region. West of Peterhof the coastal units denied them access to the sea in the Oranienbaum area and as far as Kernovo. At the same time the Finnish troops came up against the Soviet positions of the Karelia isthmus and of the river Svir. Soviet resistance hardened whilst the Germans were pausing for breath after losing numerous tanks, planes and guns. Towards the end of September they stopped, exhausted, within sight of the city. Far from being able to call upon any of the units engaged on the Leningrad front, they had to bring reinforcements up in order to maintain their positions. The Soviet troops and the Leningrad population were nevertheless in a critical situation. All routes were cut off and there was only one line of communication left and that by water across Lake Ladoga.

Abandoning the idea of storming the city, Hitler said ' Leningrad will have to surrender, it will fall sooner or later. No one shall relieve her, no one will be able to break through the lines that surround her '. With an insane

[1]Altogether the forces originally engaged in the manoeuvre against Leningrad, both through the Baltic States and through Finland, consisted of forty-eight divisions, twelve of which were Finnish (say 300,000 men), over 1,000 tanks and over 1,000 planes.

fury the Germans subjected the city to air attacks and artillery bombard-
ments[1] every day in the hope of breaking down the defenders' morale.
Jdanov, a member of the Military council and representing Stalin on the
Leningrad front, replied to these attacks, ' The severe ordeals inflicted upon
Leningrad have stiffened our will to fight and conquer. They have strengthened
our decision to overcome all difficulties in order to achieve victory over
Hitlerite Germany. They have kindled even more our hatred of the enemy
and our eagerness to fight . . .'.

In October and November the Germans took up the offensive again in
the direction of Tikhvin and Volkhov in order to reach the river Svir and
link up with the Finnish troops. In this way would they complete the encirclement of Leningrad in the east by cutting off the communications
through Lake Ladoga. To begin with, although at the cost of heavy losses,
the Germans pushed back the Soviet troops, took Budogoch and reached the
approaches to Volkhov. Despite a reinforcement of fresh divisions, however,
they were on the defensive by the end of November. Then the Volkhov front
under General Meretskov took the offensive, beat General Schmidt's units
and on 9th December recaptured Tikhvin after destroying the 12th Armoured
Division, the 18th Motorized Division and the 61st Infantry Division. The
Germans left 7,000 dead and considerable material. At the same time General
Fediuninski's 54th Army stopped German forces which were attempting to
cut the railway and reach the south bank of Lake Ladoga, in the region of
Voibokale. The 11th and 269th Infantry Divisions, together with two regiments of the 254th Infantry Division, left 5,000 dead on the field. The rest
of the 11th and 254th Divisions and the 21st Infantry Division were completely
defeated at Volkhov.

Although this Soviet counter-offensive momentarily saved Leningrad
from being completely surrounded the situation remained none the less
precarious, the north railway line being under German fire as the Germans
were masters of Schlusselburg. In order to ensure the essential supplies for
the troops and the civilians Jdanov mapped out a route across the ice of
Lake Ladoga which the people of Leningrad called the ' life-giving road ',
through which food, arms and ammunition poured ceaselessly.

The population bore their losses and privations heroically. During the
worst days of winter, in intense cold, Leningrad, underfed, without light
and attacked by shells and bombs, worked for the front. The bread ration,
consisting mainly of substitutes, went down to $\frac{1}{4}$ lb. Men, women and children
died in thousands and consequently, in the depth of winter, part of the
population was evacuated towards the interior of the U.S.S.R. across the ice
of Lake Ladoga. People left, piled up in supply lorries which were returning
to bases east of the lake, surrounded by blizzards and under the German
Air Force bombing. Through its heroic defence and by containing important
forces Leningrad had contributed to the Moscow victory. Moreover, the
Red Army had, with the very effective help of the population, saved the city
from certain destruction. In a note from the ' Secret Chancery of the Chief
of Staff' we read indeed, ' Hitler has decided to wipe the city of Petersburg
off the face of the earth. After the defeat of the Red Army there will be no
further reason to allow that large mass to exist. Finland has also stated her
lack of interest in the preservation of that city in the immediate vicinity of
her new frontier. We have considered blockading it tightly and then shelling

---

[1]According to Soviet reports, between September 1941 and January 1944 the Germans
dropped 150,000 shells and 102,000 incendiary bombs on Leningrad.

it by artillery of every calibre and crushing it to the ground by aerial bombardment ... For our part, in this war to the death, we have no reason to preserve
even part of the population of that large city.'

Like the Battle of Moscow, that of Leningrad revealed the weariness of
the German armies, exhausted by severe losses, spread out over an immense
front and fighting in the depth of winter thousands of kilometres away from
their bases. On the Soviet side the Army and the whole population, carried
away by an ardent patriotism, rose in a supreme effort against the invader.

1942—The Situation in the Course of the Winter and Spring

HITLER'S INTENTIONS

The victory won by the Red Army at Moscow in December 1941 was
followed by a series of Soviet attacks along the whole front.

In the Crimea, while the siege of Sebastopol was going on, Soviet troops
landed on the east of the peninsula and took Kertch and Theodosia. Timo-
shenko attacked in the direction of Kharkov and recaptured Bielgorod.
North of Moscow the Vieliki-Luki, Rjev railway was reached and passed.
South of Lake Ilmen, towards Staraia-Russa, six divisions of the XVIth
Army were encircled.

The chief ' chevaux de frise ', Kharkov, Orel, Vieliki-Luki, Vitebsk and
Smolensk, remained untouched but the German divisions sustained heavy
losses. There was no lull to allow them to reform and reinforce.

In April the Germans counter-attacked, in the south to give Kharkov
breathing space and in the north to free the XVIth Army. In May, Timoshenko attacked again towards Kharkov which he outflanked from both
the north and the south. Just as he reached the outlying districts of the city
he was violently counter-attacked on both flanks, in the north by von Kleist's
armour and in the south by von Paulus'. The Germans claimed 240,000
prisoners. In the Crimea the German counter-attack upon Kertch succeeded.
The Germans claimed 40,000 prisoners.

On 1st June von Manstein launched an attack in force on Sebastopol.
His powerful artillery included amongst other weapons the new 615 mm
mortars. By turning the whole of his artillery and air force on each different
sector in succession he succeeded in capturing the town on 2nd July at the
cost of heavy German and Rumanian losses. The Black Sea Fleet evacuated
the remains of the Soviet garrison.

However the decisive battle had not yet begun. Hitler would attack when
his sorely tried units were reconstituted and when the good weather made the
vast southern plains practicable for tanks. He hoped to attain in 1942 the
decisive result which he missed in 1941. Both the winter and the spring
campaigns had used up a large part of his reserves but he estimated that they
had also exhausted the enemy.

Since 22nd June 1941, according to German propaganda, the Red Army
had lost nearly 4 million prisoners, 24,000 tanks, 35,000 guns and 20,000
planes. On the basis of these figures Hitler believed it incapable of resisting
a new large scale offensive. In his mind it was only a question of dealing the
death-blow to an army which was already beaten. Without the Ukraine and
the Donetz, even with the industries of Moscow and the Urals, the Soviets

would not be able to make up their losses of material, even if, in spite of continual attacks on shipping, the western aid was becoming apparent.[1]

Moreover the loss of new territory would render the shortages, already felt in the U.S.S.R. during the winter of 1941-42, more acute. The collapse of the population's morale was also a possibility.

Actually the Germans were beginning to find it difficult to replace both personnel and material. But improvements in armaments brought about a reduction of the strength of large units without reducing their fire-power. Infantry divisions were reduced from 12,000 to 8,000 men ; panzer divisions numbered 200 tanks instead of 250 by which means the number of divisions was maintained and even increased. That of the divisions of satellite armies grew as well. Sure of his success, Hitler reckoned to draw them into the wake of the German armies whose flanks they would cover.

But, as always, it was from his armoured divisions that Hitler expected victory to come. Out of twenty-six at his disposal he committed twenty-two against the Red Army in 1942.

Two army groups were to launch the offensive in the southern part of the front :—

Von List's Army Group ' A ', deploying the XIth and XVIIth Armies, the Ist Armoured Army and the Ist Rumanian Army between Taganrog and Orel

Von Bock's Army Group South, comprising 3 German armies—von Paulus' VIth facing Kharkov, von Weich's IInd facing Kurks, von Hoth's IVth Armoured supporting the other two—and 3 allied armies, one Rumanian and one Italian on the Donetz and south of Kharkov, plus one Hungarian Army.

The Battle of Stalingrad

THE GERMAN PLAN

The aim remained the same as in 1941—crush the Red Army and take Moscow. The first failure had shown that it was impossible to sustain simultaneous divergent efforts on a vast front. Hence the following decision —an offensive south of Moscow in order to reach the Volga, then come up the right bank of the river in order to outflank Moscow widely from the east and cut it off from the Urals ; finally link up with the forces coming from the West, take Moscow and destroy the bulk of the Red Army. An action upon Baku was also being considered, which was intended to draw out the enemy's strategic reserves, get hold of the Caucasus oil and provide Hitler with a jumping off point for his future swoops upon India and the Near East. In the north there was to be one operation only to take Leningrad.

To carry out this plan the OKW had 240 divisions on the east front ; 179 German (or 70 per cent of the existing 256), 61 Allied, of which 22 were Rumanian, 14 Finnish, 10 Italian, 13 Hungarian, 1 Slovak and 1 Spanish. At the beginning of summer the main part, over 3 million men, was concentrated on a five hundred kilometre front between Orel and Lozovaia. Above all, the enemy was not to be allowed to re-establish itself on a succession of lines as in 1941 and the rhythm of the advance was fixed in advance—10th July, Borissoglebsk, 25th July, Stalingrad, 10th August, Saratov, 15th August,

---

[1]On 11th June 1942 the U.S.S.R. and the U.S.A. signed the lend-lease agreement for an amount of 11,293,831,000 dollars.

18

Kuibichev, 10th September, Arzama, 25th September, Baku. In October and November, the decisive action would take place somewhere near Moscow.

But once again the Red Army's resistance was to give the operations a very different turn and the campaign developed into four main phases—the German offensive, 28th June-19th November ; the encircling of two German armies near Stalingrad, 19th-30th November ; the German attempts to free the encircled troops, December ; finally the destruction of those forces, 10th January-2nd February, 1943.

THE GERMAN OFFENSIVE

(28th June-19th November, 1942)

1. *Failure of the action on Voroneje* (Sketch No. 7)

Coming from the Kursk-Kharkov front towards Voronjee with the intention of reaching the Volga and the rear of Moscow by the shortest possible way, the Germans engaged thirty-five divisions, of which six were armoured and four motorized, supported by 1,500 tanks and over 1,000 planes. They aimed to encircle and annihilate the Red forces in the Livni Time, Korotcha, Stari-Oskal and Kasternoi area in two or three days, then to fall upon Voroneje and the Volga.

As early as 28th June they encountered fierce resistance. The Voroneje front, set up in the midst of the battle under Rokossovski's command, was given the mission of defending the city which was being attacked by crack troops—the ' Gross Deutschland ' Division, the 24th Armoured Division, the 3rd and 16th Motorized Divisions. These units crossed the Don on the 6th and 7th July. The battle raged in Voroneje which was defended by Tcherniakhov's tanks, Ulutin's infantry and a regiment of the NKVD.[1]

Between the 2nd and 8th July the Soviet forces engaged in the area between the Kasternoi, Stari-Oskal and the Don, escaped being encircled and withdrew east of the river. On 8th July the Germans went over to the defensive at Voroneje. A counter attack by the Red Army south of the city cost the 75th German division over 5,000 men.

2. *Offensive upon Stalingrad* (Sketch No. 8)

After the Voroneje failure the Germans directed their efforts towards Stalingrad. If they held the city they would be able to cut off Central Russia from the Caucasus and to work on the rear of Moscow in the north and on Baku in the south.

With superiority in tanks and planes the Germans broke through south of the Don. Through the gap the VIth Army and the IVth Armoured Army moved forward into the bend of the river and reached the Bokovskaia, Morozovsk, Millerovo, Kantemirovka region. Further to the right the German thrust made for Novorossisk-Piatigorsk-Mozdok.

In the face of this threat the Soviet Command created the Stalingrad front with the mission of keeping the enemy out of the city. It drew from its reserves the 62nd and the 64th Armies which, on 10th July, it pushed on to the left bank of the Don, towards Kletskaia, Sourovikino, Vierkh-Koursnoiarskaia. These armies numbered only ten infantry divisions as against twenty-nine German divisions, of which four were armoured and three motorized, a powerful artillery and Richthoffen's IVth Air Fleet with 900 planes. In spite of their lower numbers and while yielding ground, these two Soviet armies

---

[1]N.K.V.D. Commissariat of the People of the Interior.

19

gave the Soviet Command time to reinforce the Stalingrad defences and to bring up new reserves.

The German plan was to attack the flanks of the forces covering Stalingrad, to encircle them, to cross the Don and take the city. On 28th July their attempt from the north against the 62nd Army failed. Hitler then gave orders to attack from the south-west along the Tikhoretsk railway with five divisions of the IVth Armoured Army (of which one armoured division and one motorized division were together at Abganerovo, seventeen kilometres south-west of Plodovitoie). At the same time the VIth Army would mop up the west bank of the Don. Indeed, the Red forces fell back east of the river from the 7th to the 17th August, but thanks to the entry of reserve anti-tank units, they checked the advance of the Abganerovo group. This was followed by simultaneous attacks from north and south ; in the north ten divisions (of which six were infantry, two armoured and two motorized) started from the small bend of the Don and marched upon Vertiatchi, north-west of Stalingrad ; in the south six divisions (of which three were infantry, two armoured and one motorized) made for the southern outskirts of the city ; in the centre three other divisions were attacking, starting from Kalatch.

Thanks to its air support the north group crossed the Don, broke through towards Vertiatchi, reached the Volga near Rinok and Erzovka, thus cutting off the city from the Russian forces on the right. Then, in order to bring supplies for the defence of Stalingrad, it was necessary to cross the river in full view of excellent observation posts, under fire of artillery and an air force with mastery in the air.

The other two German groups pushed the Soviet troops back on to the line Spartakovitz (three kilometres south-west of Rinok, Orlavka)—left bank of the Rassochka and the Tchervlienaia, Cavrilovka, Largvrod. Then at the end of August a German break through forced the defence as far back as the immediate vicinity of the city. From the 3rd September the Germans brought up division after division and masses of tanks and planes. In ten days they lost 24,000 killed, 185 guns and 200 tanks, but they broke through towards Elechanka and reached the Volga south of the city. Then the fight began for the conquest of the city. It was to last until 19th November.

3. *The defence of Stalingrad* (Sketch No. 9)

On 12th September, General Eremenko, commanding the Stalingrad front, entrusted the 62nd Army, now under General Tchouikov, with the defence of the city. This army held the following front : Rinok, Spartokovetz, Orlovka-Minima suburb, Elchanka, Kuporosnoi, hugging more or less closely (two to ten kilometres) the border of the city which stretched for more than fifty kilometres along the river. Its right came up against the Germans of the Rinok, Erzovka salient, its left linked with the 64th Army. Everywhere there was close contact, incessant attacks with tank and air support, the air force making as many as 2,500 raids a day from 25th August. The city was ablaze.

Being reinforced by the VIIIth Italian army the IIIrd Rumanian Army and the 4th Rumanian Cavalry Corps, the Germans deployed forty divisions for the Stalingrad manoeuvre and could concentrate twelve divisions, over 100,000 men, 500 tanks, 1,400 guns and 1,000 planes, upon the town. These forces were grouped in the north towards Goroditche, Goumrak and in the south towards Verkhi, Elchanka, Pestchanka, Zelenaia, Peliana.

The danger increased every hour. The Germans entered the city and each block of houses, each house, each factory, each workshop was fought for. The civilian population entered the fight. Tchouiakov, district Party Leader, controlled the Defence Committee and issued the followed proclamation : ' To-day, as it did 24 years ago, our city is living through an unhappy time. The bloodthirsty Hitlerites hurl themselves upon our sunny city on their way to the great Russian river. We shall not give up our native city to German indignities. Let us all arise as one man for the defence of our beloved city, of our birthplace, of our families. Let us fill up the streets with barricades! '

The inhabitants responded to this appeal. 150,000 went out every day to organize defence positions. The factories worked for the front under bombing and shelling. Tanks were no sooner finished than they went into action, driven by the very men who made them. Labourers, clerks and scholars went to reinforce the ranks of the 62nd Army, formed themselves into new units and anti-tank detachments. The hardest battles took place in the centre and south of the city. With seven divisions (295th, 76th, 71st, 94th Infantry Divisions, 24th and 14th Armoured Divisions, 20th Motorized Division) the German Command had reckoned to reach the Volga in two or three days. It took thirteen days with colossal losses to take the southern part on 26th September. In the north it failed before the Mamaiev Kourgan. In the centre General Rodimtsev's Guards Division denied them access to the Volga.

From 27th September to 4th October the enemy relentlessly attacked the factory sector. From the 4th to 8th October it tried to break through abreast of the ' S4 ' tractor factory. It took four days to advance three or four hundred metres. In a letter Captain Biedermann wrote : ' All that is left of my battalion is one officer, three NCOs and twenty-nine men.' On 14th October a new attack supported by artillery, aircraft and 150 tanks was launched. After four hours fighting the Germans broke through and rushed tanks, covered with infantrymen, into the gaps. By the end of the day they had taken the factory and reached the Volga. Under command of Colonel Gorokhov some units of the 62nd Army were detached and held out heroically on the banks of the Volga until the Soviet counter-attack was launched.

From mid-October onwards the Germans fiercely attacked the ' Barricades ' and ' Red October ' factories. At the end of October the Red Army units took the initiative and compelled the enemy to be on the defensive.

During the whole of the battle outside and inside the city, the German air force, in sole command of the air despite Soviet attempts, dropped over a million bombs totalling 100,000 tons. Together with the artillery it never stopped harassing the craft carrying personnel and supplies from one side of the Volga to the other.

For its part the Soviet artillery had killed 30,000 men, destroyed 420 tanks, 24 batteries and 1,000 vehicles.

The German divisions relentlessly thrust against Stalingrad suffered enormous losses. Some had practically ceased to exist, others, like the 14th and 24th Armoured, had to be reformed several times both in men and vehicles. During the course of the first three days the 79th and the 305th lost nearly all their men. From the 1st to the 16th September the 29th Motorized registered 1,157 dead, 4,846 wounded and 185 missing. On 17th September the Commander of this division reported to the Commander of the VIth Army that both his infantry regiments were practically destroyed. As early as 7th October out of his 220 tanks he had only 42 left. After two months' fighting and without achieving the capture of the city the Germans had lost 59,000 killed, 525 tanks, 280 guns and 4,070 mortars.

German soldiers' letters reflected their morale following these butcheries. Gefreiter Walter writes : ' Stalingrad is hell on earth. It is another Verdun, a red Verdun with modern weapons. Each day we attack. If we gain twenty metres in the course of the morning the Russians throw us back in the evening.'

General von Gablentz, commanding the 389th German Infantry Division writes : ' We are going through a grave crisis. In my humble opinion it resembles what happened at Moscow a year ago '.

Morale deteriorated more quickly still in the Allied Army, particularly so in the Rumanian Army where discipline was getting lax. A German staff officer seconded to the 4th Rumanian Infantry Division reported to his chiefs : ' The men's morale is very low. Both men and officers fail to understand why they must take part in the Volga Battles. The division's fighting capacity is somewhat limited '. On the other hand the will to conquer only increased in the Soviet ranks. It was expressed in a letter written to Stalin by the officers and men of the Stalingrad front on the occasion of the 25th anniversary of the October Revolution. ' We are writing to you at the height of the battle amid the deafening noise of gunfire, the roaring of aircraft and in the light of fires on the steep banks of the great Russian river Volga. We are writing to tell you and through you the whole Soviet people that our morale is stronger than ever and our will firm. Our arms are never tired of beating the enemy. We are determined to hold on till death before the walls of Stalingrad. In fighting before Stalingrad we realize that we are not fighting for the city of Stalingrad alone. At Stalingrad we are defending our Country, we are defending everything we hold dear and without which we could not live. Here at Stalingrad this question is being decided for the Russian people : to be free or not to be free. In sending you this letter from the trenches we swear to you that we shall defend Stalingrad to the last drop of our blood, to our last breath, to our last heartbeat. We shall not let the enemy reach the Volga '.

Stalin replied to this letter by his proclamation of 7th November, 1942 listened-in to by the defenders of Stalingrad which recalled the one he made a year before in Red Square to the troops which a few hours later were going to face the enemy at Moscow. ' The enemy has learnt at its expense the Red Army's capacity for resistance. It still has to meet its smashing blows '.

Vassili Zaitsev, a crack shot, on receiving a medal said, ' For us soldiers of the 62nd Army there is no land beyond the Volga '. These words were to become the password of the 62nd Army whose many heroic deeds became legendary. Thirty-three men under Lieutenant Strekov and political instructor Eftifeiev, unaided, stopped an infantry attack supported by 70 tanks, One hundred and fifty Germans were killed, 27 tanks detroyed. Aleinikov, Boloto and Samoilov, soldiers of Belikov's Guard, repulsed an attack by 30 German tanks and destroyed fifteen. Quartermaster-sergeant Khvostantsof, having destroyed four tanks, rushed at a fifth with a grenade and was blown up with it.

According to Colonel Boldiriev, German losses at Stalingrad from mid-July to 19th November amounted to 180,000 killed, 1,500 tanks, 1,000 guns and 1,337 planes.

Envelopment of the IVth Armoured Army and the VIth German Army in front of Stalingrad

1. *Preparation*

During the whole of the defence of Stalingrad, the Soviet Command, making a rough plan of its future manoeuvre, had kept in mind the possibility of an offensive launched from the two vast bridgeheads of Serafimovitch and Serotinskaia on the south bank of the Don, north-west of Stalingrad, which they still retained. As early as September it was, in fact, getting forces ready intended for this action. The problem of their concentration was difficult if it was not to jeopardize the maintenance of the defensive battle by means of the only two available railroads, Saratov to Kamichine and Baskountchak to Akhtouba. Certain units were brought by water on a journey of three to four hundred kilometres. To maintain the element of surprise the absence of cover demanded night travel, a strict discipline and thorough camouflage. About mid-November the set-up was complete, the Germans had noticed nothing.

2. *The enemy* (Sketch No. 10)

Over a stretch of five hundred and fifty kilometres, from Verkh Mamoun on the Don to Our Menderte, a hundred kilometres south-east of Khanata, the Germans had forty-eight divisions : thirty-six infantry divisions, five armoured and three motorized divisions, four cavalry divisions and Richt-hoffen's IVth Air Fleet, 4th, 6th and 8th Air Corps. The disposition was characterized mostly by the concentration of two German Armies, the VIth and IVth, before Stalingrad and to the north-west of the city, whereas the allied troops guarded the flanks, the IIIrd Rumanian Army and the VIIIth Italian Army in the north, the 6th Rumanian Army Corps and the 4th Rumanian Cavalry Corps in the south. Let us note also the weakness of the reserves, eight divisions, three of which were armoured, behind the IIIrd Rumanian Army, and the VIIIth Italian Army. Despite the scope of the Soviet's preparations these troops did not expect an attack ; had not a proclamation from Hitler stated in October ? 'The Russian Armies, now considerably reduced after the recent battles, will not be able to engage forces during the winter 1942-43 on the same scale as they did last year '.

3. *The Soviet plan* (Sketch No. 11)

Two representatives of the Headquarters Staff, Generals Zhukov and Vassilevski, had perfected the plans and directed the preparations. General Vassilevski was to conduct the operation. He deployed on three fronts—on the left the Stalingrad front with General Eremenko ; in the centre the Don front with General Rokossovski ; on the right the newly constituted south-west front commanded by General Vatoutine.

The plan consisted of a double attack on the north-west and in the south of Stalingrad to encircle the main body of German forces. The main break-through was to be south of Serafimovitch, entrusted to Vatoutine's left with three armoured corps and three cavalry corps, and a second between Stalingrad and Lake Barmastsak, carried out by two motorized corps and one cavalry corps. After the break-through the tanks would link up at Kalatch. Outside the sectors of attack the troops would contain the enemy.

4. *The break-through and the encircling manoeuvre* (Sketch No. 12)

The attack was launched at 0830 hrs on 19th November in the north and on the 20th in the south. In the north the artillery preparation lasted seven and a half hours, there were 70 guns to the kilometre, including heavy mortars. The troops showed an extraordinary enthusiasm. The 76th Infantry Division attacked to the sound of the division's band. As early as the first evening, tanks, armoured vehicles and cavalry poured into the breaches and on the 22nd, after fighting their way over a hundred kilometres, the tanks were fighting the enemy for the Don passages.

In the south also the break-through succeeded on the 20th and mobile units rushed into the breach. The left reached a point between Lake Tsatsa and Lake Barmantsak, overthrew the enemy's reserves, covered a hundred kilometres and advanced to the Sovietski area. On the 23rd the mobile forces of the south-west front and those of the Stalingrad front linked up towards Kalatch, Sovietski. Behind them the infantry consolidated the positions and completed the encirclement. The covering units on the flanks fought stiff battles against the German reserves on the rivers Tchir (south-west front) and Aksai (Stalingrad front). Until 23rd November the fighting continued in the defence zone against the units which had been overtaken or encircled. At the same time the right of the Don front fought fiercely to cover the left of the south-west front. Four and a half days after the launching of the offensive the goal was reached and twenty-two German divisions (330,000 men) with a huge amount of material were surrounded.

The actual operation had destroyed fourteen divisions (eleven infantry divisions, two armoured divisions and one cavalry division) and cost the Germans 95,000 casualties, 7,200 prisoners, 1,780 tanks, 2,830 guns and 134 planes.

From the 24th to the 30th November the Soviet troops tightened the circle, and by the beginning of December its line ran through Kouporosnoie, Elkhi, Popov, Tsibenko, Rakotino, Sovietski, Marinovka, Hills 121, 3-135, 0, Erzovka Rinok. Now the Soviet long range artillery could reach all round the twenty-two divisions concentrated in an aera of 1,500 square kilometres.

From forty to a hundred and forty kilometres separated the encircling line from the remainder of the Soviet front set up on the rivers Krivaia, Tchir and Aksai. Minefields and barbed wire entanglements had been established round the circle to prevent any sorties and marked a kind of immense concentration camp. The Soviet Command intended to prepare a methodical liquidation of the surrounded troops and to protect itself against any eventual attempt to liberate them. Until 10th January, therefore, it did not undertake any major operations but contented itself with wearing down these forces while improving its own bases.

GERMAN ATTEMPTS TO LIBERATE THE ENCIRCLED FORCES

(Sketches Nos. 13 and 14)

As his plan rested on the possession of Stalingrad, Hitler had to re-establish contact with the surrounded units as soon as possible, not with a view to withdrawing them but to keep the ground already conquered. His Order of the Day to his armies in December was categorical : ' The Stalingrad battle has reached its apex. The enemy has opened a lane for himself behind the German units and is trying desperately to recapture the Stalingrad fortress which is of so much importance to him. Under the command of generals of outstanding ability you must at all costs retain the Stalingrad position which it has cost so much blood to conquer. It must be your unshakable decision. I will do everything in my power to support you in your heroic struggle '.

The Germans assembled an impressive force together to open a way towards Marinovka, in the Tormocin, Morzovski area, five divisions (three from the Luftwaffe brought from Germany by air (7th, 8th and 9th), the 11th Armoured Division and the 306th Infantry Division) ; around Kotelnikovo, three divisions (the 6th Armoured Division brought from France, the 23rd Armoured Division from the Caucasus, the 17th Armoured Division from Briansk and the remains of six Rumanian divisions destroyed in November south of Stalingrad. But at this same moment, in order to liquidate these German reserves, the Soviet Command launched a powerul offensive from the South-West front and the left flank of the Varoneje front coming southward from Novaia, Kalitva and Monastirchina.

So two offensives were going to take place simultaneously—the German offensive of Kotelnikovo and Tormocine under General von Manstein, beginning 12th December, and the Russian offensive launched on 16th December.

The latter gradually drew the Tormocine group and prevented it from linking its effort with that of the Kotelnikovo group. Indeed, breaking through the enemy's defences, the South-West front and the Voroneje front troops advanced behind the German and Allied forces which held the large bend of the Don.

On 30th December the south-west front reached a line covering Kautenirovka, Millerovo, Morozovski, after having advanced some one hundred to one hundred and fifty kilometres and having destroyed the remains of the VIIIth Italian Army and the IIIrd Rumanian Army as well as several German divisions, either reserves of the South Army Group or brought from Western Europe.

For its part the left of the Voroneje front, reinforced with artillery and tank units, had accomplished its task in four days, had reached Kantemirovka seventy kilometres from its start line, destroyed the 5th Italian Infantry Division, the Black-shirt Brigade ' March 23rd ', the 318th German Infantry Regiment and defeated the reinforcements sent up—the 38th German Infantry Regiment, the 27th German Armoured Division, the 14th and 15th German Police Regiments and the Italian Infantry Division " Julia ". There were 15,000 prisoners. The capture of Kantemirovka cut an important strategic railway running parallel with the front from Millerovo to Ostrogojsk.

The Voroneje front's victory had the most serious consequences for the von Manstein group in spite of the latter's initial successes. It had, indeed, on 12th December after a heavy bombardment by artillery, aircraft and mortars, engaged some hundred tanks along a narrow front and pushed back the Soviet forces north of Kotelnikovo. The motorized infantry and 200 tanks were thrown into the breach and the next day advanced along the railroad towards the north-east. On 15th December the Soviet troops re-established themselves on the river Aksai. Then the forces surrounded at Stalingrad re-grouped in order to link up with those of Kotelnikovo.

Fierce fighting compelled the Soviet troops to fall back on the river Michkova but counter-attacks, supported by artillery and tanks, checked the German advance which progressed at the rate of only three or four kilometres a day. The intervention of reserves halted it on the Michkova. At this time the South-West front troops had reached the Millerovo, Tatsinsakaia, Morozovski line and were threatening the communications of the Kotelnikovo group. Von Manstein had to fall back towards the south-west with the Guard Units chasing him and causing heavy losses. This pursuit was later to change into an offensive which brought about the fall of Rostov.

During this second fortnight of December, both in the Don bend and towards Kotelnikovo, the Germans and their allies lost :—

    22 divisions destroyed (15 infantry, 4 armoured, 2 tank and 1 motorized)
    80,000 killed
    62,500 prisoners
    280 tanks, 2,200 guns, 400 planes, 7,700 vehicles.

The forces surrounded at Stalingrad had no further hope of being liberated.

Destruction of the German Armies surrounded at Stalingrad

1st January-2nd February, 1943

(Sketch No. 15)

The forces of Field Marshal von Paulus numbered twenty-two divisions : fifteen infantry divisions (fourteen of which were German—44th, 71st, 76th, 79th, 94th, 100th, 113th, 295th, 297th, 305th, 371st, 376th, 384th, 389th—and one Rumanian—20th) ; three motorized divisions (German, 3rd, 29th, 60th) ; three armoured divisions (German, 14th, 16th, 24th) ; one cavalry division (Rumanian, 1st). Nineteen were in the front line, two armoured divisions in reserve—the 14th towards Pitomnik and the 24th towards Gorodiche. One, the 384th Infantry Division, was dissolved in December. He also had at his disposal 300 tanks, six artillery regiments and two mortar regiments. The trap also closed on major transport formations, bridging units and Todt organization workers. These were to be drawn on to complete the fighting units.

At the beginning of January 1943 the situation was becoming tragic. For the last month the circle had been tightening, the efforts made to bring supplies to the troops and evacuate casualties had lost 600 planes destroyed by Soviet fighters and AA.[1] The ceaseless bombardment by artillery, mortars and planes caused heavy losses. Cold and hunger added to the suffering, the thermometer fell to 28° C. below zero. Rations were reduced to 100 grammes of bread and 30 grammes of fat. As early as 1st January all the horses of the 1st Rumanian Cavalry Division had been eaten then, regardless of hygiene, dogs and carrion were consumed. The men were riddled with vermin and typhus took its toll. By the 10th the numbers had gone down from 300,000 to 250,000 men.

Ammunition had to be used sparingly, except that of small calibre artillery and small arms which were still plentiful. Leaflets dropped by plane undermined the morale of the troops. The commander of the 376th Infantry Regiment threatened all those who dared to mention capitulation with the firing squad. In an Order of the Day Field Marshal von Paulus said : ' We all know the fate which awaits us if the Army gives up resisting : certain death, either from enemy bullets, or cold, or hunger and suffering in degrading captivity. There is no alternative but to fight to the last round '.

The attack group comprising two or three infantry divisions and all available tanks, concentrated in December in the Pitomnik, Novo Alexeievski area, was dissolved at the beginning of January, while the 14th Armoured Division remained near Pitomnik and the 24th Motorized Division returned

---

[1]Twenty transport groups bringing a daily supply of 80 tons alone lost 300 planes.

to Gorodiche. The defeat of the Kotelnikovo and Tormocine groups had been concealed from the troops.

The Soviet Command, anxious to recover the troops engaged in the surrounding of the Germans and wishing to liberate Stalingrad which was of the utmost importance for the link up with the Caucasus, decided to make a decisive end to the German troops.

It entrusted Artillery General Voronov with the conduct of operations which had been prepared by the Don front General Staff in December. Before launching them, however, General Voronov, representing High Command and General Rokossovski commanding the Don front, sent the following ultimatum to Field Marshal von Paulus on 8th January :—

' The VIth German Army, some units of the IVth German Armoured Army and the reinforcing units attached to them have been completely encircled since 23rd November, 1942. The Red Army units have enclosed this group in a solid circle. None of your hopes to save your troops by an offensive coming from the south or the south-west has been realised. The German troops sent to your rescue have been defeated by the Red Army. The remains of these troops are beating a retreat towards Rostov. The German air transport, which was bringing you starvation rations, munitions and fuel is often obliged, owing to the spirited advance of the Russian Army, to change its ground and use bases far away from the surrounded forces. Moreover this air force sustains considerable losses from the Russian air force both in machines and crews. The help it brings to the surrounded forces is illusory. The situation of your troops, encircled, is difficult. They are suffering hunger, disease and cold. The hard Russian winter has only just begun. Heavy frosts, icy winds and snow blizzards are yet to come. Your soldiers are without winter clothing and live under insanitary conditions. You yourself, as well as all the officers of the surrounded troops, realize that you have no real possibility of breaking the encircling lines. Your situation is hopeless and it is senseless to resist any longer.

' In the dead end position which is now yours, and in order to avoid unnecessary bloodshed, we offer you the following conditions of capitulation :
1. Cessation of all resistance.
2. All men, armaments and material in good condition to be placed at our disposal.

' To all officers and men giving up resistance we guarantee life and security and, after the war, return to Germany or any other country where the prisoner of war may wish to go.

' To all troops which surrender we shall leave their army uniforms, their markings and medals, their personal belongings and their valuables and to superior officers their side arms.

' To all those who surrender, officers, N.C.O.s and men, normal rations will be issued.

' Medical attention will be given to the wounded, the sick and those affected by frost-bite.

' We expect your written reply by 10 o'clock on 9th January. We warn you that if our surrender terms are turned down, the Red Army troops and the Red Air Force will be obliged to proceed with the destruction of the surrounded German troops and that the responsibility will be yours.'

This ultimatum having had no effect, the next day the Soviet Command launched the prepared attack.

1. *The Soviet Plan*

The plan aimed at splitting up the encircled forces in order to destroy the separate portions successively.

The main effort was to bear from west to east, from the Vertiatchi, Iliaronovski area towards Baburkin, Gontchara, Stalingrad. This move threatened the group which previous operations had reduced the most, both materially and morally (76th, 44th, 376th, 384th Infantry Divisions and 14th Armoured Division). These units occupied positions summarily set up after the Don battle, whilst the best troops were holding the north sector, which had been built up over a period of four months.

This plan also avoided crossing the deep west-east ravines which score the area west of Stalingrad.

Out of three planned phases the first two aimed at destroying the west and north-west groups, then the Petschanka (three kilometres south of Voropanovo), Stalingrad and Gumrak forces, while the third would liquidate isolated resistance. On the axis of the main effort, in the direction of Rogatchik, starting from Vertiatchi, Iliaronovski, the density of artillery and heavy mortars was to be, initially 165 per kilometre rising ultimately to 300. A secondary action, joining the main action, was to come from the Popov, Tsibenko, Kravtsov front towards Basarguino and Novi Rogatchik. 300 planes were to support the attack. Concentration took place between the end of December and 9th January.

On the right of the South-West front the Voroneje front was given the mission of holding the forces opposite it and, by a new offensive, liberating the Liski, Kantemirov section of the railway line.

2. *Destruction of the West Group* (Sketch No. 16)

On 9th January at 0805 hours two thousand artillery guns and over three thousand mortars opened fire while fighter and bomber squadrons appeared in the sky. The preparation lasted 55 minutes and at 9 o'clock the tanks, carrying and followed by infantry attacked. Crossing the first line they penetrated the German front. Resistance, however, increased with the advance. Outflanked bases were cleaned up with bayonets, hand grenades and incendiary bottles.

Relentless fighting went on until 13th January, the Germans offering a particularly stubborn resistance at Marinovka, Dmitrievka and Karpovka. Repeatedly the attacking troops were counter-attacked by infantry and tanks crossing from Vorochilov and Dmitrievka. Finally the west group, being threatened with encirclement, evacuated Vorochilov and Karpovka and withdrew eastwards. On 13th January the first phase of the operations was ended. The Germans, reinforced, endeavoured to re-establish themselves on the east bank of the Rassochka upon old positions used during the retreat towards Stalingrad. Success also crowned the secondary action in spite of a fierce resistance. The Soviet troops broke through the enemy defences in the Elkhi, Rakotino sector gaining five or six kilometres northwards. The Germans stubbornly defended the villages of Tsibenko, Kravtsov and Raketino. The Tsibenko garrison, surrounded, refused to surrender and was annihilated. Several times the German infantry, supported by tanks, counter-attacked. A whole German battalion was destroyed by the Guard's mortars north-east of Tsibenko.

The break-through in this sector was a direct threat to the rear of the group established on the east bank of the Rassochka. At the same time units of the 62nd Army were mopping up several districts in the vicinity of the ' Red October ' factory.

By 13th January German losses totalled 30,000 killed or wounded, 3,500 prisoners, 620 guns, 1,650 machine guns, 320 mortars, 180 tanks and 3,600 vehicles.

3. *The Battle of the Rassochka. Advance towards Stalingrad*

On 13th and 14th January the Soviet troops advancing from the west and south took the defence points of Rakotino, Skliarov, Bereslavski, Stari, Rogatchik (two kilometres south of Novi Rogatchik) and Jirnokleievka. In the Elkhi, Novo Alexeievski sector the Germans were driven out of their shelters into the desolate waterless steppes at a temperature of $-28°$ C.

On the morning of 15th January, after a short artillery barrage, the Russian troops renewed the attack. By the middle of the day they had broken through the former Soviet positions of the Elkhi, Zapadnovka sector. The enemy losses in this sector were 6,000 killed or wounded and, despite their orders, they surged back towards Stalingrad. It was only here and there that some rear-guards, utilising former defence works, attempted to contain the Soviet onrush. Rumanian units were losing morale. In one single day the Soviet troops captured over 1,200 prisoners, 200 guns, 300 tanks and 3,000 vehicles. The rate of progress had now reached eight to twelve kilometres per day. On the 16th the airfield south of Belchaia, Rassochka was captured together with 250 planes. In this hurried retreat the Germans deserted their hospitals which were full of wounded and frost bite cases.

Deeply impressed by this catastrophic withdrawal of its troops, the German Command withdrew the maximum number of reserves from round Stalingrad, including certain services, reformed the retreating units after a fashion, and with all haste made them occupy the positions which had previously constituted the Stalingrad belt. On 17th January the Soviet troops came up against these positions on the Pestchanka, Gontchara line.

4. *Destruction of the surrounded armies*

By linking-up and bringing their artillery closer together the Soviet troops took Gontchara, Borodkine and Kouzmitchi on 21st January. On the 22nd the advance started again all along the front. With artillery support the Soviet troops broke through the enemy's defences and took Voropanovo. The Germans, decimated, left the fortified Stalingrad belt and fell back on the town. On 24th January the Soviet troops reached the outskirts. The next day violent street fighting began. During the night 25th/26th January General Pfeffer, commanding the 4th Army Corps, left the divisional and regimental commanding officers free to take any measures which the situation necessitated, including surrender. By the evening of the 26th the part of the city south of the Tsaritsa was cleaned up.

Having broken down the enemy's resistance north-west of Stalingrad the Soviet troops reached the Mamaiev ' Kurgan ' and there joined up with the 62nd Army task force which had come to meet them. The main German group was now split in two ; the south units, towards the centre of the city and the north units towards the ' Barricades ' and ' S.T.Z.' factories.

The Red forces now reached the ' Red October ' factory, the Vichnieva ravine and the river Mokraia Metchetka.

Whole units surrendered on the initiative of their commanders : on 25th January the 20th Rumanian Infantry Division and the 297th German Infantry

Division; on 26th January the Army Transmission Regiment; on 27th January, in the centre of the city, the 44th German Infantry Division and the 1st Rumanian Cavalry Division; on 29th January the 376th Infantry Division. The 100th and 371st Infantry Divisions no longer existed. On 28th and 29th January alone, 12,000 officers and men surrendered. During the morning of the 31st Field Marshal von Paulus surrendered with all his staff. At 1300 hours the south group (113th, 44th, 295th and 71st Infantry Divisions) the remains of the 14th Armoured Division and the 29th Motorzied Division, led by General Reske, surrendered. On 1st February, following a concentration of artillery and mortar fire, the north group in its turn gave up resistance. It included the 389th, 94th, 76th, 305th and 79th Infantry Divisions, some units of the 113th Infantry Division, of the 16th and 24th Armoured Division and of the 60th Motorized Division. The battle of Stalingrad was over.

On 2nd February Artillery Marshal Voronov, representing High Command Staff and Army Corps General Rokossovski commanding the Don front, sent Stalin the following report :—

'Executing your orders, the troops of the Don front have, on 2nd February, 1943, at 1600 hours, completed the destruction of the surrounded enemy group.

Completely destroyed and partly captured are :—

The 11th Army Corps, 8th Army Corps, 14th Armoured Corps, 51st Army Corps, 4th Army Corps, 48th Armoured Corps—in all twenty-two divisions—the 44th, 71st, 76th, 79th, 94th, 113th, 376th, 295th, 297th, 305th, 371st, 384th, 389th Infantry Divisions, the 100th Light Division, the 3rd, 29th, 60th Motorized Divisions, the 14th, 16th, 24th Armoured Divisions, the 1st Rumanian Cavalry Division and 20th Infantry Division. The following supporting units have also been destroyed :—

(a) 42nd, 44th, 46th, 59th, 61st, 65th, 72nd Artillery Regiments; 1/97th, 43rd, 639th, 733rd, 855th, 856th, 861st Artillery Groups; 293rd Group of self-propelled guns; 2nd and 5th Regiments of six tube mortars; 9th, 12th, 121st, 30th, 37th, 91st AA Groups belonging to various regiments.

(b) The 45th, 71st, 294th, 336th, 652nd, 672nd, 685th, 501st Engineer Battalions and one engineer battalion without a number.

(c) 7th and 8th Artillery Reconnaissance Groups.

(d) The 6th and probably the 594th Transmission Regiments.

(e) The 21st, 40th, 540th, 539th Building Battalions.

(f) Numerous bridging units and other service formations.

91,000 prisoners have been taken, among which one Field Marshal and two Army Corps Generals.

The liquidation of the encircled troops being completed, operations have ceased both in the city and in the region of Stalingrad. The checking of war booty is proceeding.'

This account for the period 10th January to 2nd February was to be as follows :—750 planes, 1,550 tanks, 6,700 guns, 1,462 mortars, 8,135 machine guns, 90,000 rifles, 61,000 machine pistols, 7,369 motor cycles, 480 tractors and transport vehicles fitted with tracks, 320 wireless sets, 3 armoured trains, 56 steamships, 1,125 train carriages, 235 ammunition and arms dumps.

As early as 2nd February, Stalin sent the following Order of the Day to Artillery Marshal Voronov and General Rokossovski : ' I congratulate you as well as the Don troops on the occasion of the complete annihilation of the enemy forces surrounded at Stalingrad. I express my gratitude to all the soldiers, to the chiefs and to the political workers of the Don front for their magnificent deeds of valour.'

5. *The Offensive on the Voroneje Front*

While the destruction of the German armies at Stalingrad was being completed, the partisans' activity on the Voroneje front was brilliantly carrying out its allotted task. Spread over four hundred and fifty kilometres, facing twenty-six infantry divisions, one armoured division, one brigade and one tank group, it launched its attack from the 12th to 14th January. After breaking down the German defences in a day and a half, it reached all its objectives in ten days, destroying eleven divisions (three German, five Hungarian and three Italian), taking 106,000 prisoners and capturing an enormous amount of material. 70,000 German and Allied dead were left on the field.

During the whole of the Stalingrad battle, the partisans' activity had manifested itself more and more widely in the rear of the German armies. As early as August, Stalin had personally received Kovpak and the heads of the partisan movement and ordered them to prepare the famous raid in West Ukraine. On 6th November, 1942, these partisans crossed the Dnieper and on 18th November, the Pripet. This daring action could only take place within the general framework of the Soviet plan.

The Caucasus

While the VIth German Army and the IVth German Armoured Army were sweeping down upon Stalingrad across the Don steppes, the XVIIth Army, on their southern flank, were taking Vorochilovgrad and, on 23rd July, Rostov.

Timoshenko fell back to avoid being surrounded. Having crossed the Don the ' A ' Army Group invaded the Kuban from where it sent its armour towards the Caucasus, pushing some units southwards along the coast of the Black Sea. Across the steppes of the North Caucasus the armour covered some fifty kilometres a day. Stavropel was reached on 4th August, Krasnodar and Maikop on the 20th, Mozdok on the 25th, then the German vanguard camped two hundred and fifty kilometres from the Caspian. On the 26th the German mountain troops climbed the Elbrouz, 5,000 metres high. On the Black Sea progress was slower. Novorossisk fell on 10th September.

In the wake of von Kleist's armour, and with the greatest secrecy, came the ' Z.B.V.F.' (Zur Besonderen Verwendung) detachment under General Felmy. This force, created in Germany as early as August 1941, numbered 300 Germans who had served in the French Foreign Legion and several hundred orientals who had lived in Germany. Comprising elements from all arms, it was intended to serve as a nucleus for the German forces which were to drive the British out of the East. After serving in Greece it remained standing by for several months. Then, in August 1943, its presence north of the Caucasus was revealed through prisoners taken by the Soviet cavalry. In accordance with Hitler's plan, which looked to the Tigris and the Gulf of Persia, its action obviously linked with that of the Rommel Corps centred upon Alexandria and the Suez Canal.

The Stalingrad battle, compelling the German Command to recall part of the forces from the Caucasus, followed by the drive of the Soviet armies towards Rostov, which threatened von Kleist's communications, put an end to Hitler's dream. It was no longer a question of conquering the East and reaching India in order to offer a hand to Japan, it was now necessary to give up the Caucasus and its oilfields with all haste.

After failing in his attempt to help Stalingrad, Manstein fell back on the river Manitch, thus permitting the German armies in the Caucasus to disperse. The Ist Armoured Army and part of the XVIIth Army went via Rostov and the bulk of the XVIIth Army towards the Taman peninsular which he was given the task of holding while covering the Crimea.

Comments

A comparison between the 1942 campaign and that of 1941 is called for. In 1941 the German Armies attacked on the whole Soviet front and made their effort in three directions simultaneously—Leningrad, Moscow, Rostov. In 1942, worn out by the previous year's fighting, they could attack along 600 kilometres only, making their effort first on Voroneje, then on Stalingrad, falling back towards the Kuban and the Caucasus in the south.

In 1942, as in 1941, the Red Army was at first compelled to yield to the superiority of the enemy's resources, and waged deep delaying battles without hesitating to sacrifice the richest provinces momentarily. The chief concern of the Russian Command was to save the Army from disaster while inflicting the maximum possible losses upon the Germans. In its duration, its bitterness and its consequences, the battle of Stalingrad resembled that of Moscow, which was also a battle of attrition. As in the previous year, Hitler, for reasons of prestige, refused to admit defeat and through his obstinacy doomed his troops to disaster.

Launched on a front 600 kilometres long, the struggle ended in a cul-de-sac on the outskirts of a city whose factories and houses stretched in a straight line over 50 kilometres along the Volga. The ruins, which piled up after a few days of bombardment and fires, made a continuous anti-tank obstacle. Protected by the river, which prevented any out-flanking move by the German armour, the Soviet artillery was getting more and more powerful and better and better organized. It crushed the German divisions which exhausted themselves in frontal attacks a hundred times renewed. Winter was coming and Hitler, as in the previous year, had reckoned on finishing before the severe weather set in and had not provided his troops with winter clothing. While von Kleist's armour marched towards the Caucasus, as a year earlier that of Guderian, diverted from Moscow, had marched upon Kiev, Hitler entrusted the cover of his northern flank to unreliable troops, Italian and Rumanian, who were already weary of the war. Was he not aware that the centre of gravity of the Red Army was situated towards Moscow, that is to say north of that flank so dangerously spread along the Don over several hundred kilometres?

However, as in 1941, the Red Army not only made up for its losses, but never ceased to form new units even better equipped and better armed. For, on the Volga, Stalin won not only a battle of strength but also a battle of material. A well-supplied Soviet artillery it was which, after relentlessly breaking the German attacks upon Stalingrad, opened the way for the infantry and tanks at the time of the counter-attack. It owed its power to the immense effort on the part of the country's industry which had intensified even more since the beginning of hostilities. Had it not been for the Urals factories, set up according to five year plans in provision for the war and duplicated during the preceding year thanks to the plant and personnel in reserve in the Ukraine and the Donetz, the Red Army would have collapsed at Stalingrad.

The Soviet air force, outclassed at first as in 1941, was also issued with new material and in the thick of the battle secured the mastery in the air as in the previous year.

On the other hand the Red Army Command had used the experience gained in 1941 to good advantage. It prepared the November counter offensive with consummate skill. In spite of the tragic position of the Stalingrad defenders it was careful not to fritter away its reserves prematurely. In spite of all the difficulties it managed to conceal the position of its resources from German agents. The surprise was complete and, at the precise moment when, after exhausting their reserves, the Germans thought the last game of the year had been played, the unbeatable Soviet counter offensive was launched on 15th November, 1942, with the same suddenness and violence as on 6th December, 1941. But it would not come amiss to pay another tribute to the Red Army soldiers. As in 1941, nothing lowered their morale, neither the long and arduous retreat, nor the daily losses, nor the sight of destroyed cities, nor the lamentable exodus of the population. A year earlier they were stiffening in their supreme effort to keep Moscow from the clutches of the enemy ; at Stalingrad it was with superhuman heroism and under still more difficult conditions that they broke down the German's desperate attack.

At Stalingrad the initiative passed over. On 14th October, 1942, Hitler expressed his conviction that the Red Army, diminished through the losses it had sustained, could not undertake important operations during the winter. Now, from 10th November, 1942 to 31st March, 1943, not only were two German armies annihilated at Stalingrad, but the Soviet counter offensive extended over the whole front, winning everywhere, liberating the Caucasus and the Kuban in the south, throwing the Germans from their bases at Rjev, Gjastsk and Viazma in the centre and breaking the Leningrad blockade in the north.

The assault troops which the German Command had used and sacrificed in its stubborn effort to take Stalingrad, the key to Moscow and the Caucasus, were its best. Although able to reconstitute them it could not restore their offensive value.

In Europe and throughout the whole world, Stalingrad, after Moscow, dealt the final blow to the myth of the invincibility of the Hitlerite armies. Italians and Rumanians, crushed beside the Germans at Stalingrad, began to realise the mistake made by their leaders in linking their fate to Germany's. The hope of sharing with her the spoils of victory was replaced among the satellites by the certainty of defeat and the fear of punishment.

At the same time the Axis armies, defeated in Tunisia and driven back to the coast, were to meet the same fate as the Stalingrad armies.

The bombing of the vital centres of Germany and Italy was intensified. The conviction grew that a landing of Allied forces in Western Europe would achieve success. Very soon the German army, beaten with its allies on the Russian front by the Red Army alone, would have to fight on two fronts in Europe. Whatever she did Germany would no longer be able to escape defeat.

The European people under her yoke were shaking with impatience. Everywhere resistance movements intensified their activity. Attacks and acts of sabotage multiplied. Hostages fell in thousands before firing squads and the blood of the victims called for revenge. Before them and behind them the German soldiers felt the growing hatred of the people rising to defend Freedom.

PART TWO

The Upsetting of the Equilibrium

I.   The Situation in the Spring of 1943

THE SOVIET'S WINTER OFFENSIVE ON KURSK-KHARKOV
THE GERMAN COUNTER-OFFENSIVE (JANUARY-MARCH)

(Sketch Map 17)

THE RED ARMY had not waited for the battle of Stalingrad to finish before undertaking a series of offensives along the whole front. It had fresh reserves available which the Germans lacked both to take Stalingrad and later to save von Paulus.

In January Vatutin (South-West front) and Golikov (Vonronesh front) redisposed themselves to attack facing West. The former took Rossoch on 17th January, the latter crossed the Oskil and destroyed 2nd Italian Division. Kursk fell on 7th February and Bielgorod on the 9th. The line from which the German offensive against Stalingrad was launched had now been reached.

Further, after capturing the remains of the VIIIth Italian Army on 19th January, Vatutin's troops on the left crossed the Donetz towards Izium. They were at Lezevaia on the 10th February, Kharkov fell on the 16th ; further south Soviet armour reached Krasnograd and Pavlograd on the 20th February in Manstein's rear.

The German High Command reacted to this threat : Manstein withdrew his troops from Rostov and deployed them on the river Mius. Fresh divisions arrived from France, Germany and Italy. There were twenty of these, seven or eight of which were armoured, which concentrated for a counter-attack starting from Stalino and Dniepropretrovsk on 21st February. Popov's armour was thrown back beyond the Donetz but the Soviet troops held a bridgehead at Izium. Kharkov, attacked from the southwest and outflanked in the north was recaptured on 15th March. There again the Soviet troops had to withdraw across the Donetz but after three weeks the Germans claimed only 20,000 prisoners.

The Situation before Leningrad.   The Russians in Leningrad and Volkhov had held up the German troops facing them and the Germans were forced to give up their plans for Leningrad (Sketch map No. 6). To the rear of Leningrad the partisans waged an incessant and merciless struggle. In eight months they had derailed a number of trains, killed 15,000 Germans, destroyed 90 aircraft, nearly 100 tanks and numerous dumps. While defending the city for seventeen months under the rigorous conditions imposed by the blockade, the Leningrad troops had prepared for an offensive to restore land communications with the outside.

On 12th January, 1943, the German salient east of Leningrad was attacked on both flanks. The Leningrad front under General Govorov, supported by the Baltic fleet, crossed the Neva over the ice and captured Schlusselburg. On its way to meet it, the Volkhov front under General Meretskov attacked south of Lake Ladoga. With the aid of powerful artillery and air force the Soviet troops broke down the German defences, and in spite of very stubborn resistance took the fortified centres of Marino, Moskovskaia-Doubrovka and Siniavino station. On 18th January, the sixth day of their offensive, the two fronts linked up thus breaking the Leningrad blockade. Once more, after seventeen months, rail communications ensured normal supplies for the troops and civilian population. Besides 13,000 killed, the Germans had lost 400 guns and heavy mortars.

During January, February and March, by a series of local operations the Leningrad front improved its positions and contained in front of it the largest possible number of troops. At other points, the Russians recaptured Velikie-Luki on 1st January, 1943 and in February reduced the Demiansk salient south of Lake Ilmen. In order to maintain its strength in the Ukraine battle, the German High Command had been forced by Soviet pressure to evacuate Rjev on the 3rd March, Gjatsk on the 6th and Viajma on the 11th. On 5th March the front appeared to settle down. The thaw and wind hindered operations and both sides needed to rest before the summer.

In four months the Germans had lost 150,000 men and a large part of their equipment. Total mobilisation was proclaimed in January, and yielded another million men, whose place in the factories and on the land was taken by the foreign workers of the STO and by female labour.

Instead of bringing his existing divisions up to strength Hitler created new SS units whose loyalty to the regime was less doubtful. The High Command was very uneasy owing to the brutal measures taken against commanders who had become unpopular with Hitler.

Ultimately some forty divisions, about twenty of which were armoured, were able to launch the summer offensive. To bolster up the morale of battered Armies and civilian population it was announced that new more powerful and heavily armoured weapons would be put into service : the Tiger tank (T6), and the Ferdinand self-propelled gun to support the tanks.

For its part the Red Army continued to grow stronger. To the equipment produced in the Urals it was now beginning to add that which was provided by the Soviet-American agreement of 11th July, 1942. The Allies had delivered it under great difficulties either by way of the Arctic or across Persia. The Stalingrad victory, the relief of Leningrad and the recapture of some of the territory lost in 1942 had raised the morale of the whole nation.

Hitler expected a powerful Soviet offensive in the south and decided to forestall it. He was delayed until 5th July by the reconstituting of his armoured units, by which date the Red Army had also completed its preparations.

The German dispositions were then as follows :—

' A ' Group of Armies (Vòn Kleist), from Taganrog to the east of Kharkov with the XVIIth Army (Ruoff) and the Ist Armoured Army (von Mackensen).

South Group of Armies (von Kluge) with IXth Army (Model) south of Orel, IInd Armoured Army (Schmidt) north-east and north of Orel, IVth Army (Heinrici) north-east of Smolensk and the IIIrd Armoured Army

(Reinhardt) between Smolensk and Veliki-Luki. Von Kluge had had to stretch his front to the utmost, the average sector of each division being as much as 18 kilometres.

North Group of Armies with XVIth and XVIIIth Armies.

The means available enabled the German High Command no longer to attack on so vast a front as in previous years : 2,000 kilometres in 1941, 600 in 1942. In 1943 the two attack sectors were not more than 120 kilometres, 60 of which were for the armoured divisions. Moscow remained the strategic objective. In 1943 Hitler could no longer delude himself that he would gain a speedy and complete victory over the Red Army, but he believed the latter to be exhausted and wanted to forestall its offensive.

The Soviet salient at Kursk pointing towards Kiev between the German salients at Orel and Kharkov (Sketch 17) was an obvious sector from which to attack. From Kursk the Red Army would be able to turn Orel and Briansk in the north and in the south to outflank Kharkov and invade the Ukraine.

On the other hand, despite the defences which had been building up for three months, it seemed possible to cut off the salient from both the north and south flanks. The destruction of the forces in the sector would considerably weaken the Red Army and would make it easier than in 1942 to advance eastwards. For this operation von Kluge had at his disposal some forty divisions, sixteen or seventeen of which were armoured.

The OKH gave the following table of Soviet formations and units identified in June, 1943.

	Infantry Divisions	Infantry Battalions	Cavalry Divisions	Armoured Divisions	Armoured Brigades	Armoured Regiments
Available ..	460	234	34	?	173	87
On East Front	381	179	28		138	85

This included the NKVD and naval troops. The OKH admitted that a large number of units had melted away in the recent battle.

On the Soviet side, six fronts rearranged after the Spring offensive (Sketch No. 18) were taking their stand : in the south, enclosing the Kharkov salient, the South-west front (Malinovski), the Steppe front (Koniev), the Voroneje front (Vatutin) ; in the north, enclosing the Orel salient, the Central front (Rokossovski), the Briansk front (Popov), the West front (Sokovski).

Marshal Vassilevski, Chief of Staff to the Commander in Chief and Marshal Zhukov, assistant to the Commander-in-Chief were frequently used by Stalin to co-ordinate the actions of these fronts.

The Soviet Command had twice conquered its enemy, at Moscow in 1941 and Stalingrad in 1942, by wearing him down in defensive battles. They reckoned that in spite of the increased German power they would once more break the latter's attacks and then take to the offensive themselves. They had prepared positions facing the probable lines of attack and they were prepared to face the armoured onslaught. The forecast was to prove correct.

The battle started on 5th July and went on relentlessly until 23rd August. Between 5th-17th July the German offensive could only push back the Soviet lines north and south of Kursk 15 or 20 kilometres and this only at the cost of heavy losses. As early as the 12th the counter-offensive against Orel was launched and the town fell on 5th August. The battle for Kharkov began on 3rd August and finished on 23rd with the liberation of the city. Thoroughly beaten the German armies surged back towards the west. They withdrew up to 500 kilometres in the centre and 1,300 kilometres in the south.

II. The Summer Battle of 1943

THE GERMAN OFFENSIVE AGAINST KURSK

The German Plan (Sketch No. 19)

At the beginning of the summer 1943 three German armies enclosed the Soviet salient of Kursk. In the west, the IInd Army (von Weichs) stretched to over 200 kilometres was to hold up the enemy's forces. In the north, the IXth Army (Model) which was to attack from Orel towards Kursk included twenty divisions amongst which seven were armoured, two motorized and eleven infantry. On its main axis it had concentrated towards Glazunovka, Taguino, the 41st and 47th Armoured Corps, 5th Armoured Division, 1st Motorized Division, 5th Infantry Division, in all 1,500 tanks amongst which were a number of Tigers, and 3,000 guns on a stretch of 32 kilometres. The density per kilometre went up to 4,500 men, 40 to 50 tanks, 70 to 80 guns ; the 23rd Army Corps covered it in the east towards Maloarkhangelsk. In the south, attacking from Kharkov towards Kursk, the IVth Armoured Army (von Hoth) entrusted its main effort to the SS Armoured Corps, 48th Armoured Corps and 52nd Artillery Corps. Spread over 80 kilometres eighteen divisions were engaged ; ten armoured, one motorized and seven infantry divisions, in all 1,700 tanks and 2,000 guns.

On the Oboian road alone there were six armoured divisions and two infantry divisions making an average density per kilometre of 3,000 men, 42 tanks and 50 guns. It was covered in the east by an attack by the 11th Army Corps and the 3rd Armoured Corps from Bielgorod towards Korotcha.

The 1st, 4th and 8th Air Corps of Marshal Richthoffen's IVth Air Fleet supported this mass of 430,000 men, 3,000 tanks, 6,500 guns and 3,200 mortars. The Germans' hope to take Kursk on the 9th July, the fifth day of the offensive, was based on this large number of tanks and planes.

Soviet's Preparation for the Defence. Between March and July the Central front and the Voroneje front had been resuming their defence against this powerful force of tanks. Defence lines were disposed over a depth of 100 kilometres, cross-roads, towns and villages were fortified. In three months hundreds of kilometres of trenches were dug—70 for one division—anti-tank ditches, barbed wire and wire entangelments erected over 100 kilometres and in places there were as many as 2,000 anti-tank mines and 17,000 anti-personnel mines per square kilometre. Units and weapons were all dug in. Expecting the attack on the flanks of the salient, the High Command placed its reserves accordingly, giving the troops the maximum possible support from artillery, anti-tank guns and AA guns. Its reserve of tanks were so grouped to make the best possible use of movement. Under the personal supervision of Marshal Zhukov and Marshal Vassilevsky the units were taught to get used to the noise of mortars and gain confidence in their fighting equipment by seeing tanks passing to and fro over them while they were in their trenches.

Ceaseless reconniassance crowned these three months' day and night labour by exposing the enemy's intentions and the approximate date of attack. On 2nd July a telegram from Marshal Stalin expected the attack within three to six days. Its imminence was revealed by the Germans working to open lanes through their own obstacles and the Soviet mines. At last during the night 4th/5th some prisoners announced it as due to start in the morning. Immediately counter-attacks were prepared in the threatened sectors, the co-operation between infantry and artillery took the Germans by surprise on their start lines causing heavy losses. Another result was that the enemy's artillery was neutralised and could not destroy the Russian anti-tank defences.

Such was the beginning of the attack that on the 4th July Hitler was announcing to his troops ' a general offensive on the eastern front . . . of a decisive importance, a land mark in the . . . last battle for a German victory '.

The Operations. They took place simultaneously on both flanks of the salient ; the attack from Orel towards Kursk (sketch maps Nos. 19 and 20), seven armoured divisions and ten groups of self-propelled guns, three times as much armour as Guderian had against Moscow in 1941, attacked on a front of 10 kilometres. This formed the centre of the battles which took place between 5th and 17th July in the north of the salient aiming at Olkhovatkha. The 46th Armoured Corps in the west worked from Taguino towards Gnilets and the 23rd Army Corps in the east worked from Pokhvalnoie towards Maloarkangelsk to cover it.

First Phase. Under protection of all their artillery and air force the Germans attacked at 0530 hours on 5th July towards Maloarkangelsk, at 0730 hours towards Olkhovatkha and at 0930 hours towards Gnilets. Against Olkhov-atkha the attack concentrated three armoured divisions and four infantry divisions, in all over 500 tanks, amongst which were some 100 Tigers. The latter came in groups of 10 to 15 followed by Ferdinands ; then the medium tanks in sections of 50 to 100 ; and finally the motorized infantry. Under massive artillery fire the tanks tried to breach the Soviet defences. They hit the mines. Four times repulsed the Germans left on the field hundreds of dead and dozens of tanks. The fifth attack cut into the Soviet defences and broke through several lines of trenches gaining 6 to 8 kilometres. On the flanks the secondary attacks failed entirely. German losses on General Pokhov's front alone amounted to 1,500 killed or wounded, over 100 tanks and 106 planes.

On the 6th, fresh reserves renewed the attack at the very moment when General Rokossovski commanding the Central front decided to counter-attack. The fighting was relentless and the Germans lost 10,000 men, 110 tanks and 113 planes. Bewildered by the counter-attack and by the losses, the Germans did not commit their last reserves, the 11th Armoured and the 10th Motorized Divisions.

In the second phase on the 7th and 8th July, the Germans continued their efforts towards Olkhovatkha and Poniri. Before Poniri, an important centre of resistance on the Kursk railway, the units which, on the evening of the 7th had reached the northern outskirts, were thrown back on the morning of the 8th by a counter-attack. German losses mounted to 42,000 men and over 800 tanks or self-propelled guns. With their offensive capacity destroyed and their local reserves exhausted, the Germans returned to the defensive on the evening of the 8th.

In the third phase, from the 9th to 15th July, the Central front prepared a counter offensive, which was launched in the early morning of 15th July. With strong artillery and air force support, the right flank of this front reduced the salient made by the German advance and recovered its original positions. This action was helped by the offensive on the West and Briansk fronts, launched towards Orel on the 12th July.

The Attack upon Bielgorod-Kursk (Sketch No. 21). The battles of the IVth Armoured Army went on without a break from the 4th to the 23rd

July and stretched over a front 100 kilometres long and 35 kilometres deep. The SS Armoured Corps, the 48th Armoured Corps, and the 52nd Army Corps led the attack and came from Borissovka, Tomarovka and Kazatskoie on the Bielgorod, Oboian road. They first met Marshal Tchistiakov's Guard units and then General Katukov's tanks. In the east another group, consisting of the 3rd Armoured Corps and the 11th Army Corps attacked from Bielgorod towards Korotcha and met General Choumlov's Guard units. In the west four armoured divisions and two infantry divisions were engaged on a stretch of 40 kilometres around Krasnopolie. The main battle consisted of small battles as follows : from the 4th to the 9th, battles in the direction of Oboian and Korotcha ; from the 10th to the 12th, the battles of Prokhorovka; from 13th to the 15th battles towards Leski, Gostitchevo and Chakhovo ; finally from the 17th to the 23rd there was a Soviet counter-offensive which restored the situation. On the 4th July at 0016 hours and after 10 minutes' preparation a German division, supported by 100 tanks attacked Tomarovka. The battle continued during the night and on the morning of the 5th, the main forces started with 1,000 tanks, 700 of which were on the Oboian road. This attack met General Tchistiakov's troops whilst their units advanced upon Korotcha. In spite of the heavy forces in the action, no result was reported from either side. Everywhere artillery fire, dug-in tanks, grenades and fire bottles destroyed tanks, at one point as many as 12. The Germans gained only 3 to 4 kilometres in their first effort and this advance cost them 10,000 men, 200 tanks and 180 guns. On the 7th and 8th July, having received new reinforcements they renewed their attacks on Sirtsevo, Iakovlevo, Loutchki front. They now met General Katikov's armour, and photographs taken at 1615 hours on the 7th July showed 200 German tanks in flames.

On the 8th July the Germans committed the SS Armoured Corps and 48th Armoured Corps on a new attempt to break through towards Oboian. After five days fierce fighting they had advanced 35 kilometres and reached Gertsovka, Zacidivka, Sirtsevo, Kotchetovka, Bororaditskoie line. Nowhere did they come across unoccupied ground. Each night the Soviet reserves occupied previously prepared positions so that next day the Germans would have to fight another battle to attempt a break through. Also the Soviet troops often attacked the flanks and rear of the German main body. To meet these threats the Germans were obliged to divert troops that would otherwise have been used in the main attacks. In the evening of the 9th, pausing for breath, the Germans gave up the idea of breaking through direct to Kursk via Oboian. All the reserves of the IVth Armoured Army had been used.

Before Korotcha the same sort of resistance under General Chonnilov fiercely defended each height, ravine and kolkhoz against the 3rd Armoured Corps and 11th Army Corps. As early as 8th July the Germans contented themselves with widening the Melekhovo pocket towards the east.

In the second phase the German Command modified its plan and tried to break through in a double attack ; one towards Prokhorovka with the force originally directed on Oboian and the other starting from Malekhovo with the 3rd Armoured Corps and 11th Army Corps originally going for Korotcha. Marshal Vassilevski from the Headquarters staff commanded all the Russian troops in the Prokhorovka area.

On 11th July after slight progress from the south and east towards Prokhorovka the Germans intended to try again the next day, but in the course of the morning the Russians launched a powerful counter-attack with General Rotmistrov's Guard units. Over 1,500 tanks and a large number of aircraft fought a battle of unprecedented fury. During the day over 400 German tanks were destroyed, and the offensive had been definitely checked. On this 12th July, a crucial date in the summer campaign of 1943, the Red Army, taking the initiative, went over to the offensive in the direction of Orel.

In the third phase, from 13th to the 15th the Germans wanted to widen the pocket created by their advance and tried to surround the Soviet units in the salient south of Chakhovo. They failed and on the 16th they went on the defensive on the Voroneje front.

In the fourth phase, early on the 17th the left flank of the Voroneje front attacked the forces which had breached the Soviet defences and by the 23rd had completely recovered the ground which had taken the IVth German Armoured Army ten days' fighting to win.

The unsuccessful offensive against Kursk from the 5th to 23rd cost the Germans 70,000 men killed or wounded, nearly 3,000 tanks, over 1,000 guns of which 850 were self propelled, 1,400 planes and over 5,000 vehicles. The 3rd Armoured Division at the beginning of the attack numbered 300 tanks, and 180 men to each motorized company and, according to prisoners, it now had only 30 tanks, and 40 men per company. The 17th Armoured Division engaged on 16th July had only 60 tanks left and the 19th had fewer still. These losses were greatly to influence the operations of the Red Army in the neighbouring sectors.

The Voroneje front and the Central front had brilliantly accomplished the mission given them : ' Wear down the enemy from already prepared positions and prevent any breakthrough until the West, Briansk and other Fronts have resumed the offensive '. On 12th July this offensive was launched with the aim of reducing the Orel and Kharkov salients and destroying the main German forces.

The Soviet offensive against Orel and Kharkov. The Soviet offensive against Orel and Kharkov was not so much a battle as a continuous series of battles between Armies and Groups of Armies fought between 12th July and 25th August on a 600-kilometre front and which finally sheared off the two salients which were manned by insufficient reserves worn out by the offensive and were attacked on every side. The battles always took the same form : powerful artillery and air bombardments broke the German defences at several points, armoured and motorized forces were thrown into the breaches on converging ones, German *cheveaux de frise* were outflanked, encircled and reduced in spite of counter-attacks. In this way Bolkhov and Mtsensk fell in the north, Tomarovka, Bielgorod and Perissovka in the south and finally Orel and Kharkov.

Hence the battle for Kharkov was similar to that of Orel and the Bielgorod manoeuvre similar to that at Bolkhov. The offensive methods of the Soviet were in general the same as those of the Germans but differed in one important aspect ; the ideas of the Soviet High Command were commensurate with its resources.

The offensive towards Orel (Sketch No. 22). The Orel salient formed for the Germans a base for the attack on Moscow as the triangle Bolkhov, Mtsensk, Orel allowed good deployment. Orel itself, a rail and road centre, played an important part in the battle against Stalingrad in 1942 and in 22 months the Germans had made the whole salient a strongly fortified area.

First there were several lines of trenches covered by barbed wire entanglements and concealed minefields with scattered fire positions and shelters Then there was the main position five or six kilometres deep. This consisted of fire trenches and communication trenches connecting centres of resistances provided with a new device, the crab. The crab was a steel chamber fitted for firing or observation with wireless, pedal ventilator and periscope. Obstacles were cleared for fields of fire, villages and edges of woods were made into strong points. Three similar positions were built in succession by the forced labour of the local population. They all depended on the north-south courses of the rivers Vijebet, Volna and Desna which themselves constituted major obstacles. The Germans awaited the attack from the Russian left flank and had grouped twenty divisions from Orel to Kursk, eleven infantry, seven armoured and two motorized. Nine others came from other sectors and were to join the battle, notable the SS ' Grosser Deutschland ' Division coming from Bielgorod.

The Soviet plan for the offensive against Orel and Kharkov had already been made before the Germans attacked Kursk and the following forces were to be involved : the left flank of General Bagramian's West front towards Glinivaia, Ojigovo ; General Belov's left flank in the Gorodiche area ; on the Briansk front the adjoining flanks of Generals Gorbatov and Kolpatchka each side of Novosil ; finally the right flank of the Central front with Generals Poukhov and Romanenice.

Bagramian was to break through in the Glinivaia, Ojigovo sector, reach the Kaprivna, Sorokono line, continue south-west towards Bolkhov, there to join Belov's troops coming from Sred-Rostoki and with them to destroy the German Bolkhov group. During this movement Bagramian and Belov were to work their way on to Orel from the North. The city was to be captured by Gorbatov and Kolpatchka, the former breaking in towards Izmailovo, Viaji, pushing on towards Otrada to march southwest along the west bank of the Oka. The latter was to break through towards Viaji and Orlovka, to work on to Stanovoi, Kolodex and outflank Orel on the south-west. Pukhov, on the right of the Central front, was to break through the Kamenka, Taguino front, push his right towards Nesterovo, his left towards Kromi and link up with Galanine's troops so encircling Orel in the south.

The attack was thoroughly prepared and strict security measures were enforced. Land and air reconnaissance probed the German defences, and the boundaries and reserves of their forces. Rehearsals were held on ground similar to the attack sectors. Sappers cleared 3,000 anti-tank mines, 12,000 anti-personnel mines and on Bagramian's front alone they cleared 238 lanes for tanks and infantry. All operations and other movement took place at night. Finally, extensive political action instilled the password : ' An impregnable defence and a decisive attack '. On the evening of 11th July, despite the fierceness of the battles in progress, Bagramian, Gorbatov, Kolpatchka were ready on their start lines while Pukhov was preparing to throw the Germans back to their former positions before swooping on Kromi.

Bolkhov Operations. General Bagramian's Advance (Sketch No. 23). On 12th July an artillery and air bombardment was launched against the main position. It started at daybreak and pounded the German defences for two hours forty minutes. At 0605, tanks and infantry attacked behind a barrage and cleaned up trenches and strongpoints whose survivors offered no resistance. At 0700 hours after breaking through the first line the tanks overtook the infantry and broke through the second line on the Fomina. The infantry followed the tanks and by 1000 hours the main position had fallen.

In the afternoon the Germans had recovered from the surprise and had pulled themselves together. Some retreating units tried to re-establish themselves on the Jeliabovo, Staritsa, Retchitsa, Slobodka line where they were joined by reserves while the air force attacked the Russians. They even organized local counter-attacks. Towards evening the remains of 211th and 293rd Divisions were forced to retreat to take up a position to the rear which they attempted to hold with the help of part of 5th Armoured Division and reserves of the 53rd Army Corps. Bagramian then engaged his tanks in the gap north-east of Retchitsa and ordered the attack of Oulianovo with a view to gaining ground towards Kaprivna. His reconnaissance in these directions was stopped by darkness. During the first day he had broken the front over a distance of 14 kilometres, broken through the second position, advanced 10-14 kilometres and reached the rear position.

Breaking the rear position 13th July. Relying on the strongpoints Medintsevo, Oulianovo, Staritsa, Retchitsa, Dournevo and Slobedka, the Germans tried to check the Soviet advance. Staritsa was attacked by General Fedounkine and Oulianovo by General Vorobiev. The position was well covered by obstacles and the ground was good for defence. Fediounkine's forces progressed in spite of heavy German fire and counter-attacks and entered Staritsa from the east. The garrison fought in the streets before attempting to flee towards Medintsevo but perished, being outflanked by the Russians, who took them in the rear. The fall of Staritsa hastened that of Oulianovo which Vorobiev attacked first from the west and then from the north-west with tanks. He exterminated the garrison. Now the last position had been forced, the road to the south was open and only the remnants of units were still clinging to a line running through Jeliabovo, Poustoi and Medintsevo. The Soviet High Command took advantage of this success by throwing a powerful force of tanks into the breach. Part of the force took Vesnini, Kaprivna and drove on towards Jagodnaia, the remainder, with the aid of infantry took Medintsevo and pursued the Germans who fell back on Dudorovskii. Meanwhile Bagramian's left flank forced the Vitebet thus widening the breach towards the south-east. In the evening of the 13th they occupied Dolgaia, Dournevo, Debri and Slobedka.

In two days Bagramian's troops had broken through the German defences to a depth of 25 kilometres on a front of 23 kilometres destroying the 211th, 239th Infantry Divisions, 5th Armoured Division and other units which had been rushed in as reinforcements. It was now possible to advance towards both Bolkhov and the Orel-Briansk railway, thus threatening the communications of the whole enemy group at Orel.

The breach widens. (Sketch No. 28). While by the evening of the 13th Bagramian reached the Tchernitchino, Medintsevo, Vesnini, Kaprivna line and Jhukovo on the Vitebet, Belov's troops had broken through north-west of Bolkhov and marched towards the south-west. Reacting to this movement which aimed at encircling Orel, the Germans withdrew fresh troops from elsewhere and threw them into this sector. So on the 14th some units of 321st, 339th, 183rd and 110th Infantry Divisions arrived and also the 9th, 18th and 20th Armoured Divisions and some other units. These troops tried to stop the Russians reaching Bolkhov by holding them at Melekhovo, Afonasova, Jagodnaia and threatening the flanks of the Soviet advance at Khatikovo to

Moilovo and Sorokino to Oukolitsi. These threats made the Russians reinforce their flanks but it did not prevent them from maintaining their advance.

Battles of Jagodnaia and arrival at Bolkhov (Sketch No. 24). The offensive against the Bolkhov Germans, directed towards Jagodnaia reached the Vitebet on 14th July after forcing the Afonasovo, Melekhovo line. On the river it came up against previously prepared positions held by the remnants of the units already defeated, and also Army Corps reserves as well as the 18th and 20th Armoured Divisions. This German resistance west of Jagodnaia covered the north-east of Bolkhov. The Soviet Command surrounded Jagodnaia from north and south, closed the ring round it while a special group forced the river towards Chvanova and pushed south-east towards Uzkoie, Gnezdilovo in order to cut the Bolkhov, Khotinets road. Tanks and infantry were thrown towards Gorodok and blocked all the gaps. The Germans fled throwing down their weapons, leaving equipment and wounded behind. Meanwhile at Jagodnaia the Soviet troops annihilated the garrison and collected rich booty.

Battle of Sorokino (Sketches Nos. 25 and 28). On the 14th General Xenophontov launched an attack similar to that of Kaprivna on Volkhov. Having repulsed a counter-attack on Retchitsa, the Soviet troops forced the Vitebet and on the morning of the 15th stormed Sorokino and liquidated its garrison. In the evening they overcame the fierce resistance at Oukolitsi and pushed on towards Kireikovo which fell on the morning of the 17th. Chasing the retreating Germans towards Sereditchi the Soviet troops arrived on the 18th on the Machok, on the right bank of which was the line which covered the north of Bolkhov. This thrust in the south-east towards Bolkhov was covered by the movement of Bagramian's right flank which was widening the breach in the south-west. Still further west General Boldino's left flank after attacking towards Zikevo reached the Paliki, Nemetski, Alekseievski line on the 18th.

Battles of Karatchen (Sketch No. 28). After their break through, Fedioun-kine's troops advanced through the wooded region between Reseta and the Vitebet where there were very few roads, roughly in the direction Vesnini, Elensk and then Khotinets. They did this to cover General Malidieu's advance in the west and south-west. Because of their shortage of troops the Germans were only able to block the roads and were surprised either on their flanks or in rear by Fediounkine's troops which moved off the road and attacked each position separately. In this way he captured the centres of Dolina, Elensk, Trosna and Klen on the 14th. Forcing the pace on the 19th his troops reached the Boukinski, Zavod, Joudre, Ilinskoie, Nizina line which with great boldness they penetrated to a depth of 75 kilometres, thus covering from the west the main forces engaged towards Bolkhov. They also threatened the Orel-Briansk railway which was vital for the Germans.

Battles South-west of Bolkhov. On the morning of the 18th, to guard against this latest threat the Germans brought the 18th and 20th Armoured Divisions into the sector with various reserve units equivalent to more than a division. The 9th and 10th Armoured Divisions arrived during the next few days. Owing to their local superiority, favourable ground and the lack of Soviet infantry which had been left behind by the tanks, they were able to push the armour back from Kamenka. Elsewhere they failed and were only able to hold up the Russian advance at the cost of heavy losses.

On 17th July General Xenophontov's troops were to thrust into the Kamenka region, their tanks aiming towards Gnozdilovo, Bogoroditskoie to cut off Orel from Briansk. Another strong armoured force was to attack towards Borilovo linking up with Belov's troops to surround and destroy the Germans in Bolkhov.

As early as the night 17th/18th a few tanks had made a daring raid to reach Krasnaia-Nov, seven kilometres south of Khotinets, and cut the Orel-Briansk railway before returning to their base. On the 18th the tanks broke through. In the evening they reached Mivrino, Boukino, Visokoie, Proletarski, and on the 19th Pechkovo, Krasnikovo. Also on the 19th Soviet troops operating towards Borilovo cut the Bolkhov to Khotinets road in the region of Roudnevo, Sourianino. The Germans counter-attacked, supported by over 1,500 air strikes but made no impression on the Soviet positions. They lost 2,000 men and 67 tanks in the Dolbilo, Sourianino region alone.

Results of Bagramian's Offensive 12th-19th July. In one week these troops had broken through the German defences to a depth of 70 kilometres, outflanked Bolkhov to the west and south-west and threatened to surround the city. Belov, who had reached Ragozina, Milchina, Novoloutovinski, Kolitcheva, Azarovo line turned the Bolkhov position to the east and south-east. The Germans had sustained heavy losses : 211th and 293rd Infantry Divisions and the 5th Armoured Division has been destroyed, the 4th, 8th and 20th Armoured Division which had been used as reinforcements were greatly reduced.

Advance of General Belov's troops. (Sketches Nos. 26 and 27). After thorough artillery and air preparation, Belov attacked on the morning of the 12th, at the same time as Bagramian, making his effort on the left from Tolkachevo to Bolkhov. By noon, after overcoming a stubborn resistance, the Soviet troops had gained two to four kilometres. Special reinforcements intended to throw the Russians back beyond the Oka only pushed them back a little. The battle lasted all day and night, each side receiving reinforcements, until a powerful attack by Soviet tanks towards Krivtsovo, Bagrinovo threw the Germans back to the south-west, threatening their second line along Rakovski, Kichkino, Novomoskovski and Korolevka. Finding themselves held up by air attacks and anti-tank defences Belov's armoured units turned on the 16th towards Doubrovski, Antchakino. In the evening they took Odnopitok, Novomoskovski and then came up against some well established German units supported by strong artillery. However they had advanced 12 kilometres and cut through the whole defences to threaten Bolkhov from the east and south-east.

Also on the 16th July, Belov's right flank taking advantage of Bagramian's left flank which was rolling up the German front before it, pushed rapidly towards the south-west. Chasing the retreating enemy they reached the Machok near Ragozina, Cherbovo. On the 18th and 19th the German efforts to throw the attackers back across the Oka had local successes only. Belov improved his positions and took Novoloutovinski, Azarovo and Slobodka.

In a week, Belov had broken through 80 kilometres of front to a depth of 20 kilometres, outflanked Bolkhov in the north and east and inflicted heavy losses on five divisions. These were the 34th, 112th and 208th Infantry Divisions, the 25th Motorized Division and the 12th Armoured Division. It was now possible, in conjunction with Bagramian, to surround the Bolkhov forces and start doing the same at Orel. The advance of his left flank also enabled his neighbour Gorbatov to attempt the destruction of the German group at Mtsensk.

On the morning of the 20th the Germans counter-attacked in force south-west of Bolkhov. The Russian infantry, supported by tanks, put up a stubborn resistance against the Germans who in the Roudnevo region were twice as strong in tanks and infantry. They yielded only slightly. During the day the Germans lost 64 tanks, 18 self-propelled guns and 20 armoured cars. The Germans committed six divisions on the next day with no more success.

Belov reaches Bolkhov and Loutovinovo. While Bagramian's left flank fought some hard battles to the south-west of Bolkhov, Belov who had over-come a dour resistance pushed on towards the south and south-west. On the 22nd he reached the city from the north and north-east. Rather than attack frontally he did so from three directions after a heavy artillery and air pre-paration. Some units reached the north and east outskirts of the city whilst others entered from the south-east. The Germans counter-attacked over and over again. Some districts changed hands several times.

Capture of Bolkhov (Sketches Nos. 26 and 28). On the 25th General Badanov's tanks were concentrated in the Gorodok, Sereditchi, Peredel, Lagoduaia region and attacked at the same time as Bagramian's left. They broke through the German defences and by evening had reached the rivers Tskan and Ors and the north-west outskirts of Bolkhov. On the 30th, having broken all resistance they reached the line Brejnevski, Bonkino, Borilovo. On the 26th Belov's troops renewed their attacks on Bolkhov from the north-east and south-east. On the 28th they captured Loutovinovo, an important centre in the south-east approaches to Bolkhov.

Being threatened with encirclement the Bolkhov forces resisted desperately. Being well fortified in buildings they met the Soviet attacks with heavy fire and violent counter-attacks. On 27th July they tried to throw the attackers out of the eastern and southern outskirts. However, the Soviet forces con-tinued to gain towards the centre and gradually annihilated the German units. On the 29th the city had been cleaned up. The next day, Belov's troops, chasing the remnants of the German troops reached the line Borilovo, Pavlovski, Podtchernevo.

Battles of Karatchev (Sketch No. 28). At the same time the west front was fighting some hard battles towards Karatchev. There the Germans had concentrated 5th Infantry Division and the ' Grosser Deutschland ' Armoured Division to throw back the Soviet forces northwards and remove the threat to their communications with Orel. Despite all these attempts, the Soviet forces held firmly on to the line Grontovski, Liessozavod, Moskovski, Jivkini-Dvori, Mal Semenovka, Alekhino, Izmorozn. They also threatened a considerable length of the Orel, Briansk railway thus holding up important forces.

Balance Sheet of the Bolkhov Operation. Between the 12th-30th July, Bagramian's left flank and Belov's troops had taken the fortified city of Bolkhov. They were threatening the essential communications of the German forces concentrated towards Orel. In these battles the Russians had inflicted heavy losses on fourteen German divisions, consisting of several thousand killed and 3,000 prisoners to General Bagramian's troops. The Soviet forces had captured 100 tanks, over 600 guns and nearly 1,000 motor vehicles. Much important equipment had been destroyed.

45

The Advance of Generals Gorbatov and Kolpatchka (Sketches Nos. 27 and 28). In the centre and on the left of the Briansk front Generals Gorbatov and Kolpatchka, on the same day as Bagramian and Belov, attacked the German forces in Orel and Mtsensk.

Gorbatov was detailed to break through the Izmailovo, Viaji front. First, he was to cross the Zoucha and reach the Dobrovodi-Protassovo region and then to direct his right flank northwards to Doumtchino to join Belov's left and liquidate Mtsensk. His left was to follow the Oka in the south-west to meet Kolpatchka. The latter was to break through the Viaji, Orlovka front, and reaching the Orel-Smeuka road and railway was to march on Orel from the south, covering himself on the Oka. Together Gorbatov and Kolpatchka were to take the city, which success General Panov's tanks were to exploit. In the east secondary attacks were to come from the river Optouka.

This plan demanded from the two groups a narrow front attack by their adjoining flanks which would diverge after the break through to put the 35th German Army Corps out of action and reach the Oka and the Optouka. The right of the Central front was to cover the whole operation from the south-west by attacking towards Kromi on the 15th.

The offensive was launched as arranged with heavy artillery and air preparation on the morning of the 12th. In spite of the resistance the attacking troops advanced step by step deepening and widening the breach. As early as 1100 hours they held Izmailovo, Ivan, Bol-Malinovets in the main position. The enemy retaliated with air strikes in groups of forty or fifty planes and with tank and infantry counter-attacks, slowing down the advance east of Evtekhov, Gratchevka.

On the 13th at 0800 hours a new attack by Gorbatov outflanked and took Evtekhov. He reached the Krasni, Obraztsovka line while his neighbours took Veselaia. The Russians advanced towards Jeliaboug, destroyed a shock battalion of 2nd Armoured Division and in the pursuit reached the line Kotcheti, Kolbaievka.

In the south, Kolpatchka destroyed the 484th Infantry Regiment of the 262nd Infantry Division, took Setoukna and occupied Borezovets. Taking advantage of this sucess, Kolpatchka threw his left flank towards Arkhangelskoie which he outflanked from the north-east and south. At the end of the day the infantry linked up with Panov's tanks near Trekhonetovo.

Widening the breach and the arrival on the Olechnia. By 14th July the attack by the combined flanks of Generals Gorbatov and Kolpatchka had made a breach of 30 kilometres to a depth of 12 kilometres. To re-establish itself the German Command committed some of its reserves : on the 14th some units of 18th Armoured Division and 36th Motorized Division and on the 15th, in the Souvorovo region, the 2nd Armoured Division. At the same time its air force was intensely active. Infantry and tanks hurled themselves ceaselessly against the Soviet flank. The most heavy counter-attacks were at Krasni, Obraztsovka, Kolbaievka and Arkhangelskoie. All failed with heavy losses.

By an energetic attack in the north-west, Gorbatov destroyed the 56th Infantry Division. On the 16th he reached the Olechnia between its junction and the approaches to Podmaslovo. Finally, pursuing the remnants of the units defeated at Jeliaboug he crossed the Olechnia on their heels and established a bridgehead on the left bank towards Alexandrovka.

Kolpatchka's offensive, restrained by the stiff resistance of the 262nd Infantry Division, 36th Motorized Division and the 8th Armoured Division in well prepared positions moved more slowly. Following relentless fighting his right reached the line Podmaslovo, Panikoviets on the 16th, thus widening the breach in the front to 50 kilomeres over a depth of 22 kilometres. They were now able to advance to outflank Mtsensk in the north-west and Stanovoi-Kolodez in the south-west.

The breakthrough of German positions on the Olechnia. The German Command had fortified the line of the Olechnia and on it had placed the 36th Motorized Division, the 2nd and 8th Armoured Divisions and special artillery forces. The remains of the 56th and 262nd Infantry Divisions, defeated on the main position, had also fallen back on this line. On 17th July the Soviet attack was resumed by the adjoining flanks of the Briansk and Central fronts. They were met with heavy fire, infantry and tank counter-attacks and air attacks. The counter-attacks were thrown back across the Olechnia by the Soviet forces who established a bridgehead on the left bank in the Arsenevo, Alexandrovka sector.

Offensive by the Central front (Sketch No. 28). On the 15th July the right flank of the Central front, coming from the Olkhovalka region, quickly broke through the hastily prepared German positions and pushed them northwards. The latter quickly called on more tanks and infantry, clung to each hill and village and increased their counter-attacks. All was in vain. The Central Front Command decided then to surround the Orel forces. It attacked again east of Orel to eliminate the 41st and 47th German Armoured Corps. On the 19th at 0800 hours Soviet tanks and infantry, supported by artillery and air attacks, broke through north of Podmaslovo. In three hours they reduced all strongpoints to a depth of three or four kilometres. Following up, General Ribalko's tanks, under an air umbrella, overtook the infantry at 1130 hours and fell on the Germans. Any planes which tried to bomb them sustained heavy losses at the hands of the Soviet fighters. Nearly 100 tanks with infantry counter-attacked but were repulsed, losing 28 tanks. The Germans threw reserves into the breach, priority being given to motor drawn artillery and self-propelled guns. Counter-attacks against the Soviet flanks were made ceaselessly. However by the end of the day the right wing of the Central Front had overcome all resistance and pushed on towards the Oka.

Capture of Mtsensk. On 19th July, Gorbatov reached the line Gorbountsovo, Sitchi, Podmaslovo. He attacked Dobrovodi and Protasovo and broke through the middle position on a 10 kilometre front. The salient thus created threatened both the Mtsensk group and the German forces engaged in the south against Kolpatchka.

Going on with his offensive on 20th July, he surrounded and took Dobrovodi by a clever manoeuvre. The garrison was annihilated. At 1900 hours the tanks overtook the infantry, cut the Mtsensk to Orel road and reached the Oka. The infantry followed up to consolidate the success. The air force vigorously bombed the Germans' withdrawal routes and Oka crossings.

The speedy advance of General Gorbatov's left and General Ribalko's tanks threatened the German forces at Mtsensk with encirclement so that, early on the 20th, the German Command ordered a withdrawal. Gorbatov pursued them and entered Mtsensk the same day. At 0400 hours on the 24th he cut the Mtsensk to Orel road towards Ilkovo, Piervi, Voin thus preventing any withdrawal towards the south-west. His troops cleaned up the right bank of the Oka, destroyed the surrounded forces, took many prisoners and much equipment, and counted 2,000 Germans dead.

On the 22nd their arrival was complete on the Oka and Optoukha in the Drobichevo, Derioujkino sector and bridgeheads were established. The Germans received reinforcements and fought to hold the last positions covering the east of Orel. The Russians after winning a bridgehead west of Voloubouevo towards Tchijovka and one south of Boatchovo faced a well organized resistance. They then suspended their offensive to bring up their artillery, regroup and reconnoitre the enemy's defences. Kolpatchka conformed to Gorbatov's moves and on the 23rd reached the line Derioujkino, Nikolokoie. In the south the right of the Central front attacked on the 21st, crossed the Netchouv and pushed on towards Zmevka.

So on 23rd July the left and centre of the Briansk front, after breaking through the intermediate position on the Olechnia and liquidating Mtsensk faced the last position covering Orel. On the Oka and Optoukha the Germans had the 30th, 56th, 78th, 299th and 262nd Infantry Divisions and the 2nd, 8th and 12th Armoured Divisions and other units and detachments. They reinforced the north and east of the city which they meant to hold and it was up to the left of the Briansk front to wrest it from them before the reinforcements arrived.

Crossing the Oka and Optoukha. Liberation of Orel. On the 23rd Gorbatov and Kolpatchka resumed the offensive, this time with their outside flanks, in order to outflank Orel on both sides. The Germans resisted from deeply dug positions and also counter-attacked with tanks and infantry. They employed large air forces and much artillery. Nevertheless on the 28th, Gorbatov reached Choumova, Savenko while Kolpatchka's right arrived on the line Gremiatchi, Southern edge of Stanovoi-Kolodez, Oloviannikovo. Meanwhile Bagramian and Belov on the line Borilovo, Pavlovski, Podtchernevo threatened the flank and rear of the Germans.

During the night of 31st July/1st August, the Germans began to withdraw their troops from the pocket under the protection of strong rearguards. The Russians discovered the manoeuvre and caught the Germans in a complete state of disorganization. On 1st August they reached the line Zaria-Svobodi, Viazki, Krontaia-Gora, Mikhailovka, Jouravka forming a half circle round the east, north and west of Orel. On the 3rd, dumps and buildings were blown up. During the night 3rd/4th Kolpatchka attacked from the east and south. Gorbatov did likewise the next day. At dawn on the 4th, Colonel Mikalitzine's 5th Soviet Division entered the city from the east, followed by Colonel Kerstov's 380th Infantry Division (Gorbatov's left). The 129th Infantry Division (General Pantchouk) attacked the southern edge.

The 4th was spent in street fighting. By the evening the east of the city was cleaned up and, forcing the Oka, Soviet troops entered the west districts. Meanwhile, Gorbatov's right broke through on the Niepolod, outflanked the city on the west and cut off any chance of withdrawal on that side. An attack by Kolpatchka's left from the south against Sakhanski completed the circle. For a further two days and a night the fighting continued in the city. The tanks carried sub-machine gunners. The infantry opened the way for them. Some artillery advanced among them firing over open sights destroying machine guns, mortars and tanks. The inhabitants pointed out any traps and the sappers cleared them. On the evening of the 5th, after mopping up,

Gorbatov's and Kolpatchka's troops reached the line Baklanovo, Krestianine, Sakhanski, Bolchaia-Bistraia.

Pursuit of the Germans (Sketch No. 28). Bolkhov and Orel having been liberated, the Briansk Front began the pursuit. The retreating Germans burned villages, blew up bridges and made the roads unusable with booby traps or delayed action mines. The roads were full of interminable columns of both motor and horse drawn vehicles. Groups of soldiers, leaderless, wandered through woods and across fields. To minimize the losses the German Command covered the retreat with shock troops, SS units and picked detachments from defeated divisions who clung to favourable positions.

In spite of all, the Soviet troops continued to advance. On the 8th they surrounded Narichkino and destroyed the garrison ; on the 9th they took Khotinets, a road centre. The Germans stood on the line Alekhino, Dronovo, Khotkovo. A tank detachment sent along the Orel-Briansk road broke through this position. On the right, a concentric attack on Karatchev carried the town on 18th August. The Germans fleeing westwards in small groups tried to take refuge in the Briansk forests.

On the 17th, 18th August the pursuit paused on the line Oulemets, Jourinitchi, Revni, Leski. This was done to bring up artillery, regroup and prepare for a large-scale offensive against Briansk. The right flank of the Central front had taken Dmitrovsk-Orlovski on the 12th and continued westwards.

At this stage the actions of the partisans in the Orel region must be mentioned: they destroyed bridges and railways, delayed or stopped German units, laid ambushes, acted as guides to Soviet forces for attacks behind the German lines, impeded or prevented the evacuation of wheat stocks, of supplies and even of the civilian population.

Results of the liquidation of the Orel salient. By 18th August, with the co-operation of the West and Central front forces, the Briansk front troops had, after fierce fighting, completely defeated the crack German troops in the regions of Bolkhov, Orel and Karatchev, and reduced the Orel salient.

In one month's fighting the Germans had sustained irreparable losses ; eight divisions had been destroyed (34th, 56th, 112th, 208th, 211th, 262nd, 293rd Infantry and 25th Motorized Divisions) ; eight armoured, four motorized and sixteen infantry divisions and many reinforcement units had been decimated. They had lost tens of thousands killed, 280 planes, 1,500 tanks, over 3,000 guns and mortars and 2,300 vehicles. The Briansk front troops alone had taken over 5,700 prisoners, 240 tanks, 1,700 guns and mortars. A number of Soviet towns had been liberated amongst which were Orel, Bolkhov, Mtsensk, Karatchev and Jizdra.

In an Order of the Day, Marshal Stalin, the Commander-in-Chief, conferred the title of ' Orel Divisions ' to the 5th, 129th and 380th Infantry Divisions which were the first to enter the city.

THE OFFENSIVE AGAINST KHARKOV
(Sketches Nos. 29 and 30)

The Situation. The offensive by the Voroneje and Steppe fronts took place from the 3rd to the 25th August within the following limits : in the north the line Soumi, Bielgorod, in the east the Donetz, in the south the line Zenkov, Kharkov and in the west the river Psiol.

From the German Command's point of view the Bielgorod, Kharkov salient had no less importance than that of Orel even after the Kursk failure. On the one hand it barred access to the Ukraine and on the other it covered the Donetz basin. Kharkov, a rail junction and second city of the Ukraine, was one of the most important political and economic centres of the U.S.S.R. The region was turned into a huge fortress and the city was protected in the north by seven lines of resistance and in the east by the Donetz and three lines. The defences spread over some 90 kilometres. Two fortified belts covered the immediate approaches to the city, which in its turn was prepared for street fighting. The most important points of resistance beside Bielgorod and Kharkov were Tomarovka and Borisovka, which covered the north of Kharkov, then Krasnopole, Soumi, Akhtirka, Bogodoukhov. The Germans called Bielgorod 'the impregnable north bastion of the Ukraine' and Kharkov 'the belt shutting off the Ukrainian expanse and the essential strong point of the south-east front'.

The IVth Army defending the salient faced the Voroneje front with six infantry and two armoured divisions, with in reserve, towards Trostianets the 7th Armoured Division. Also in reserve was the 11th Infantry Division near Golovtchino facing the Steppe front with seven other infantry divisions and some of the 6th Armoured Division. In all there were nineteen divisions, fifteen infantry and four armoured.

The Germans meant to hold the salient at all costs and, to do so, intended to reinforce the IVth Army with eight fresh divisions from neighbouring sectors or from the rear : 256th Infantry and 10th Motorized Divisions and six armoured divisions (Armoured SS, Gross Deutschland, Das Reich, Adolf Hitler, Totenkopf, 3rd Armoured).

Soviet preparations (Sketch No. 31). On 22nd July Zhukov presided at a conference at which he unfolded his plan. Three attacks were to break up the front after which he intended to reduce the elements one by one. The first attack was from the north-west of Bielgorod southwards in the direction of Kharkov ; the second was from the south of Krasnaia-Iarouga south-westward in the direction of Graivoron, Akhtirka ; the last from the north-east of Petchenegui towards Merefa. The main forces were concentrated in the Iakovlevo, Tcherkaskoie, Gostichevo region, consisting of the left flank of the Voroneje front (General Vatutin) and the right flank of the Steppe front (General Koniev). Their mission was to destroy the bulk of the German forces in the Bielgorod, Kharkov salient and to liberate both cities.

The Steppe front was to manoeuvre with its right on the Donetz. Generals Managarov and Krioutchenkine were to work from north to south on the right bank while General Choumilov with the Guards worked from the east. They were to surround Bielgorod, reduce the defences, take the city and push straight on to Kharkov, rolling up the German defences on the west bank of the river.

The troops of the Voroneje front which were to be committed were those of Generals Tchistiakov and Jadov with Rotmistrov's and Katoukov's tanks. After breaking through at Tomarovka and Borisovka, they were to push on to Zolotchev, Olchani, Valki and outflank Kharkov from the west. They were to be met by General Hagen of the South-West front who was coming from the east to turn the city from the south. The aim of his attack was Staro-Saltov, Martovaia, and finally Merefa.

Finally Generals Moskalenko, Trofimenko and Korzoun were to act as a flank guard to protect the west of whole operation against expected powerful enemy reactions. They were to attack south-west towards Akhtirka and Boromlia and working towards Zenkov were to widen the breach westwards and prepare further operations towards Romni and Poltava.

On the 2nd August, under cover of night the troops secretly took up their positions on their start lines : from Snagot to Bikovka for the Voroneje front, from Bikovka to Voltchansk for the Steppe front and from Voltchansk to Malinovka for General Hagen. The most difficult task was that of General Choumilov's troops who had to take up a position on a riverbank overlooked by the enemy. The Russians had concentrated superior forces and furthermore had definite information of the German defence system.

Breaking of the German defences and the destruction of the German forces of Tomarovka, Bielgorod and Borisovka

(Sketch No. 29)

Battles of 3rd August. At 0500 hours, 6,000 guns opened fire, starting the preparation on the main position. Planes in groups of twenty or thirty ceaselessly bombed and machine gunned previously located points, assembly points of reserves, and artillery. During the last five minutes the violence was such that the Germans were unable to open fire on the attackers. Isolated batteries which tried to counter were silenced.

At 0800 hours the artillery lifted its fire deeper into the German positions. Infantry and tanks, keeping close up behind the fire, carried the strong points and quickly penetrated the German defences. At 1300 hours the leading troops of the Voroneje front reached the Drasgoukskoie, Berozov line, where they were overtaken by Rotmistrov's and Katoukov's tanks. At 1400 hours the main body of armour swooped into the gap.

In General Managarov's sector and in front of Krioutchenkine's right flank the Germans were resisting from strong positions. The Soviet troops fought relentless battles amongst the trenches until 1500 hours. To speed up the attack Solomatine's armour was committed and broke through the main resistance.

By the evening of the 3rd the forward units reached the outskirts of Tomarovka and Domnine, pushed on towards Kalinina and Koulechovka and cut Bielgorod off from Tomarovka. General Rotmistrov's had gained 26 kilometres and approached the Saenkov, Dobraia Volia region. The infantry of the Voroneje front had broken through the main position, gained 10-12 kilometres and was now on the line Boutovo, Krasni Ostrojek, Stepnioe, Rakovo. The Steppe front took its objective on Hill 218, Ternovica, Petropavlovka after advancing 7-9 kilometres.

The first day caused heavy casualties to the 6th and 19th Armoured Divisions, the 67th Infantry Division and the 57th and 332nd Infantry Divisions caught during their retreat towards Bontovo.

Battles of the 4th and 5th August. By the evening of the 5th Katoukov's tanks were fighting at Klimov, Aleksandrovka, Odnorobovka, Gorodok. They had gained 50 kilometres and were threatening to split the defenders of Kharkov in two. Rotmistrov's tanks reached the Vorojbiti region, the woods north of Chtchetinovka, Verzonaki. Tchistiakov's infantry rolled up the front westwards and reached the line Zibino, Mochtchenoie, Tomarovka. At the same time, taking advantage of the tanks' success, Jadov's troops approached a line running through Strigouni, Koulechovka, Gomzino and Orlovka and Step.

On 5th August, Trofimenko and Moskalenko attacked, defeated the 57th Infantry Division, broke through the front over 26 kilometres from Visoki to Soldatskoie, advanced 8-16 kilometres and in the evening reached Staroslie, Kasilovo, Ivanouskaia-Lisitsa, Kazatchia-Lisitsa, Nikitskoie.

Finally the Steppe front (Managarov) had broken through two defensive lines in forty-eight hours and on the evening of the 5th was fighting towards Vodianoie and Krasnoie. Its mobile elements preceded it and cut the Bielgorod-Kharkov railway towards Griaznoie.

On the 4th and 5th August there was bitter fighting for Tomarovka. The Germans meant to use that area to counter-attack the flanks of the Soviet advance and left its defence to the 57th and 332nd Infantry and the 19th Armoured Divisions. Katoukov's tanks outflanked the city and invested it from the east. Under Tchistiakov's orders General Nekrassov reached the western edge and entered the city at 1700 hours on the 5th. Iachik pushing from the north-east reached the south-east. Finding themselves almost surrounded the Germans left their wounded and equipment and fell back by night towards Borisovka.

The Battle of Bielgorod (Sketch No. 32). The Germans surrounded Bielgorod with a fortified belt ; pillboxes on the fringes, fortified buildings, anti-tank ditches on the main approaches, mining of buildings and vast minefields. On the north and east approaches to the city the Soviet sappers were confronted with the problem of 16,000 mines. Also the Donetz was a serious obstacle in the east. Bielgorod was defended by 198th Infantry Division duly reinforced by artillery, mortars and tanks, yet the battle lasted only one day.

In the evening of 5th August, General Krioutchenkine, after breaking through north of Bielgorod, reached the line Oskotchnoie, Tchernaia Poliana. At the same time Choumilov's right had liquidated the strong point of Mikhailovka and reached the Donetz east of the city. One of his units coming from Starigorod crossed the river and reached the north-east edge of the town while sappers, working under fire and from makeshift resources, built one heavy and two light bridges. The main attack could then begin. Krioutchenkine carried Oskotchnoie, Iatchnev, Kolodez, Tchernaia Poliana. The 305th Russian Infantry Division pushed southwards beyond Oskotchnoie, took Arkhangelskoie about the middle of the day on the 6th and cut the road between Bielgorod and Streletskoie, Bolkhovets. Solomatine, his tanks having taken these last two centres went on towards Graznoie, cutting the Bielgorod-Kharkov road. Colonel Serouguing's 89th Division of the Guard, which had taken Tchernaia Poliana, outflanked the city in the west and Choumilov's units, breaking through on the right bank of the Donetz, burst into the south-western districts. At 1800 hours Bielgorod fell into the hands of the Soviet troops. There were a few centres of resistance which kept up through the night and only a few groups succeeded in escaping. There were 3,200 dead in the city and a number of tanks, guns and mortars left behind. An Order of the Day from Marshal Stalin conferred the title of ' Bielgorod Divisions' on the 89th and 305th Infantry Divisions.

Arrival at the German's rearmost positions (Sketch No. 29). The capture of Tomarovka and Bielgorod enabled the offensive to be continued. On 6th and 7th August the two attacking fronts defeated the rearguard of the retreating IVth Armoured Army and advanced 60 to 70 kilometres. In the evening of the 7th they approached the rearmost positions at Bogodoukhov, Zolotchev, Kazatchia Lopan, Jouravliovka, Vesieloie, where the German Command had hurriedly thrust the remnants of battered units and some detachments sent up from the rear. Borisovka, Golovtchino, Graivarone centres held out but on the 7th August Katoukov's tanks entered Bogodoukhov, a strongpoint and important centre of communications. They had covered over 100 kilometres and had overtaken the infantry by 20 to 40 kilometres. In the city they found enough petrol to refuel all the vehicles. When Bogodoukhov was reached the defences of the Kharkov salient were cut up and the communications between Kharkov and Poltava were threatened. On the same day Rotmistrov's tanks took Zolotchev, a big road junction and entered Kazatchia Lopan. Moskalenko reached the line Krasnopolie, Popovka, Slavgorod. Trofimenko, who had liquidated Borisovka and Golovtchino marched south-west along the Vorskla and took Pisarevka, another road junction. Finally Jadov's troops linking up with Rotmistrov's tanks arrived in the evening of the 7th in the Naoumovka Olkhovatka region. Meanwhile the Steppe front broke through the defences of Dolbino-Brodok on the 6th and then attacked the Mikoianovka, Volkovo front.

Destruction of the German forces at Borisovka (Sketch No. 33). While the bulk of the Voroneje front had penetrated 100 kilometres into the German defences some of its forces had remained behind to destroy the enemy at Borisovka and Golovtchino. These troops had been surrounded after battles fought on the 4th and 5th. The Soviet Command sent Rotmistrov's troops reinforced by some units belong to Tchistiakov and Trofimenko to help liquidate the Borisovka group. The troops thus destroyed belonged to the 57th, 255th and 332nd Infantry Divisions and 19th Armoured Division. The number of killed was over 5,000 amongst whom was General Schmitt, commanding the 19th Armoured Division. There were 450 prisoners taken and also 92 heavy tanks, 20 of which were repairable, 17 medium tanks and much equipment.

Development of the Steppe Front Offensive on Kharkhov. When the Steppe front reached the last position in front of the north of Kharkhov on the evening of the 7th, it had already broken through several successive lines. From the 8th to the 11th the Russians fought relentlessly against the enemy who was firmly emplaced, supported by a strong air force and who counterattacked continually. Some localities changed hands several times. Finally the resistance was overcome but only after very strong attacks supported by powerful concentrations of artillery.

On the 9th Managarov, Krioutchenkine and Choumilov broke through the Kazatchia Lopan, Jouravliovka, Vesieloie front. Also on that day the Steppe front reached the line Slatino, Liptsi, Vesieloie, thus finishing the cleaning up of the German defences on the west bank of the river as far as Roubejnoie. This move enabled General Hagen, who had taken over the South-west front under Koniev, to cross the river more easily.

On the evening of the 9th therefore Hagen crossed the Donetz at Roubejnoie and pushed as far as Peremoga, Stari Saltov. The next day he crossed the river along his whole front and stormed Petchenegui, an important centre.

The Steppe front had the difficult job of storming Kharkov's outer defence belt. On the nights of the 10th and 11th August General Koniev, commanding the Steppe front, tightened the blockade from the north-west and south-east and made several attacks. An important role was played by the artillery.

On 11th August the Soviet troops fought fiercely north of the city and conquered Rouskie Tichki and Tcher Kaskie Tichki. The 305th Infantry Division was engaged, supported by tanks and reached Rouskoie Lozovoie but its frontal attacks failed. Further east the 375th Infantry Division advanced through woods and after putting some units out of action reached Hill 215. In the evening the resistance weakened. Rouskoie Lozovoie fell after simultaneous attacks from the 305th and 375th Infantry Divisions from the north and east respectively.

Development of the Offensive on the Voroneje front (Sketch 29). While the Steppe front progressed from the north towards Kharkov, the Voroneje front continued its offensive in the south-west and west. One aim was to cut the main roads from Kharkov to the west and the other was to widen the gap in the German front as much as possible. To meet this threat the German Command hurriedly rushed reserves to the west of Kharkov. These were taken from other positions on the front and consisted of four armoured divisions (Das Reich, Totenkopf, Gross Deutschland, Viking) and the 256th Infantry Division, which arrived between 8th and 11th August. The SS ' Gross Deutschland ' had been opposite Briansk in the Orel Salient and had entrained on 4th August at Karatchev, detraining near Akhtirka. The SS Divisions ' Das Reich ', ' Totenkopf ', ' Viking ', and the 3rd Armoured Division which were brought into the Valki, Stari Mertchik, Lioubotine region came from the Barven Kovo, Kramatorskaia region and from the river Mious sector.

Offensive of Katoukov's tanks. Katoukov's tanks which had taken the Bogodoukhov region on the 7th were given the mission of cutting the Kharkov-Poltava road as soon as possible and continuing towards Koviagui. On the 8th May they were heavily engaged with units of the SS Armoured Division ' Das Reich ' and the 3rd and 19th Armoured Divisions round Bogodoukhov and repulsed all counter-attacks. North of Bogodoukhov the Russian tanks came up against some groups which had been despatched before Tomarovka, Borisovka and Golovtchino and were forcing their way south. At Nofo Sofievka a column of 35 tanks and 200 vehicles which was falling back towards Koupievakha was destroyed. On the 9th after repulsing all counter-attacks Katoukov's tanks crossed the Merla together with Jadov's infantry which had reached the line Bogodoukhov, Mironovka. Together they occupied Mourafa, Khrouchtchevaia Kikitovka, Alexandrovka. However, the Germans depending on the Mertchik managed to organize themselves at this point and prevent any further advance.

On the 10th throughout the day, fierce fighting went on along the river and reinforcements arrived in the shape of the SS Armoured Division ' Totenkopf '. At last the Soviet troops succeeded in making several crossings and forming small bridgeheads. The main units crossed during the night and Katoukov's tanks resumed the offensive in the early morning of the 11th. The Germans tried to resist along the Tchervoni Prapor, Marino line but at 0600 hours this line was broken. At 0900 hours the leading units reached Aleksievka, Visokopolie, Koviagui station and cut the Kharkov-Poltava railway. They were counter-attacked immediately and unsuccessfully by German infantry and tanks coming from Valki Kolomak. The Germans renewed their counter-attacks north-eastwards on Konstantinovka, Mourafa with tank-borne infantry and thirty other tanks. They attacked north-westwards Starimertchik, Charovka with another regiment and fifty tanks.

By the end of the day they had reached Katoukov's rear. Fighting was to continue until 15th August.

Owing to the importance of the Zolotchev-Kharkov axis the German Command decided to reinforce there with the 3rd Armoured Division and armoured trains coming from Kharkov. On 8th August Jadov and Rotmistrov acted together and gave battle to the Germans established on the line Zolotchev, Kazatchia Lopan who in their turn counter-attacked continually with tank support. On the 9th in the morning the Soviet forces broke the German resistance and in the evening they reached the line Rogozianka, Mironovka. The Germans held this line until the 12th. Rotmistrov's tanks were withdrawn from the front and concentrated towards Sennoie. Jadov's troops relieved Katoukov's left flank on the Krisine and until the 12th there were fierce battles on that line.

Offensive by the right flank of the Voroneje front (Sketch 29).   Between the 8th-11th August the right flank of the Voroneje front developed its operations in two directions. Moskalenko advanced towards Boromlia and Trofimenko towards Akhtirka. Moskalenko's troops reached the line Krasnopolie, Popovka, Slavgorod on the evening of the 7th and early on the 8th they resumed the attack and drove off the remains of the 57th and 332nd Infantry and the 11th Armoured Divisions. The Germans clung to the wooded hills and waterways but the Soviet troops advanced 8-13 kilometres during the day and captured the region Jigailovka, Petchini, Nitsakha. The Germans brought up some units of 7th Armoured Division. On the 9th Moskalenko continued to advance and his right flank took the important centre of Tchernetchina. General Burkov's tanks which were supporting Moskalenko, broke through, advanced 20 kilometres and by the end of the day they occupied Trostianets, a road junction, where they released 2,500 Soviet civilians from a concentration camp. The Soumi, Boromlia, Akhtirka road was now cut.

On 10th August Moskalenko threw back westwards the remnants of 57th Infantry Division, broke the resistance of the 7th Armoured Division and advanced 10-12 kilometres. He occupied Boromlia and Grebennikovka. At Trostianets his left flank repulsed violent counter-attacks from the SS Armoured Division ' Gross Deutschland '.

General Tchibissov, covering Moskalenko's right flank tried to break through towards Krasnopolie, Vierkh, Sirovatka on the 8th. However, on the 10th, he broke the German dispositions over a 20 kilometre front and reached the line Jelezniak, Bolchoi Bobrik.

Between the 8th to the 11th Trofimenko gained a brilliant success. Early on the 8th he pursued the remains of the 225th Infantry Division to the banks of the Vorskla and threw back units of the SS Armoured Division ' Gross Deutschland ' intended to cover Akhtirka. On the evening of the 9th he reached the line Kirikovka, Staraia Riabina, Koupievakha. On the 10th he outflanked Staraia Riabina and Iablotchnoie in the south and south-west and destroyed their garrisons, thus opening up a way towards Akhtirka and Kotelva. On the 11th General Polouboiarov's tanks burst upon the eastern outskirts of Akhtirka where violent street fighting took place. On the same day, Kravtchenko's tanks entered Kotelva whose garrison was destroyed. On the evening of 11th Trofimenko's infantry reached Petrovski, Viskopie, Parkhomovka, Krasnokoutsk having covered 50 kilometres in four days.

So the Voroneje front was positioned as follows : on the right it held the line Boromlia, Akhtirka, Kotelva, and its left cut the Kharkov-Poltava railway and was in the region of Visokopolie, Koviagiu. It threatened the German's rear at Kharkov and had opened a way towards Poltava.

Failure of the German counter-attacks upon Bogodoukhov (Sketch No. 29). Since 8th August the German Command had been concentrating important reserves before the Voroneje front to break up its main body progressing south-westwards and then to attack the Steppe front on its flank as it advanced on Kharkov. Operations developed in the Akhtirka and Stari Mertchik regions in the direction of Bogodoukhov and hence the Voroneje front was involved in fierce fighting from 11th to 23rd August.

Battles south of Bogodoukhov from the 11th to 16th August. In the after-noon of the 11th the Germans counter-attacked Katoukov's troops south of Bogodoukhov. The SS Armoured Division ' Totenkopf ' started from Konstantinovka and the SS Armoured Division ' Das Reich ' from Novi Mertchik in the direction of Charovka. They arrived behind Katoukov's units which had reached the railway near Visokopolie and surrounded them. To re-establish contact, Katoukov committed his reserves from Mourafa towards Visokopolie. Early on the 12th, after a night of fighting, his tanks threw the Germans out of some villages and pressed on towards Tchervoni Praper and Charovka which they captured by the end of the day, thus re-establishing contact with the surrounded units at Visokopolie.

From the 13th to 15th the German Command used the SS Division ' Viking' and two infantry divisions which tried to break through towards Bogodoukhov. Katoukov's tanks repulsed the German attacks. On 16th August Rotmistrov's tanks and General Tchistiakov's Guards placed themselves on the defensive.

Battles in the Akhtirka, Kaplounovka region. From 11th to 16th August Tchibissov and Moskalenko fought relentlessly against the 75th and 88th Infantry Divisions and remnants of the 57th, 255th and 332nd Infantry and 11th and 19th Armoured Divisions.

Trofimenko's right flank fought doggedly for Akhtirka which changed hands several times. Other units under Trofimenko fought south of Akhtirka on the Vorskla crossings in which they succeeded on 14th August. In the face of this failure the German Command decided on a new counter-attack on Akhtirka. It assembled the SS Armoured Division ' Gross Deutschland ' 7th Infantry Division and some units of 11th Infantry and 10th Motorized Divisions which were to be joined by the 112th Infantry Division brought from Briansk. At the same time the greater part of the SS Division ' Toten-kopf ' was concentrated south-west of Bolchaia Roublievka in order to attack towards Kolontaiev from the south. On 15th August Trofimenko's bridgeheads west of the Vorskla were violently attacked.

By now the Russians had realized the Germans' intentions and in their turn decided to attack the flanks and rear of the forces which were in the process of concentrating. The attack was left to Moskalenko's and Korzouna's troops which had previously been in reserve round Popovka, Pojnia, Slav-gorodok. They were to follow the east bank of the Psiol in a south-westerly direction. Tchibissov's troops were to attack Soumi to cover Moskalenko's right.

This offensive by the Voroneje front began at 0700 hours on 17th August after a heavy preparation. It broke through from Bezdrik to Veliki Istoro on a 30 kilometres front and by the end of the day Tchibissov, Moskalenko and Korzouna had fought their way to the line Bezdrik, Nijnaia Sirovatka, Veliki

Istoro. On the 18th Tchbissov continued his offensive and, after cleaning up the east bank of the Psiol reached Bititsa, Bolchaia Tchernetchina, Tokari. Moskalenko marching westward, spread along the Psiol between Pachkov and Bichkinue. Korzouna advanced 20 kilometres in a south-westerly direction and occupied the line Nokoselovka, Fedorovka, Grouzkoie facing south.

Disregarding this threat, the Germans attacked, early on the 18th, against Trofimenko's right flank intending to march towards Bogodoukhov and surround the Soviet forces in the Akhtirka, Kotelva, Krasno-Koutsk region. With nearly 200 tanks the Germans broke through Trofimenko's right and continued south-eastwards. At nightfall, the Germans who had penetrated deeply into the Russian positions, found themselves in a pocket. The next morning they were counter-attacked and lost Visokoie and Vesioligai and on the 20th they lost Kaplounovka. The German attempt on Bogodoukhov from the north-west was also a failure. The SS Armoured Division ' Toten-kopf' had attacked towards Krasno-Koutsk and on the 19th had taken Kolontaiev, beyond which it could go no further.

These tactical successes in the Akhtirka region had no effect on the general situation before Kharkov, and caused heavy losses. The Germans in Akhtirka were exposed to a danger which increased as the Voroneje front developed its offensive on the right.

On the 23rd Moskalenko and Korzouna pursued the Germans and took Lebedine, Veprik, Olechnica, Tchoupakovka and attacked Zenkov, after covering 40 kilometres in five days. Taking advantage of these successes Trofimenko also took the offensive. He beat off the forces which had broken through east of Akhtirka, pushed them back westwards beyond the Vorskla and recaptured Akhtirka on the 25th. Thus all attempts by the Germans to stop the Russian offensive and retain Kharkov met with complete failure. Between the 11th-20th August the German losses before the Voroneje front reached 34,000 men, 520 tanks, 530 guns, 140 planes and over 2,300 vehicles. Also the Soviet forces had captured 1,736 prisoners, 132 tanks, 485 guns and 60 mortars.

Relief of Kharkov (Sketches Nos. 29, 34). From the 12th-13th August the Steppe front fought relentless battles in and around Kharkov. The struggle was made extremely difficult for the Red Army because the Germans had surrounded the city with a closely knit defensive organization. Outside the defensive belts, to a distance of 8-14 kilometres centres of resistance were formed at Dergatchi, Tcherkaskoie, Lozovoie, Tsirkouni, Prelestni, Ioujni, Vasichtchevo and some other places. In the gaps there were strong points organized for all-round defence ; minefields, anti-tank ditches and barbed wire entanglements covered all approaches. The roads leading to Kharkov from north and south had been destroyed, bridges demolished and their approaches mined and booby-trapped, often with 50 or 100 kilogram bombs. Within the main defences of the city there was a succession of intermediate positions. To the north and west of the city, forests had been made into obstacle zones, strewn with mines and defended by special detachments armed with machine pistols.

The buildings comprised the nearmost belt of defence. Medium artillery was placed in the ground floor rooms and on the upper floors were machine guns and machine pistols. Barricades closed the approaches to the city which were heavily mined. The whole town had been organized for street fighting.

For the defence of Kharkov the Germans had concentrated the 39th, 106th, 167th, 168th, 198th, 282nd, 320th Infantry Division and some units of 3rd and 6th Armoured Divisions. Because of serious losses sustained previously these divisions had been reinforced and so regained their fighting capacity. Also a fresh division, the 355th, arriving from the Crimea was to be used in the Konstantinovka region. Finally, in view of the immediate defence of the city some SS and police detachments had arrived. The main mass of the artillery was disposed in depth to defend the north and east of the city.

On 11th August Hitler ordered Kharkov to be retained at all costs. Energetic measures were threatened against officers and men who might show cowardice. The Soviet troops were justified in expecting a desperate resistance.

The Soviet Command decided to outflank the city from the east and west. To this effect, Managarov's troops and later Rotmistrov's tanks were to proceed towards Korotitch to cut the roads leading from Kharkov to the west ; Kriutchenkin was to attack from the north and hold up the Germans there ; finally Choumilov and Hagen were to take the city from the east and south.

On ground, fortified as this was, the closest possible liaison between infantry, artillery and air force was required. Tanks must be covered by infantry.

Battles for the Outer Belt. On the evening of the 11th, Managarov, Kriutchenkin and Choumilov came into contact with German positions which they pierced on the 12th after a heavy preparation with artillery and air bombardment. By the end of the day Managarov had taken the following strong points—Cheptouchine, Zamirta and the northern part of Dergatchi. In the Cheptouchine Zamirta sector 1,150 Germans were killed and two heavy tanks burnt out. Kriuchenkin beat back several infantry and tank counter attacks and reached the southern edge of Tsirkouni.

On the 12th Choumilov had no success. On the other hand Hagen reduced the strong point at Kamennaia Iarouga and by the end of day reached the intermediate line on the west bank of the Roganka. Taking advantage of their local successes the Soviet troops continued their attacks on the 13th. After liquidating Dergatchi and killing over 500 Germans, Managarov reached Polevoie, Severni by nightfall. Kriutchenkin reduced some important centres of resistance round Tcherkaskoie, Lozovoie, Bolchaia Danilovka, killed a thousand Germans and captured 12 guns. The Russians approached the near belt and Kriutchenkin attacked Sokolnoki and took it.

Choumilov had now completed the break through across the outer belt in the Tsirkouni, Klioutchkine sector. He advanced toward Losevo and out-flanked Kharkov. His right flank reached the north-east edge of the city towards Chevtchenki whilst his left attacked Losevo.

Hagen forced the river Roganka, broke through the outer belt with his left in the Tchounikbine region and at the end of the day reached the line Gorbotchev, Fedortsi, Lialiouki, Vasichevo station, Vedenskoie.

Thus on the 12th and 13th August the Soviet troops had broken the outer belt and, in several sectors, had approached the rear belt, bringing the fighting to the very edge of Kharkov. They remained in these positions until the 17th preparing a new attack to complete the encircling and meanwhile driving back desperate counter-attacks.

On 17th August Hagen's left flank overran the following strongpoints on the north bank of the river Oudi—Ternovaie, Lizogoubovka, Vasichevo—

and broke the outer belt along the whole front reaching the line Lialiouki, Vasichevo.

Battles from the 18th to 22nd August—Kharkov outflanked from west and east. From the 18th to the 22nd August particularly violent battles took place on both flanks of the Steppe front. Anticipating success in their counter-attack at Akhtirka, the Germans desperately defended the Kharkov region.

On the 18th and 19th Managarov carried out an outflanking movement from the west and captured the forest mass west of Kharkov. On the evening of the 20th he reduced the centres of resistance on the river Oudi and on the line Peretsetchnaia, Gavrilovka, Kouriajanka. Taking advantage of these successes Krioutchenkine concentrated his forces on his right and invaded the city at the nearest points, the west and north-west. To speed up the operations Rotmistrov's tanks, which had been pushed into the wooded region south of Polevoie on the 20th, were given the task of cutting off the ways of retreat from Kharkov towards the west and south-west.

On 21st August fierce battles took place on the river Oudi in the region of Gavrilovka and Kadtotchi. The Russians ferried their tanks over during the night and attacked at dawn on the 22nd. By the evening Rotmistrov had occupied Korotitch and threatened to surround the German forces in Kharkov.

Hagen also had resumed the offensive on 18th August and the German Command, realising the danger of any new advance from that side, sent the 335th Division, only recently arrived from the Crimea, to oppose him. Despite this resistance Hagen reached the intermediary position Biezlioudovka, Konstantinovka on the 22nd August.

Attack on Kharkov. The break through of Rotmistrov's tanks in the Korotitch region and the arrival of Hagen near Konstantinovka accentuated the threat to Kharkov. The Germans now controlled only the railway and the road towards the south-west in the direction of Merefa, Krasnograd, and this was continuously bombed by the Soviet air force. At the same time the expected success of the counter-attacks from Akhtirka upon Bogodukhov did not materialize and, in fact, the Akhtirka group were themselves threatened with encirclement. German Command therefore decided to withdraw its troops from Kharkov to save them from total destruction. During the afternoon of the 22nd, Soviet observers discovered columns moving from Kharkov towards the south-west and it was decided to attack the city that same night. Krioutchenkine's right was to attack from Kouriajanka towards Zalioulino and encircle and annihilate the units defending the north-west districts. His left, starting from the Alexeiovka, Bolchaia, Danilovka region, and penetrating to the centre of the city would push on towards the south-west while Choumilov would outflank from the south-east. On 23rd August at 1200 hours Kharkov had been completely cleaned up. Street fighting had destroyed most of the defenders and remnants of units were fleeing towards the south-west behind the rivers Merefa and Mja. The German losses reached enormous proportions—22,000 officers and soldiers captured between the 11th and 23rd August by Krioutchenkin's troops alone, besides 78 tanks, 900 machines and 250 field guns. In an Order of the Day, Marshal Stalin conferred upon ten divisions the title ' Kharkov Divisions '.[1] The fall of Kharkov deprived the Germans of one of the mainstays of their

---

[1] 89th, 252nd, 84th, 299th, 116th, 375th, 183rd Rifle Divisions and 15th, 28th, 93rd Guards Rifle Divisions.

front. The Soviet troops were now able to continue their offensive towards the west and hasten the liberation of the Donetz basin. They ceaselessly pursued the retreating forces and this pursuit was later to turn into a spectacular offensive taking the victorious Red Army as far as the Dnieper.

THE ADVANCE TO THE DNIEPER. THE CROSSING OF THE RIVER
(Sketch No. 18)

The west front (Sokolovski) wasted no time in exploiting the victories at Orel and Kharkov and attacked along the axis of the Kursk, Smolensk railway. The Briansk front (Popev) marched towards Briansk and entered Karatchev on 16th August. The German Command thereupon ordered the evacuation of Briansk. South of Kursk the Central front (Rokossovski) reached the Desna and captured the Bakhmatch branch line, in the direction of Kiev, on 8th September. The Voroneje front (Vatoutine) marched upon Krementchoug.

The German forces of the Donetz, being again threatened with encirclement, made a belated retreat under the pressure of the 3rd and 4th Ukrainian fronts (Malinovski and Tolboukhine). Stalino fell on 7th September, Poltava on the 22nd, Malinovski and Vatoutine reached the Dnieper between the bend of the river and Kiev, and Rokossovski upstream from Kiev near Tchernigov.

In the north, Smolensk, directly threatened by the west front and surrounded in the north by Eremenko, fell on 25th September.

The Germans were relying on holding the Dnieper whose west bank dominated the east bank along almost its whole length. Rapids make it impassable between Zaporoje and Dniepropetrovsk. However, in the early days of October, the Soviet armies, in a surprise action, forced a crossing upstream of Kiev towards the junction with the Pripet, and downstream near Pereslaiev and Krementchoug. The counter-attacks launched against the bridgeheads were repulsed by the Soviet artillery and on 17th October Koniev's tanks, arriving from Krementchoug, drove towards the south in the direction of Krivoi Rog.

Malinovski crossed the Dnieper upstream of Dniepropetrovsk, which he captured on the 25th, and the Dnieper obstacle had given way. The Germans regrouped themselves on the line Nikopol, Krivoi Rog, Znamenka, but to do this they had to withdraw troops from the southern part of their front which collapsed under Tolboukhin's attacks. After losing Nikopol on 26th October the German troops surged back towards the west beyond Perekop. The Crimea had now become blockaded by land.

North of Kiev, Vatoutine attacked beyond the Dnieper with major forces which advanced rapidly towards the south. Kiev, having been outflanked, fell on 6th November. 20,000 Germans were taken prisoner. Immediately exploiting their successes in the south, west and north-west the Soviet troops covered some hundred kilometres in a few days and occupied Korosten and Jitomir. The Germans counter-attacked and recaptured these two cities but the Odessa-Mohilev strategic railway remained cut off.

Further north Rokossovski's troops crossed the Dnieper near Loiev and, moving upstream, reached the Berezina, which they crossed. On 25th November they entered Gomel from the west. For his part General Popov reached the Dnieper on each side of Mohilev. In the south, Marshal Koniev widened the bridgeheads of Krementchoug and Dniepropetrovsk and captured Znamenka on 10th December and Tcherkassyon 13th December. Downstream the Germans had only one point of contact with the river at Kanev.

The advance to the Dnieper, begun on the day following the Orel and Kharkov victory, had freed the whole left bank of the river in less than four months.

THE ACTION OF THE PARTISANS

In the course of the Summer 1943 the partisans in the Ukraine constantly gave the most effective help to the Red Army. Every day trains, bridges and railways were blown up, communications cut and losses inflicted on the Germans. This help was especially valuable when crossing the Dnieper. The partisans, massed in the woods in the vicinity of the bridges, prevented the last minute destruction by the German rear-guard. Sometimes also they secretly prepared the materials for the construction of rafts.

As the Red Army advanced the action of the partisans took the form of combined operations with the regular troops. They constantly harassed the Germans from the rear, setting ambushes, attacking German columns and holding traffic junctions sometimes until the arrival of the Red Army. In two sectors they derailed no less than 280 trains.

Comments

The defeat of the attacks on Leningrad, Moscow and Stalingrad put an end to the Blitzkrieg and the war of attrition was now beginning. Kursk, Orel, Kharkov were, in fact, one gigantic wearing-down battle of unprecedented magnitude as to duration, size and the resources engaged on both sides. On the eastern front, and, in fact, in the history of the Second World War, it became a decisive turning point.

This battle, initiated by the Germans on 5th July, ended with the crossing of the Dnieper at the beginning of October after lasting for three months without interruption. It began on a one hundred kilometres front north and south of Kursk, with an attack by the German IXth Army and the IVth German Armoured Army. The Soviet counter-attack developed on a six hundred kilometres front and finally the irresistible Russian pressure affected the front from Smolensk to the Black Sea.

In order to reinforce this battle each side gradually brought up all his reserves. The Germans had originally deployed 3,000 tanks (seventeen armoured divisions) at Kursk, in the end they had lost over 6,000 between Kursk, Orel and Kharkov.

One may wonder why the Germans discarded surprise as a means of attack against a salient which they knew to be formidably organized and held by the Red Army who had had such successes in the last two years. Conversely one is surprised that, despite its superior resources, the Soviet Command did not attack but left the initiative to the Germans. The answer seems obvious : Hitler counted on a new weapon, the ' Tiger ', better armoured and better armed than its predecessors, to give back to his armoured divisions their former supremacy. He saw in the Kursk salient a huge ' cauldron ' in which two Soviet groups of armies were doomed to destruction through the gap opened in the very centre of the eastern front ! The ' Tigers ' would sweep down upon Moscow in a lightning raid.

61

The Soviet Command, for its part, placed every confidence in its artillery whose resources had increased tenfold since the battle of Moscow. It remained convinced that if an attack by tanks was detected in time and came up against a defence sufficiently dense, entrenched and disposed in depth, it was doomed to failure. It was a question of reproducing, as soon as the German offensive started, the victories gained in 1941 and 1942 at Moscow and Stalingrad after hard retreats.

Hitler betted on his tanks, Stalin on his artillery. Never were there so many guns on such a narrow front. Never was there a defence system so powerful or so deep. For three months the Red soldiers had been shifting soil, digging trenches, anti-tank ditches, shelters and laying mines. The forecasts as to the direction of the effort and the launching of the attack proved to be accurate. On 5th July everything was ready.

The artillery hinged on three echelons—on the first line the anti-tank guns, reinforced by guns of all calibres, were to destroy on sight the enemy tanks as soon as they appeared ; on the second line groups ensured direct support for the infantry ; on the third line a combined action in which artillery regiments or even divisions could, owing to their range and their firing positions, concentrate their fire on any one point of the battlefield either to break a tank attack or to support a counter-attack. The density of this artillery reached 290 guns per kilometre in places. Stalin, however, did not rely entirely on his guns ; he also deployed armoured divisions which were to overcome the German armoured divisions when these had been tired by the anti-tank guns and the artillery. If the enemy tanks succeeded in breaking through the first line Soviet tank units would come in the shortest possible time to reinforce the second line, their weapons being concealed in pits already dug which constituted so many well camouflaged firing points. That does not mean to say that these tanks were sacrificed ; they remained available at any moment for local counter-attacks, whilst the general counter-attack was left to armoured corps in general reserve massed on the enemy's flanks.

On 11th July, 1,500 tanks were used by General Vassilevski south of Kursk and definitely checked the pressure of the main German group which lost 400 tanks in one day. The offensive by the IXth Army north of Kursk failed under similar conditions. On both flanks of the salient the Germans surged back on their starting bases.

The Red Army had done more than merely save Kursk, it had broken the offensive capacity of the German armoured army by destroying, in less than three weeks (between 5th and 23rd July) 3,850 tanks and self-propelled guns. Once the balance had been upset, Russian armour could rush upon Orel and Kharkov and the remaining German armour could only just manage to check it. Short and powerful artillery preparations opened breaches through which they rushed to threaten the communications of the defenders of Orel and Kharkov, the two mainstays of the Ukraine front.

In order to avoid being encircled the Germans attacked the enemy flanks with what remained of their fighting armoured formations. In this way on 20th July they repulsed Bagramian's tanks on their way to Khotinets and they were not able to resume the offensive until five days later. In the same way on 10th August at Akhtirka and on the 11th south of Bogodoukhov, some fierce Panzer counter-attacks encircled the Russian armoured vanguard for a while, but as soon as the infantry came up the attack collapsed under the combined pressure of the Soviet forces.

The picture of these operations appears somewhat muddled, their chronological report in which attack follows attack and counter-attack follows counter-attack is somewhat tedious. The Soviet attacks took place as in a well prepared scenario within the initially planned framework. There was no question of a brilliant victory revealing really new conceptions ; the Red Army had become a powerful machine with well co-ordinated parts, each section of which had been ground smooth by hard wear.

After the failure at Kursk the most violent German counter-attacks were no more than interruptions. The front had collapsed. Kharkov had only been liberated for a few weeks when the Dnieper was reached and crossed. The irreparable failure in the Summer 1943 in the Ukraine indicated how powerless the Germans now were to force the issue and even to hold the Soviet attack. Until then Hitler had been able to blame his defeats on the Russian winter—success was to return each summer, but this time his armoured divisions, decisively stopped, saw themselves forced back to their starting bases after sustaining heavy losses while the Soviet counter-attacks ceaselessly following upon German attacks, proved irresistible.

With the mobilization of January 1943, Germany had made her maximum effort. She had played all her trump cards and hopelessly lost the game on the Eastern Front. This fact forced itself upon Hitler and his satellites at the time when in Western Europe the threat of an Allied landing was becoming more definite.

Soviet superiority showed itself in every field : the enemy plans were discovered in time ; the defence system was deep and powerful and doomed the German armoured attacks to defeat ; the onslaught of the Panzers with air support, which had gained the Wehrmacht its lightning victories on every European front, was no longer sufficient to force the issue. At Moscow, Stalingrad and Kursk the Soviet guns triumphed over the Hitlerite tanks, the failure of the ' Tigers ' at Kursk in 1943 recalling to mind that of the ' Panthers ' at Moscow in 1941. The Red Army continued increasing its resources, perfecting the use of new weapons, combining speed and power, co-ordinating its weapons to the best advantage and having once regained the initiative maintained the offensive without weakening.

The Germans remained relentless in their resistance. Disliking a policy of static defence they continually counter-attacked, a policy which bought any new ground at a very high price. The Red Army, however, had the resources required to maintain an attack and launch new ones, whilst the German reserves, thrown backwards and forwards from one sector to another, got thinner every day.

Soviet strategy was based on the unquestionable superiority of resources, demonstrated in the case of the 6,600 guns supporting the attack against the northern flank of the Kharkov salient, or of Bielgorod, attacked by three Soviet divisions and defended only by one reinforced German division. The superiority of forces, tanks, guns, planes was at this time with the Red Army and remained so.

The battle of the Summer 1943 foreshadowed that of 1944 when, facing the Allied landings in the west, the German army was to receive blows from the Red Army dealt in succession not only on a six hundred kilometre front as in 1943, but on nearly three thousand kilometres from the Black Sea to the White Sea.

PART THREE

The Withdrawal
1944

Situation of the Front at the Beginning of 1944

OUTLINE OF THE OPERATIONS

(Sketches Nos. 35 and 36)

AFTER ITS VICTORIES at Kursk, Orel and Kharkov, the Red Army had advanced towards the west, gaining 500 kilometres in the centre, 1,300 kilometres in the south, liberating the Ukraine east of the Dnieper and establishing large bridgeheads in the west at Kiev and Dniepropetrovsk. The front then ran through the river Svir, Mga, Tchoudovo, Staraia Roussa, Nevel, Gomel, Obroutch, Fastov, Tcherkassi, Zaporojie and the course of the Dnieper down to the Black Sea.

According to Soviet estimates, the German army had, in 1943, lost 1,800,000 dead and a huge amount of material. In spite of its own losses the Red Army had a definite advantage. All the more so as the Germans, who since 1941 had been able to engage nearly all their forces against the U.S.S.R., now, with diminished resources, had to sustain the combined attacks of the Allies in the east, south and west against 'fortress Europe'.

The OKW had 376 divisions out of which 257 were engaged on the Russian front, i.e., 207 German and 50 Finnish, Rumanian or Hungarian.[1] Out of thirty armoured divisions twenty-five were fighting on the eastern front. The distribution of these forces was as follows :—

In North Finland, Karelia and the Karelian Isthmus—the XXth German Army of Lapland and the Finnish Army.

On the banks of the Gulf of Finland, in front of Leningrad and further south on the Uritsk, Novgorod, Veliki Louki front—the Northern Group of armies of General Kuchler comprising the XVIIIth and XVIth Armies (the sector for each division was 20 kilometres).

On the Nevel, Vitebsk, Orcha front and as far as the Pripet—the centre group of armies under von Busch comprising the IIIrd Armoured Army and the IVth, IXth and IInd Armies (the sector for each division being 24 kilometres).

South of the Pripet as far as Kazatine—the southern group of armies of Manstein[2] comprising the IVth and Ist Armoured Armies and the Ist Hungarian Army.

Further south on the Bielaia Tserkov, Kirovgrad, Kherson front—the southern group 'A' of Kleist comprising the VIIIth and VIth German Armies and the IIIrd Rumanian Army.

---

[1] A document of the OKW dated November 1943, quoted by Jodl, admits the presence on the Eastern Front of two hundred German divisions, ten Rumanian, six Hungarian—representing 4,183,000 men, out of which 3,900,000 were Germans (without counting the Finns).

[2] The southern group of armies later became the northern Ukraine group and came under General Model, while the southern group 'A' became the southern Ukraine group of armies under General Schorner.

At the rear in the Jassy region—the IVth Rumanian Army. Finally, in the Crimea—the XVIIth German Army. In all fourteen armies—eleven German (three armoured), two Rumanian, one Finnish, to which must be added the Hungarian forces and the Spanish ' Blue ' Division.

Hitler's High Command expected the Red Army to resume the offensive in 1944 against the German right flank. It therefore massed its reserves on that side.

Facing the German army the Red Army was organized on twelve fronts which, according to German data, represented 460 infantry divisions, 234 infantry brigades, 34 cavalry divisions, 173 armoured brigades and 87 armoured regiments.

From north to south the lay-out was as follows : North of Lake Lagoda—the Karelia front. Round Leningrad, holding the sector of the Karelian Isthmus and maintaining the defence west, south and east of Leningrad—the Leningrad front. Between Lake Lagoda and Lake Ilmen—the Volkhov front. From Lake Ilmen to the region east of Vitebsk—the two Baltic fronts. Between the region east of Vitebsk and the region south of Mozir—the three White Russian fronts. From the region south of Mozir to the Black Sea—the four Ukrainian fronts.

Stalin's order of 1st March, 1944, gave the Red Army the task of ' freeing the Soviet territory from the Fascist invaders and restoring the frontiers of the U.S.S.R. over their whole length from the Black Sea to the Sea of Barentz, then to follow on the heels of the wounded German beast and finish it off in its own lair to remove the threat of enslavement which weighed upon the U.S.S.R.'.

Owing to the extent of the front as well as the depth and speed of the advance, the operations were to be on an unprecedented scale. The execution of the Soviet plan entailed ten large scale operations without German Command ever being able to resume the initiative lost in 1943 after the Kursk defeat.

In January-February the relief of Leningrad brought about the collapse of the northern flank of the East front. It uncovered White Russia and the Baltic States.

In February-March the German front was split up by their defeat on the right bank of the Dnieper by the Ukraine front. This prepared the way in White Russia for the offensive towards Lwov and Jassy-Kichinev.

In April-May the defeat of the German and Rumanian Armies in the Crimea and at Odessa disengaged the southern flank of the Red Army, freed the two big Soviet ports on the Black Sea and left Rumania and Bulgaria open.

In June-July the defeat of the Finnish army of Karelia removed all danger to Leningrad and freed the communications of the U.S.S.R. with the White Sea.

In June-July also, the defeat of the German armies in White Russia opened the road to the Baltic States, Poland and East Prussia.

In July-August the victory of the 1st Ukrainian Front and the left of the 1st White Russian Front over the Northern Ukraine group, freed West Ukraine and part of Poland. The Soviet troops reached the Vistula and set up a bridgehead, the starting base of the 1945 offensive.

In August the victory of Jassy, Kichinev brought about the defection of two satellites of the Axis, Rumania and Bulgaria. It opened a road for a new encirclement of the German right flank and placed the southern German ' glacis ', Hungary, Austria, Czechoslovakia, within reach of the Red Army.

In September-October the defeat of the Northern Group in the Baltic States completed the liberation of Soviet territory and drove 30 German divisions back to the sea between Toukoum and Libau.

Between September and December the battle of Hungary put that country, Germany's last ally, out of action. It also enabled the Red Army to go to the help of Czechoslovakia and Yugoslavia, to reach Austria and attack Germany from the south after depriving her of a large part of her industrial resources.

Finally in October the defeat of the XXth German Army of Lapland deprived Germany of the two naval bases of Petchanga (Petsamo) and Kirkenes, from which the Arctic supply route to the U.S.S.R. had been threatened.

Ten Battles of Destruction

1. THE RELIEF OF LENINGRAD (JANUARY-FEBRUARY 1944) (Sketch No. 37)—THE SITUATION AT THE END OF 1943

During the summer the Germans expected to attack from Siniavino, reach Lake Ladoga and close the blockade. Having been warned, the Russians launched a preventive attack in July to destroy the German reserves and improve the position of Siniavino. Although the Germans reinforced the seven divisions already in the sector with four new ones (in all one third of the forces deployed between Leningrad and Novgorod), the Soviet troops achieved their objective, the German losses numbering 45,000 men. The Baltic fleet had sunk 54 German transports and in nine months fighter planes of the Leningrad front had brought down 1,000 planes. At the end of 1943 the front presented the following aspect :—

West of the city, on the Gulf of Finland, a strip of land, known as ' the small ground' was retained thanks to the heroic resistance of the coastal forces. It included Oranienbaum and extended westwards as far as Kernovo on the Gulf of Kopor, and eastwards to the outskirts of Peterhof. To the east the front was arc-shaped, running through Ligovo, Pulkhovo, Iam-Ijora, Kvanovskoie and then following the north bank of the Neva : further east it went through Godorok. Beyond this the Volkhov front held the Markovo, Viniagolovo, Smerdino, Miagri, Grousino, Komintern, Spaskaia-Polist, Iammo, Kholinia, Tchavnitzi (north bank of Lake Ilmen) line.

The offensive on the Leningrad and Volkhov fronts was to meet the XVIIIth German Army, twenty-six divisions strong (thirteen infantry divisions, two light divisions, five air force, one S.S. police, three S.S. grenadiers with tanks, one armoured division and the Spanish ' Blue' Division), a large artillery force including some 380 heavy guns and several batteries of 406 mm intended for the bombardment of Leningrad.

The Germans considered their Leningrad positions as the northern bastion of the front and had been continuously reinforcing them during the twenty-seven months since September 1941. The positions, disposed in depth, consisted of one main position and several successive ones, dotted with numerous works, often concreted. The second position stretched obliquely from Ropcha to the river Luga, along the right banks of the river Ijora, Souida and Oredoj. The third followed the Luga from its mouth as far as

Chimsk, included the fortified zone of Kinguissep and numerous resistance centres. The fourth rested on the Narva, the lakes of Tchoud (Peipous) and Pskov. An important network of railroads and roads facilitated the movement of reserves.

The country, being generally wooded and crossed with rivers and marshes, was favourable to the defenders.

The Soviet offensive began in mid-January, but following an unusually mild winter, the ground was only partly frozen making traffic difficult off the roads. The forests were blocked by numerous abattis, all of which were mined. Very dense minefields prevented access to all the roads and to the strips of land between the marshes.

The Soviet plan proposed to ' annihilate the German forces in the Leningrad area, liberate that region and prepare a later offensive intended to liberate the Soviet Republics of Esthonia, Latvia and Lithuania '.

The Leningrad front, under General Godorov, was to carry out two concentric attacks in the direction of Ropcha, starting from the ' small ground ' in the west and from Poulkovo in the east, the advance being resumed afterwards in the direction of the south-west and the south. This action had to be co-ordinated with an offensive from the Volkhov front under General Mereskov against the German right in the general direction of Novgorod-Luga.

On this front the Soviet forces had only a slight superiority but their flexibility gave them a clear advantage in troops and material on the main axes of attack. The attack was launched on 14th January and continued until 29th February over a front of three hundred kilometres and a depth of two hundred and seventy kilometres. In the first phase, from 14th to 27th January, the German positions in the Strelna, Ropcha, Krasnoie-Selo region were broken and the main German forces defeated. In the second phase the Soviet troops forced the Luga positions. In the third phase, from the 15th to 29th February, they completed the liberation of the Leningrad region and destroying the XVIIIth German Army.

First Phase, 14th-27th January, *Collapse of the German Front.* The attack on the Leningrad front began on 14th January south of Oranienbaum after over an hour's artillery preparation. Despite counter-attacks the advance gained three to four kilometres on the very first day. On the 15th, after artillery and air preparation lasting over two hours, the attack was resumed in the east in the Poulkovo sector. It came up against the 126th, 170th and 215th Divisions which, despite their losses, continued to resist. By the afternoon, however, the Germans, having exhausted their local reserves, committed their main reserves from Gatchina. In the evening of the 15th the Soviet advance had reached from one to four kilometres. The struggle went on relentlessly deep into the most powerful centres of the sector.

On the 19th the Soviet troops stormed Krasnoie-Selo, which had been made into a fortress. The same day, troops arriving from Oranienbaum captured the road junction of Ropcha, an important centre of resistance. Both attack groups linked up. On the 21st the general advance was directed south-west and south to cut off the German retreat towards the Narva, the main effort being towards Volosovo-Gatchina. Caught in the net, the Germans lost 25,000 killed, 265 guns (including 85 heavy guns ranging from 152 to 406 mm), 30 tanks and 160 mortars in five days. The Soviet troops took about 1,000 prisoners.

The Volkhov front's offensive also developed with full success. After forcing the river Volkhov north of Lake Ilmen, the left of this front broke through long established defences north and south of Novgorod and, on 20th January, stormed the old Russian city and annihilated the forces surrounded in the forests west of the city. In dead alone, the German losses reached the 15,000 figure. The advance was threatening the communications of the XVIIIth Army which, having exhausted its reserves, had to withdraw troops from the centre in the Mga region.

On the 21st, the left of the Leningrad front and the right of the Volkhov front, linked up, broke through the defences of the Peski-Gorodok sector and on the same day took both the town and the station of Mga and pressed on towards Tosno, which they were to take on the 27th.

On the 24th, after an outflanking manoeuvre, the Leningrad front took Pavlovsk (Sloutsk). During the night of the 25th/26th January it stormed the important rail junction of Gatchina (Krasno-Gvardieisk) which had been reinforced with concreted works.

On the 26th, the front attacking south of Leningrad had advanced one hundred kilometres. The German forces, split up and threatened with encirclement, fell back.

The troops of the Volkhov front, for their part, resumed the attack on the 26th. Coming from the Viniagolovo, Smerdino sector and moving in a south-westerly direction they cut the Leningrad-Tchoudovo railway north-west of Lioubane on the 27th.

So, as early as 27th January, the Soviet attacks had disrupted the German organization on a front of three hundred kilometres. On the Leningrad front they had defeated ten divisions, sorely tried two others, killed 40,000 Germans, taken 3,000 prisoners and destroyed 158 tanks, 200 guns, 250 mortars, captured 620 guns, 410 mortars, 20 SP guns, 60 tanks and 1,360 machine guns. The advance had reached between sixty-five and a hundred kilometres.

Second Phase—28th January-15th February, Advance of the Leningrad Front. In order to finish splitting up the German forces defeated at Leningrad, it was necessary to reach the fortified line along the Luga as soon as possible before the Germans had time to establish themselves firmly. The right of the Leningrad front, coming from Volosovo in a westerly and south-westerly direction, reached the Luga on 31st January. It had advanced between 15 and 20 kilometres each day across wooded and marshy country, and outflanked and surrounded the centres of resistance. At the same time, the extreme right of the Leningrad front, after mopping up the coast between the Gulf of Koper and that of Narva, arrived from the north upon the Narva.

On 31st January violent battles took place at Kinguissep and on the Luga corridors north-west and south-east of this town. After two days' relentless fighting it was surrounded and stormed on the morning of 1st February.

On 3rd February the Soviet forces forced the Narva in several places and secured small bridgeheads on the other side of the river, north and south of the city of Narva.

Opposite the centre and the left of the Leningrad front, the Germans, protecting themselves with ruined buildings, abattis and minefields, tried to gain enough time to make their retreat. In spite of these obstacles, the Soviet units, marching day and night, covered ninety kilometres and on 30th January they also reached the Luga. They immediately established small bridgeheads on the south bank towards Poretchie and Gostiatino.

On the 31st they crossed the river, turned and cut off the centres of resistance. On 4th February they reached the Plious and occupied Diadi.

Fearing a Soviet move upon their communications with the east of the Luga, the Germans made a thrust south-east of Diadi on the south bank of the Plious with the 154th and 220th Infantry Regiments, the 158th Artillery Regiment of the 58th Infantry Division, the motorcycle battalion and the engineer battalion of the 12th Armoured Division and heavy artillery groups.

The Soviet Command, speedily moving its artillery forward, intended putting the 58th Division out of action, then outflanking the Germans on the Luga from the south. Its troops therefore crossed the river Plious on both flanks of the 58th Division west of Zaroudine and towards Ihgomel. On the first day the units of the right cut the roads behind Diadi and those on the left completed the encircling from the east. On 14th February the German troops were caught in the Zaroudinie-Griekhovo net and annihilated. On 15th February the 220th Regiment of the 58th Division, surrounded between Lake Tchornoie and Lake Chirskoie, also disappeared.

The left of the Leningrad front, coming from Gatchina on the Gatchina-Luga railroad and road axis, met with strong resistance towards Siverski, an important traffic junction covering Luga and where the Germans had brought units of the 12th Armoured Division. On the third day, after violent street fighting, the German garrison was overpowered, as also were other units surrounded at Rojdiestveno on the same day.

The units defeated in the capture of Siverski comprised the 320th, 212th, and 44th Regiments of the 11th Infantry division, the 29th Tank Regiment of the 12th Armoured Division, not to mention five infantry battalions, two tank companies and two artillery groups destroyed.

Covered by their rearguard, the Germans fell back on the river Luga and by means of counter-attacks vainly tried to prevent its being reached.

On 10th February the Soviet troops took Tolmatchevo, crossed the river and pressed on without a break towards Luga, a strongly organized traffic junction. Outflanking the city from the west and from the east, the Soviet troops stormed it on 12th February, capturing 42 guns and 60 mortars.

Having conquered everywhere, the Leningrad front had now reached the Narva, Lake Tchoud (Peipous) and Lake Pakov, and completely defeated the left of the XVIIIth German Army.

Advance of the Volkhov front. During the first phase of the offensive, the ten German divisions and the Spanish ' Blue ' Division facing the Volkhov front had sustained heavy losses. On 26th January, after defeating the Germans at Poddoubie, north-west of Novgorod, and at Suekhovo, south-west of that city, the Soviet troops moved rapidly towards the west and south-west. The right flank was directed towards Finev-Loug and Oredej to cut off the retreat of the troops which were resisting further north at Lioubane and Tchoudovo. On 30th January both these places fell freeing the Leningrad-Moscow railway entirely. At the same time the left flank was fighting hard towards the source of the Luga. On 12th February they seized Batitskaia station and the same evening reached the Luga.

The Germans still facing the right of the Volkhov front made their withdrawal under flank attacks from the Soviet forces and with heavy losses. For instance, the artillery regiment of the 121st Division left thirty guns in the hands of the Russians at Apraksi Bor on 1st February.

Between 31st January and 8th February violent fighting took place east of the Oredej-Batitskaia-Tchtorgoch railway against German reserves which had been brought into the area. Localities changed hands several times. In the south the fighting was just as violent on the rivers Mchaga and Chelon where the Germans tried to stop any advance towards the Luga-Pskov railway. A Soviet unit, supported by partisans, threw back superior forces south of Lakes Vrevo and Tcheremenetskoie and cut the Luga-Pskov railway and road towards Gorodets and north of Zapliousie.

Third Phase, 15th-29th February, The thrust towards Narva and Pskov. The Leningrad and Volkhov fronts, while pushing back the remains of the XVIIIth German Army, pursued their offensive. The right of the Leningrad front forced a crossing of the Narva and secured a bridgehead thirty-five kilometres wide by fifteen deep south of the city of Narva. Advancing upon Aouvere they cut the Narva-Talim railway.

The centre of the Leningrad front advance from Louga towards the south-west along the Luga-Pskov railway, captured the fortified junction of Strougui-Krasnie on 23rd February and at the end of the month arrived at Pskov from the north-east.

The left of the Leningrad front occupied Chimsk on 18th February. It was reinforced by the Volkhov front with which it amalgamated and, after linking up with the 2nd Baltic Front, took the railroad junction of Dno on 24th February.

On the left of the Leningrad front the 2nd Baltic front had taken the offensive against the XVIth German Army south of Lake Ilmen on 17th February. It took Staraia Roussa, was engaged in the capture of Dno and, at the end of the month, reached the Novorjev-Poustachka line.

Thus had the Leningrad and Volkhov fronts advanced one hundred and fifty to three hundred kilometres to the west and south west in the depth of winter, in particularly unfavourable weather conditions, across a fiercely defended wooded marshy region. They had completely defeated the XVIIIth German Army and inflicted considerable losses on the left of the XVIth Army. Between 14th January and 19th February the Germans had lost 7,200 prisoners. The material destroyed included 97 planes, 275 tanks, nearly 2,000 guns, over 2,500 mortars and more than 3,600 machine guns. Besides which, the Soviet troops had captured 190 tanks, 1,850 guns and 2,500 mortars.

The released Leningrad-Moscow railway ensured a base for further progress towards the west across the Baltic States.

THE GERMAN DEFEAT IN THE UKRAINE (FEBRUARY-MARCH, 1944)

The situation in the Ukraine at the beginning of 1944 (Sketch No. 38). At the end of December the 1st Ukrainian front (Marshal Zhukov) was firmly holding a bridgehead two hundred and sixty kilometres wide and one hundred and twenty deep in the Kiev region. The one which the 2nd and 3rd Ukrainian fronts had established towards Krementchoug and Dniepropetrovsk was four hundred kilometres wide and seventy deep. Strictly speaking they were more like deep wedges on the right bank of the Dnieper. While the Leningrad and Volkhov fronts were preparing, the 1st Ukrainian front attacked in order to clean up the west bank of the Dnieper and occupy a more favourable base for the next offensive.

On 24th December the attack was launched along one hundred and fifty kilometres. West and south of Kiev it met with a desperate resistance supported by armoured formations. From 24th December to 13th January the Red forces advanced westwards and inflicted enormous losses upon the Germans—over 100,000 killed and 2,500 tanks, 2,000 guns and nearly 1,000 mortars destroyed or captured. They liberated Jitomir, drove the Germans back three hundred kilometres towards the west and cut the Vilna-Lvov railway. By the end of January the front ran through Sarni, Berditchev, Bielaia Tserkov. The German flank west of the Dnieper was now exposed to a north-south attack.

The 2nd Ukrainian front also attacked at the beginning of January and defeated three armoured divisions, one motorized division and one infantry division round Kirovgrad, an important, strongly fortified centre, which it captured.

The Ukrainian fronts' task. Let us recall that at the end of January 1944 the following groups of armies were spread from the Pripet to Vinnitsa— the south group with Marshal von Manstein (IVth and Ist Armoured Armies and Ist Hungarian Army), the south group ' A ' with Marshal Kleist (VIIIth and VIth German Armies and IIIrd Rumanian Army) and in reserve round Jassy, the IVth Rumanian Army.

The Soviet plan gave the Ukrainian fronts the task of defeating the enemy on the west bank of the Dnieper and liberating the Ukrainian regions on that bank. The first phase divided the objectives as follows :—

Korsoun, Chevtchenkovski ... 2nd front and left of the 1st front.
Nikopol   ...   . 3rd and 4th fronts.
Rovno, Loutsk   ...   ... right of the 1st front.

First Phase, February, 1944. The offensive was to take place during the muddy Spring season which usually put a stop to operations. The four Ukrainian fronts were to carry out their tasks in rain, on waterlogged ground and impassible roads and against large swollen rivers—the Boug, the Prout, the Dniestr and the Seret.

1. ANOTHER STALINGRAD—THE KORSOUN-CHEVTCHENKESKI DISASTER
(Sketches Nos. 38 and 39)

Situation. At the end of January the 1st Ukrainian front had reached Sarni on its left deep into the German position. Its north flank was covered by the Pripet and the marshes of Pinsk ; it could therefore use all its strength against the German salient stretching from the south of Kiev to Kanev on the Dnieper which was also threatened from the south owing to the recent liberation of Kirovgrad.

The Germans hoped to use this salient, the centre of which was in the Korsoun-Chevtchenkovski area, to attack the 1st Ukrainean front's communications in the north. They had made good use of the ground which was furrowed by ravines and rivers, wooded in places and generally favourable to defence, and had packed it with centres of resistance. On the right bank of the Dnieper, where the VIIIth Army had concentrated major forces, the Kanev heights offered long ranges of observation on all sides.

This salient was to be reduced by the 1st Ukrainian front starting from Bielaia Tserkov and the 2nd front starting from Kirovgrad who were advancing to meet towards Zvenigorodka-Chpola. The first period, from the end of January to 3rd February, was the double break-through until the junction of both fronts had been achieved ; the second, from the 10th to the 17th February was the destruction of the surrounded forces.

71

First phase. After an effective artillery preparation in thick fog, the infantry advanced through the mud and made a wide break through in both sectors of attack. Immediately outflanking points of resistance, the tanks charged forward followed by the Don Cossacks, ensuring their link up with the infantry. The latter advanced five to ten kilometres daily, reducing the strong-points which the tanks and cavalry had by-passed. On 3rd February the mobile forces of the two fronts met, but as yet they had only narrow corridors, both flanks of which were exposed to enemy counter-attacks.

Second phase. These attacks were increased in an effort to break the surrounding line. Eight armoured divisions and several infantry divisions were concentrated round Ouman ready to attack on 5th February. But the Soviet artillery massed in the corridors facing south repulsed all the counter-attacks, while in the north the Cossacks tightened the net and spreading westwards overran the centre of resistance at Olchane where they destroyed three infantry regiments.

Third phase. The 2nd front was then amalgamated with the 1st under the command of Marshal Koniev. In order to annihilate the surrounded forces he planned to split them up by a series of co-ordinated attacks : from Smela towards Orlevets and Gorodiche ; from Mechni towards Drabovka and Korsoun-Chevtchenkovski ; from Kanev towards Tagantcha and Korsoun-Chevtchenkovski ; from Begouslav towards Volkhovets ; from Nikolaievka towards Vigraev and Korsoun-Chevtchenkovski ; from Tolstaia towards Oichane and Gorodiche ; from Tserkovo towards Gorodiche and Orlevets.

These attacks were mostly directly against centres of communications which were indispensable to strategic rail movements in the rear. It was now no longer a question of breaking through a continuous front as in the first period, but of breaking down quickly some hurriedly prepared defence points and of driving back the counter-attacks which the encircled forces had to launch to try to break out. The German Command attempted to send supplies by air, but the A.A. and fighter planes made air transport ineffective. On 9th February Marshal Koniev sent the besieged troops an ultimatum but at the same time Hitler promised them prompt help and the ultimatum was rejected.

The Soviet offensive started on 10th February and was characterized by numerous attacks following on top of each other so that the Germans had no time to recover and concentrate their forces either to defend themselves or to counter-attack.

On the 14th, by means of a daring outflanking move, the Soviet forces took Korsoun-Chevtchenkovski. The surrounding line now just took in the Steblev, Chanderovka, Komarovka region. Taking advantage of a snow blizzard, rid of their impedimenta and fortified by a triple ration of alcohol, the Germans tried a sortie in full force in various sectors. Artillery fire greeted the infantry columns and tanks. Infantrymen were slashed down by the mounted Cossacks and crushed by the tanks. At Kamarovka alone 2,000 died. The surrounded ·forced had now ceased to exist and the few isolated detachments concealed in the ravines and woods south-west of Chanderovka were wiped out the next day.

The VIIIth German Army units which had been destroyed comprised the 11th and 42nd Army Corps consisting of the 12th, 88th, 82nd, 72nd, 167th, 168th, 57th, 332nd Infantry Divisions, 213th Protection Division, S.S. ' Viking ' Division and the S.S. Motorized Brigade ' Valonia '. Out of a total strength of 80,000 men, 53,000 had been killed and 18,200 taken prisoner. Among the dead was Artillery General Wilhelm Stommermann who had commanded the encircled forces.

The material destroyed included 430 planes, 155 tanks, 60 SP guns, 270 mortars and 900 machine guns. The Russians had captured 40 planes, 115 tanks, 620 guns, 50 SP guns, 270 mortars and over 10,000 vehicles, all in good condition.

Right to the end the German Command renewed its attacks in order to break the ever tightening circle isolating the VIIIth Army, from the outside. One was aimed at Chpola, the other at Zvenigorodka. The latter, having superior forces, achieved some slight progress south of the town without however breaking through the Soviet line. Between the 5th and 21st February it cost the Germans 27,000 killed, 330 planes, 830 tanks and 450 guns destroyed, and 115 tanks and 270 guns captured.

The German defeat in the Korsoun-Chevtchenkovski region had serious consequences for them. It had cost them about ten divisions and from a morale point of view it had increased the haunting fear of being surrounded. It also enabled the Red Army to split up the southern group of armies.

The Soviet troops fighting in the mud, in the rain and often in heavy snowstorms, once more showed their worth. So, in an Order of the Day, Stalin called this victory ' another Stalingrad '.

2. LIBERATION OF NIKOPOL AND KRIVOI ROG

(Sketch No. 40)

While the battle of Korsoun-Chevtchenkovski was in progress the 3rd and 4th Ukrainian fronts, under Marshals Malinovski and Tolboukhine respectively, defeated the German divisions at Nikopol.

Nikopol and Krivoi Rog were two important industrial centres ; the former specialising in the quarrying and treatment of manganese and the latter rich in iron ore deposits. In order to retain them at all costs the Germans devoted three armoured divisions and ten infantry divisions of the VIth Army to their defence.

During the three months following the fall of Dniepropetrovsk the Germans had been organizing five positions in depth. Moreover, south of Nikopol they had a bridgehead on the left bank of the Dnieper one hundred and twenty kilometres wide and thirty-five deep. Off the roads, the mud made the country impossible for vehicles.

The 3rd front, detailed for the main effort, was to attack north-east of Krivoi Rog ; the 4th front was to reduce the bridgehead on the south bank of the Dnieper and then, together with the 3rd front, to proceed to capture Nikopol.

After fifty minutes of artillery bombardment the 3rd front attacked. With efficient artillery support during the whole day and the following night, the infantry fought fierce battles within the German positions, outflanking the centres of resistance and taking them one after the other. The next evening, after breaking through, the tanks and infantry pressed on towards Apostolovo.

Driving back renewed counter-attacks supported by groups of ten tanks, the Soviet forces took Apostolovo on 5th February after a night attack, and cut off the communications of the Nikopol forces with the west. After three days of fighting off fierce counter-attacks the Soviet troops took Cholokhovo, north-west of Nikopol. After four days' fighting the 3rd front had defeated three armoured divisions and four infantry divisions, advanced sixty kilometres through mud and cut off Nikopol from Krivoi Rog.

Meanwhile the 4th Ukrainian front had attacked the eleven divisions firmly established in the bridgehead south of the Dneiper, broken through on several points and driven the Germans back to the river. This success facilitated the task of the 3rd front which stormed Nikopol on 8th February. On 22nd February, Krivoi Rog also fell after being attacked from the north, east and south-east.

By the end of February the 3rd front had reached the upper and middle course of the Ingoulets and was preparing for a new operation to destroy the main forces of the VIth Army. For its part, after reducing the bridgehead on the Dnieper and defeating seven divisions, the 4th front prepared to liberate the Crimea.

3. LIBERATION OF ROVNO AND LOUTSK

(Sketch No. 41)

While the left flank of the 1st Ukrainian front was attacking towards Korsoun-Chevtchenkovski, the right flank was preparing its offensive against Rovno, Loutsk.

The waterlogged ground, interspersed with forests and marshes and numerous rivers flowing south to north (Gorine, Oust, Stoubel, Karmine, Styr, etc.), was favourable to defence in depth. The Germans had strengthened the defence of localities and practicable passes between the marshes, but north of the Rovno-Loutsk road and railway the defensive organization was somewhat summary, as the German Command regarded the large wooded masses which covered the area as unsuitable for large scale operations.

The Soviet Command attacked west of Sarni to outflank the most important centres, Loutsk and Rovno, from the north.

The attack was launched just as the German Command had directed its reserves towards Korsoun-Chevtchenkovski and Nikopol. Taken by surprise, the Germans were driven out of their positions. On 5th February Loutsk and Rovno fell. At the same time, an attack coming from Gecha, south-west of Rovno, broke through the German positions. The counter-attacks against Rovno and Loutsk failed. In both these cities the Red Army captured important dumps.

This success in the north-west protected the 1st Ukrainian front which was about to attack Tchernovits.

At Korsoun-Chevtchenkovski, Nikopol, Loutsk and Rovno the three fronts had entirely accomplished their tasks and during the month of February had defeated and destroyed major German forces and prepared the liberation of those parts of the Ukraine west of the Dnieper.

Second Phase—March, 1944. At the beginning of March the 1st, 2nd and 3rd Ukrainian fronts re-grouped in order to strike in new directions. At the same time large units of cavalry and mechanized formations, abundantly provided with self propelled and field artillery, were being organized.

The right of the 1st Ukrainian front marched southwards from Chepetovka and splitting the group of Southern Armies in two, reached the spurs of the Carpathians. The left, attacking in a south-westerly direction from Berditchev and Kazatin, was to cover the advance of the right in the south, and drive the Germans from Proskourov, Vinnitsa, Jmerinka, Kameneiz-Podolski.

The 2nd Ukrainian front was to split up the Southern Group ' A ' between Ouman and the mouth of the Dnieper, then reach the frontier on the Prout. This front faced the VIIIth Army, reinforced by numerous armoured divisions diverted from other sectors.

The 3rd Ukrainian front would proceed towards Kichinev to liquidate the VIth Army which, together with the VIIIth Army constituted the Southern Group ' A '.

On 4th March the offensive was launched on all three fronts. It was to reach all the objectives in twenty-seven days.

1. *Offensive against Tchernovits* (Sketch No. 41.) The action of the 1st front (Marshal Zhukov) developed in the Volhunie-Pedolie area and in the approaches to the Carpathians. The area was bordered in the west by the Kremenets mountains, in the south by the ramifications of the Carpathians and in the north by Southern.Polesia. It was intersected with numerous steep-banked rivers, tributaries of the Boug and Dniestr, which each formed an obstacle, besides which, the spring mud had made traffic difficult even on the roads.

The Soviet Command knew the strength of the German defences and had concentrated a mass of guns towards Chepetovka which ensured superiority in the main direction of attack.

The preliminary bombardment caused the Germans enormous losses. Then the infantry under Generals Tcherniakhovski and Gretchko achieved a break-through and the armoured forces of Generals Leliouchenko and Ribalko rushed through. After two days' hard fighting, in spite of counter-attacks, the tanks and infantry had broken the front to a distance of one hundred and eighty kilometres in width and twenty-five to fifty in depth. Four armoured divisions and eight infantry divisions were completely beaten and lost 15,000 killed, 200 tanks, 250 guns, 400 mortars and 2,000 vehicles. Besides which the Soviet forces captured 120 tanks, 200 guns, numerous dumps and 3,000 prisoners. In their advance towards the south, Tcherniak-hovski and Leliouchenko overran Volotchisk on 6th March, thus cutting the Tarnopol-Proskourov railway and separating the Germans of Proskourov-Vinnitsa from those of Tarnopol. For his part, Ribalko and his tanks, supporting others of Tcherniakhovski's formation advanced towards Proskourov, while Gretchko neared Konstantinov.

Counter-attacks from Tarnopol, Trembovlia and Proskourov created a relentless battle around Zbaraj-Voletchisk and Koupel which lasted until 20th March. The Russians finally repulsed these and resumed their advance, while General Poukov, who had been detailed to cover the main offensive in the west, launched his attack and, scoring successes at Doubno and Kremenets, reached Brod.

The left of the 1st Front made a still more important advance—on 18th March Moskalenko stormed Jmerinka, a large railway centre, and liberated Vinnitsa on the 20th.

On the 21st the 1st Front resumed the attack after a powerful artillery bombardment and disrupted the front between Tarnopol and Proskourov. Leaving the infantry to reduce the resistance, Katoukov's and Leliouchenko's tanks rushed southwards. On the 24th, Katoukov reached the Dniestr and forced a crossing at several points near Zaliechtchiki. The same day,

Leliouchenko overran Goussiatine and attacked Skala. Tcherniakhovski outflanked and surrounded Tarnopol. Attacking west of Proskourov, Gretchko's troops and Ribalko's tanks penetrated the German defences while Generals Jouravliev and Meskalinko, coming from the north-east, neared the river Ouchitse, south of Proskourov.

Four days' fighting had thus split up the front north of Tchernovits. Katoukov reached the outskirts of this town, while the flanks of the 1st front had, by a pincer movement, cut off the westward withdrawal routes of major forces between Proskourov and Kameneiz-Podolski.

Breaking the resistance at Skala, Leliouchenko's tanks rushed upon Kameneiz-Podolski and prevented the Proskourov forces, now encircled, from withdrawing southwards. Tightening the circle, Gretchko took Proskourov.

The surrounded force, some fifteen divisions, vainly tried to fight free. They were split up and annihilated one after the other. At the same time the progress towards the west and south continued. On 30th March the Russians took Kolomia and Tchernovits and reached the approaches to the Carpathians.

Such was the end of an operation which was eventually to have an important bearing on the war. Marshal Zhukov's 1st Ukrainian front had brilliantly fulfilled its task.

From 4th to 31st March the balance sheet of this victory reads : important centres, such as Kameneiz-Podolski and Tchernovits, liberated ; twenty-nine divisions, among which eleven armoured and two Rumanian, entirely defeated; 208,000 killed or taken prisoner ; 2,810 tanks and armoured vehicles, 4,600 guns, 2,600 mortars, 8,500 machine guns, 54,000 vehicles captured.

2. *Defeat of the German forces at Ouman* (Sketch No. 42). General Koniev's troops had barely finished the Korsoun-Chevtchenkovski battles when they started re-grouping towards Ouman where the Germans were reconstituting some thirty sorely tried divisions, ten of which were armoured, and who were banking on the spring mud to prevent any major operations. In spite of the very unfavourable condition of the ground, the Soviet Command, having achieved a great superiority of resources, resumed the offensive on 4th March at 7.50 am after an hour's artillery bombardment. The 2nd Ukrainian front (Koniev) crushed the defenders in their positions, broke through over thirty-five kilometres and repulsed all counter-attacks. In five days the Soviet forces, with mud up to their knees, widened the breach to one hundred and seventy-five kilometres, advanced forty to seventy kilometres and broke down the powerful defences on the river Gorni-Tikitch.

This unexpected and catastrophic defeat cost the Germans seven infantry divisions, six armoured divisions and one artillery division destroyed and 500 tanks in good condition, including 200 'Tigers', 'Panthers' and 'Ferdinands' left near Potach station. The triumph of the Soviet armour over the German armoured and motorized divisions was evident all over the battlefield north and south of Gorni-Tikitch where, for dozens of kilometres columns of tanks, guns and vehicles were sinking in the mud and abandoned material lay everywhere.

On 10th March a chance battle gave the Soviet troops Ouman, a centre of communications of the first importance. Pursuit detachments were immediately constituted with tanks, motor cycles, tank-borne infantry, sappers, artillery and Don Cossacks, which outstripped the Germans in their retreat to the Boug. Only a few elements without any equipment managed to escape. Keeping close to the tanks the infantry speeded up the pace over fifty kilometres of mud and were often the first to cross rivers and secure bridgeheads from which the tanks could start again. Vaniarka fell on the 15th, depriving the Germans of the Odessa-Jmerinka railway. Two days later the Soviet tanks took Iampol on the Dniestr and also forced a crossing of the river. With the help of the infantry they overran Soroka and then Beltsi in the north of Bessarabia. By the end of March the 2nd front had reached the Soviet-Rumanian frontier on the Prout which was crossed at several points. Only the debris of defeated units of the disrupted front reached Rumanian territory. Over 62,000 dead Germans littered the Ukrainian plain. The material lost or destroyed included 600 tanks, 1,270 guns, 750 mortars and 21,000 vehicles.

Marching and fighting through mud, the Soviet troops had covered over four hundred kilometres and crossed such rivers as the Boug, Dniestr and Prout with only makeshift equipment. Their tanks, having wider tracks, had been able to drive over waterlogged ground in which the German armoured vehicles were sinking. Everywhere the Ukrainian population assisted the advance, providing transport and even carrying supplies on their backs when roads were impassable to vehicles.

3. *Encirclement and destruction of the VIth German Army at Bereznegova-toie, Sniguiriovska (Sketch No. 43).* The 3rd Ukrainian Front (General Malinovski) attacked at the beginning of March at the same time as the 1st and 2nd fronts. Its task was to destroy the VIth German Army established on the Ingoulets and to free the Southern Ukraine after linking up with the 2nd front.

After losing Nikopol and Krivoi Rog, the Germans had set up a defence between the Boug and the Ingoulets which was helped by the rivers flowing north-south, the Visoun, Ingoul, Gremokleia and Gniloi-Elianets, which had been swollen by the spring rain. The VIth Army had gathered there the remains of the units defeated at Nikopol, Krivoi Rog and in the bridgehead of the Dnieper south of Nikopol. It numbered twenty-five divisions, twenty-one infantry, three armoured, one motorized and a number of reinforcement units. Planning an attack from the right starting from Krivoi Rog, the Soviet Command had concentrated its mobile tank and cavalry units there.

After the preliminary air and artillery bombardment the infantry attacked and forced several points along the Ingoulets. The cavalry and tanks of Generals Pliev and Tanastchichine immediately crossed the river. The extent of the front prevented the Germans from recognising where the main effort lay. On the fourth day both cavalry and armour reached Kazanka and Novi Boug, cut off the communications of the VIth Army with the VIIIth (which was now being attacked by the 2nd front) and set up a huge bridgehead west of the Ingoulets. After fierce trench fighting the Soviet troops penetrated thirty to sixty kilometres into the German dispositions on a one hundred and seventy kilometre front.

Three armoured divisions and six infantry divisions lost, in four days, over 8,000 killed, 67 tanks, 175 guns, and over 2,000 vehicles after fruitless counter-attacks to stop the Soviet advance.

In addition to the main effort, other units of the 3rd front crossed the Dnieper, took Berislav, outflanked the VIth Army from the south, liberated Kherson on 13th March and pressed on towards Nikolaiev while the Soviet advance in the north, after crossing the Ingoul, moved southward preventing the Germans from retreating towards the west. The main body of the VIth Army, finding itself encircled, increased its attempts to re-establish contact with the VIIIth Army by attacking in dense columns amongst which the artillery wreaked havoc. It lost in this way 10,000 killed and 4,000 prisoners. On the 16th, concentric attacks by all arms destroyed the remains of the VIth Army, that is, nine infantry divisions and one armoured division. Eight infantry divisions, two armoured divisions and one motorized division, which had escaped encirclement, had lost all fighting value. Only four sorely tried infantry divisions remained useable. The total losses of the VIth Army amounted to 50,000 killed or wounded, 275 tanks, 190 SP guns, 1,200 guns, over 1,000 mortars, over 3,000 machine guns and more than 16,000 vehicles.

During this annihilation of the VIth Army, the 3rd front continued its advance westward, occupied Novaia Odessa on 16th March and after re-grouping reached the Boug on a wide front where it broke through the defences of the west bank on the 28th.

During March and April the second phase of the operations west of the Dnieper had cost the Germans some 500,000 killed or taken prisoner, 5,000 tanks or SP guns, 10,000 guns, 130,000 vehicles. Ceaselessly fighting in rain and through mud the three Ukrainian fronts had advanced two hundred and fifty to three hundred kilometres. Never had such a large scale spring offensive been seen. Their success was to enable the Soviet Command to liberate Odessa, the Crimea and then invade Rumania and Hungary.

3. THE DEFEAT OF THE GERMANO-RUMANIAN ARMIES IN THE CRIMEA AND AT ODESSA, APRIL-MAY, 1944

The third offensive of 1944 led by the 3rd and 4th Ukrainian fronts and the Independent Coastal Army, freed the whole coast of the Black Sea from Kertch to the Dniestr estuary and the two great Russian ports of Odessa and Sebastopol.

The Odessa operations (Sketch No. 44). These took place from 28th March to 16th April under command of General Malinovski. After destroying the bulk of the VIth German Army the 3rd Ukrainian front had reached the Boug in the Konstantinovka, Novaia-Odessa, Nikolaiev, Stanislav sector. From the Boug to the Dniestr the high water had made the smallest rivers and estuaries into as many serious obstacles to say nothing of the waterlogged ground, impassable off the roads. Covered by the advance of the 2nd front now in Rumania on the Jessy, Ribnitsa, Ananiev line, the 3rd front was to cross the Boug, liberate Odessa and reach the Dniestr. The effort would be made through the right, from Konstantinovka, Voznesensk towards Tiraspol in order to split up the enemy forces and drive the main body to the sea. This mission was given to General Pliev's Cossacks and General Jdanov's tanks.

On the morning of the 28th the Soviet troops attacked, crossed the Boug between Konstantinovka and Voznesensk and secured a bridgehead on the west while the left flank liberated Nikolaiev, an important and strongly fortified port at the mouth of the Boug on the Black Sea, and the next day established a bridgehead at Novaia-Odessa. On the morning of the 30th, after crossing the Boug along all its course from Konstantinovka to Nikolaiev, the mobile forces rushed into the gap towards Domanevka, attacked Isaievo and Berezovka and completed the break up of the front.

On the 31st the left captured Otchakov on the coast. In four days the 3rd front had gained sixty to seventy kilometres on a front one hundred and sixty wide. On 31st March it lined up along the river Tiligoul in the Troitskoie, Berezovka, Koblevo region. Its advance had maintained a steady rhythm of fifteen to seventeen kilometres per day in spite of flooding and impassable roads. The Germans fell back behind the Dniestr but intended to defend Odessa as a bar to access into Central Rumania. This, however, the Soviet Army was to prevent.

Indeed, on 1st April, in spite of alternate rain and snow, Pliev's Cossacks and tanks overthrew the rearguard on the Tiligoul, set off in pursuit, took Razdelnaia and Strasbourg on the 5th and cut off the Odessa Germans' retreat towards Tiraspol. On the 6th they drove back the Germans counter-attacking north-west of Odessa and after surrounding them annihilated them on the 8th. In this way the remains of five or six divisions perished ; 7,000 dead remained on the field and the Soviet forces took 3,200 prisoners, 45 tanks and 300 guns.

In order to isolate Odessa from the west, Pliev's Cossacks continued southward along the Dniestr, occupying Beliaievka and Maiaki on the 7th, while the infantry, coming from the east, reached the Kouialnik estuary. The battle began in front of the positions covering the city on the land side. On the evening of the 9th the Soviet infantry reached the northern outskirts, advanced by infiltration under cover of darkness and began street fighting while the Cossacks held the western edge. After one night's fighting the mopping up ended inside Odessa on 10th April at 1000 hrs.

Continuing the pursuit the right of the 3rd front occupied Tiraspol on the 12th, crossed the Dniestr further south and towards Kopanka set up the bridgehead from which the August offensive was to start. The VIth German Army, which had lost its main forces in March, disappeared entirely here. While sinking in the mud, manhandling the guns and with the population carrying shells on their shoulders from village to village, the Soviet troops covered two hundred kilometres in sixteen days at the rate of twelve to fourteen a day and prevented any recovery of the enemy. This success allowed the liberation of the Crimea to be undertaken on 8th April.

The Crimea Operation (Sketch No. 45). By occupying the Crimea the Germans were able to threaten the left flank of the Red Army in its advance westward, deprive the Red Fleet of the ports on the Black Sea and the Sea of Azov and to maintain their pressure on Rumania, Bulgaria and Turkey. The German XVIIth Army, in charge of the defence of the Peninsula, had therefore been reinforced with two divisions and sixty battalions.

Now the summer and autumn offensives of 1943 had brought the Soviet troops to the Sivach and the Bay of Karkinitok, shutting twelve German and Rumanian divisions into the Crimea. In November the 4th Ukrainian front had even established a bridgehead of a hundred square kilometres south of the Sivach towards Tchijan-Ourjine, while the Independent Coastal Army, having forced the Straits of Kertch, had gained a foothold in the Crimea. All the counter-attacks launched against these bridgeheads had failed.

During the five months blockade the German and Rumanian forces had erected new fortifications and modernized the old ones, especially in the north at Perekop, Ichoun, Tchongar, in the pass between the marshes south of the Sivach and in the Kertch peninsula. Towards Perekop three lines of defence were disposed in succession over thirty to fifty kilometres—the main one consisted of three series of trenches supporting the Turkish rampart, the second utilized the Ichoun positions and the third the course of the Tchatirlik. In the Kertch isthmus the depth reached seventy kilometres as the town was covered by three positions. Finally, inside the Crimea intermediary lines were based on the rivers Boulganak, Alma and Katcha. The XVIIth Army comprised twelve divisions and several dozen independent regiments, battalions and detachments, 3,000 guns and heavy mortars and 600 planes.

In the Soviet plan a double attack, from the north towards Perekop-Sivach and from the east towards Kertch, was to prevent the enemy from using the interior lines. The 4th Ukrainian front (Tolboukhine) was to break out from the Sivach bridgehead and make the main effort in the south-east working in three directions—Topalovka, Djankoi-Simferopol, Djankoi-Seitler-Karassoubazar—while the attack upon the Perekop isthmus was to take second place moving from Vorontsovka towards Ak-Netchet and Eupatoria. This move ensured surprise as the Germans had their main forces towards Perekop. The five simultaneous attacks aimed at dividing the front in order to destroy each group separately. The part played by General Eremenko (Independent Coastal Army) consisted in breaking through the Kertch defences and pressing on quickly towards the west thus preventing the enemy halting on any of his successive positions or evacuating from the ports of the south east coast. In addition, the Black Sea Fleet and the air force ensured the blockade of the Crimea with Marshal Vassilevski in charge of co-ordinating the combined operations of the Army and the Navy.

The battle began on 8th April with the attack by the 4th front. For two and a half hours a thousand guns or heavy mortars and several hundred bombers battered the defences in the Perekop isthmus and on the south bank of the Sivach. At 1030 hrs while the artillery were still pounding the first lines the infantry and tanks rushed to the attack.

Despite a desperate resistance, General Zakharov's troops took Armiansk on the Perekop isthmus during the day. Overrunning the German lines one after the other and driving back numerous counter-attacks, he advanced twenty kilometres. On 10th April he met with stubborn resistance at Ichoun.

At the same time, General Kreiser's troops concentrated south of the Sivach, broke through the defences and advanced into the Tomachevka pass. The first day they overran three lines of trenches ; on the 9th they drove the Germans from Karanku and on the 10th from Tomachevka, thus carrying the last German position. On the 11th the armoured forces were sent into the gap ; they advanced towards the south-east and at the end of the day took the town and station of Djankoi, an important communications centre, and captured 2,000 prisoners. Meanwhile the infantry attacking from Tomachevka in the south-west had reached Voinka and arrived at the rear of the Germans engaged near Perekop. Being attacked on their flanks the Germans fell back in disorder and abandoned Ichoun. In order to reinforce further towards Perekop and Sivach, the German Command removed the 73rd Infantry Division from Kertch. On the morning of the 11th Eremenko launched his attack. By 0600 hrs he held Kertch. In the evening he reached the Adjibai-Sultanovka line and penetrated the second position. The Black Sea Fleet and the Flotilla of the Sea of Azov made the operations easier by landing some units on the flank of the German troops.

By the evening of the 11th the advance had gone twenty kilometres deep into the Perekop isthmus, sixty south of the Sivach, and thirty at Kertch. It was now possible to advance over clear country.

On the 13th the pursuit detachments rushed towards the south. On the same day, in the west, General Zakharov liberated Eupatoria ; on the 14th Ak-Netchet and Saki. On 15th April he forced a passage across the Boulganak, the Alma and the Katcha. That very evening he reached the Belbek on the outer belt of Sebastopol where once again he met organised resistance.

Kreiser's troops and the armoured forces of the 4th front worked simultaneously towards Topalovka, Djankoi-Simferopol and Djankoi-Seitler-Karassoubazar. At Seitler they destroyed the remains of the 10th and 11th Rumanian Divisions and near Bioukoular-Sarabouzi some units of the 111th and 336th German Divisions. The pursuit troops outflanked the rearguard, pressed on towards Toupalevka and, on 13th April, cut the Simferopol-Saki road. The tanks outflanked Sarabouzi from the south-west and entered Simferopol which they cleared. On the 14th, after hard fighting over mountainous, wooded ground, the mobile units occupied Bakhtchisarai and Alouchta where they cut off the last line of retreat from Kertch towards Sebastopol. On the 15th, together with Kreiser's troops, they reached the outer belt of Sebastopol north of Choula.

The Coastal Army advanced so rapidly after the break-through of the 11th April that the Germans gave up all thoughts of an orderly retreat. On 12th April, after advancing forty kilometres, Eremenko overran the Ak-Mokai positions. On the 13th he liberated Feodosia and Krim Station. On the 14th he annihilated five thousand Germans encircled at Karassoubazar. On the 18th, after occupying Baidari and Balaklava, he arrived on the outer belt also. Some units had covered fifty to eighty kilometres a day and the Soviet troops had covered the distances from Perekop and Kertch to Sebastopol that is, two hundred and fifty and three hundred kilometres, in five and six days.

The Germano-Rumanian forces had lost tens of thousands of killed in the Crimea, 37,000 prisoners and a large part of their equipment. The remaining troops had been driven back to the sea in the south-west corner in an area of two hundred and fifty square kilometres. Having completed this first phase the Soviet troops had only to take the fortress of Sebastopol and destroy the last enemy forces.

Liberation of Sebastopol (Sketch No. 46). Hitler had decided that Sebastopol must be retained at all costs and, on 3rd May, he took the XVIIth Army away from General Joeneke, relieved several army corps commanders of their duties and replaced them with officers who still believed in the possibility of resisting to the last man without yielding an inch on the outer belt and the heights of Balaklava. The defence comprised three successive zones, hundreds of concreted works, thousands of kilometres of trenches, tens of kilometres of barbed wire entanglements, with, on Mount Sapoun alone, six lines of trenches and, in front of the city, two anti-tank ditches. Finally, between 24th April and 7th May ten provisional battalions arrived by sea and air to supplement the defenders.

In the Soviet plan Zakharov's left was to attack from the north towards the Mekenzia Mountains, Kreiser's troops from the east from Mount Sapoun, the key to the outer belt, and the former Independent Army from the south-west, following the coastline. These last two thrusts were to provide the main effort. The fleet and the air force were to tighten the blockade to the maximum.

On 7th May the attack began with two hundred guns per kilometre and hundreds of bombers opening the way for the infantry. The resistance collapsed at several points. Zakharov took the Mekenzia, Kreiser the Sapoun and the Independent Army the Karan coast. On the evening of the 8th fighting had reached the outskirts of the city. From the northern heights long range guns sank on sight the ships in the bay. Fighting went on by day and night and on the evening of the 9th Zakharov and Kreiser took the city from which the remnants of units fled towards Cossacks Bay and Cape Chersonese, but the tanks soon caught up with them and they surrendered. So the fortress fell, it had taken the Germans two hundred and fifty days in 1941-42 and cost them 30,000 killed or wounded—the Soviet troops took five days. This time, Sebastopol, the last German strong-point in the Crimea had cost them 20,000 killed and 24,000 prisoners, including two generals.

The Crimean operation ended in overwhelming defeat for the Germano-Rumanians—twelve divisions annihilated in 35 days, 111,500 killed or taken prisoner, an enormous amount of material lost and 190 troop and supply ships sunk by the Russian fleet and air force between the 8th and 12th May. The XVIIth shared the fate of the VIth Army and was annihilated and the two big ports were returned to the U.S.S.R., thus helping her in the attack on Rumania and Bulgaria—a crippling account. All the more so as the bridge-head of the 3rd Ukrainian front west of the Dniestr gave the Soviet armies access to Bessarabia and Rumania.

The Situation at the beginning of the Summer Campaign (Sketch No. 47). At the beginning of Summer in 1944 the three Winter and Spring offensives of the Red Army had defeated the German forces at Leningrad, on the right bank of the Dnieper, in the Crimea and at Odessa, liberated nearly the whole of the Ukraine, Moldavia, the Crimea, the Moscow and Kalinine regions and part of White Russia, given back to the U.S.S.R. the industrial centres of the south, the ore quarries of Krivoi Rog, Kertch and Nikopol, the fertile lands of Western Ukraine and finally carried the war into Rumanian territory. These operations had also entirely destroyed the XVIIIth, XVIIth, VIth German armies, inflicted losses on the Ist and IVth Armoured Armies, the XVIth and VIIIth Armies and prematurely exhausted major formations intended as reserves for future battles. They had allowed the Germans no respite to reinforce, regroup and prepare for the Summer campaign.

Having upset all German forecasts by uninterrupted attacks, the Red Army held, by June, the Narva, Pskov, Veliki Louki, Mozir, Kovel, Kolomia, Orgueiev, Tiraspol-lower Dniestr front. This line lent itself to converging attacks against the German centre in White Russia ; it was also favourable to an operation in the Baltic States in the north and on the flank of the Germano-Rumanian armies in the south.

By engaging the main forces and wearing down the strategic reserves of the enemy, the Red Army greatly facilitated the Allied operations in Western Europe. The German dispositions were as follows : in the north the armies of Finland and Karelia ; on the Narva, Pskov, Idritsa front the Northern Group of Armies, Lindemann (the Narva Army, XVIth and XVIIIth Armies reconstituted) ; on the Podolsk, Vitebsk, Jlobine front as far as the Pripet and Kovel, the Centre Group of Armies, von Busch (IVth, IXth, IInd Armies, IIIrd Armoured Army) ; between the Pripet and the Dniestr, the Southern Group of Armies, changed in July to Northern Ukraine Group of Armies, Model (Ist and IVth Armoured Armies, 1st and 2nd Hungarian Armies) ; on the Kolonia, Jassy, Dniestr, Black Sea front, the Southern Group ' A ', changed in July to Southern Ukraine Group, Schoerner (VIIIth and VIth German armies, IInd and IVth Rumanian Armies).

The Germans anticipated an initial attack upon Lwov from the south of the Polesia marshes, intended to separate the centre group from the Ukraine Armies, then a double offensive, one in the Balkans, the other upon Warsaw, to drive the centre and northern groups to the Baltic. The first assumption was based on the political aims attributed to the Soviets to get the Balkans under their influence before the arrival of the British, the other upon the identification of certain concentrations in front of the Northern Ukraine group. Consequently they reinforced the latter to the maximum, bringing in all available armoured divisions and leaving but few reserves for the other groups—three armoured divisions to Southern Ukraine, two to the centre, two or three infantry divisions to the northern—the rest of the forces being held up in the west, in Italy and on the West wall by the threat of an Allied landing.

Certain German generals favoured falling back on the Pinsk, Baranovitchi, Vilna, Dvinsk, Riga line, short and easy to hold with diminished forces. Hitler, however, decided to wait where he was for the Soviet attacks.

4. THE FINNISH DEFEAT IN KARELIA, JUNE–JULY, 1944

(Sketch No. 48)

The defeat of the Finnish troops opened the Summer campaign of 1944. The Soviet attacked in the Karelia Isthmus. With the help of the Germans, the Finns had for two years been preparing three powerful positions in the Karelia Isthmus : the first, on the Vankhaia-Ama, Moustalovo, Raiaiski line, reached completion in 1941 ; the second and most important, on the Metsiapirti, Lipola, Kivennapa, Miatsiakioulia line, consisting of twelve to fourteen concreted emplacements and some twenty shelters per kilometre ; the third, the famous ' Mannerheim ' line, was marked out by lakes Souvanto-Larvi, Bouioksi-Iarvi, Muola, Soumma, Mourila. Behind these positions Viborg, a road junction, a big port and a military base equipped for a prolonged defence, was surrounded by a double fortified belt. In front of the positions there were obstacle areas—granite blocks, minefields, scarps, anti-tank ditches and barbed wire entanglements. Everywhere in Karelia and the isthmus, woods, marshes, river and numerous lakes linked to each other were favourable to the defence. The advance could only be made through narrow passes, between lakes and marshes or across woods, heavily mined and strewn with abattis.

The defence of the isthmus was left to the Finnish troops of the south. In Karelia, between Lake Sieg and Lake Ladoga, there was the Army of Karelia, with the Maselskaia group between Lakes Sieg and Onega and the Olonets group between Lakes Onega and Ladoga. The Onega and Ladoga coastguard brigades, belonging to the Navy, held the banks of both lakes.

General Govorov's front of Leningrad was to break through the first position in the isthmus in the direction Bielo Ostrov, Viborg-Kivernnapa road. A secondary attack was to follow along the railway towards Teriyoki-Berke (Koivisto).

The right of the front would take advantage of the break-through on the left to outflank the first position and reach the second as early as the third or fourth day at the same time as the Southern Group. Once the first position had been broken, the main attack would veer slightly left towards Kouter-selka, Soumma. The units detailed for the main effort were to break through the second position, then, exploiting their success, and without stopping, break the Mannerheim line and take Viborg. This incessant pursuit would prevent the Finns from holding on to the successive positions. The main effort fell to General Goussev's troops supported on their left by the Baltic Fleet.

In order to break through positions such as the above the Russians had carried out intensive aerial reconnaissance. They had dug attack trenches one or two hundred metres from the Finnish lines and prepared perfectly camouflaged places to shelter both personnel and equipment prior to the attack.

On 9th June, the day before the attack, the artillery, mortars and planes dropped thousands of tons of missiles upon the Finnish defences and communications. Then the mortars proceeded systematically to destroy fortified positions. Part of the artillery, particularly that of heavy calibre, fired straight on to the first line blockhouses, both the day before and during the immediate preparation for the attack. The same guns also opened passages through the network of supporting defences.

Soviet fighters cleared the sky of Finnish planes and under their protection the 'Stormoviks' attacked the advanced position. The bombers completed the action of the artillery upon the batteries, the immediate rear and the enemy communications. Finally powerful formations bombed the defences in depth.

An artillery and air bombardment lasting three hours immediately preceded the attack and the Finns, shaken by the barrage, the bombing and their enormous losses, could not offer any serious resistance to the onrush of the infantry, tanks and SP guns.

The infantry advanced resolutely and adroitly through the first line works and obstacles which were now almost totally destroyed and the units of which had lost 70 per cent of their strength. Supported by the tanks, artillery, air force and fleet, it broke through the whole depth of the first position in three hours without stopping. The second day the advance into the powerful Finnish defences was forty kilometres wide and twenty-four deep. The Soviet troops had taken Toriyoki and a large number of fortified points.

Finnish Command, alarmed at the rate of withdrawal, brought in its reserves and vainly tried to check it on the intermediate lines.

The second position was broken through near Moustamiski, Kouterselka on the sixth day. The advance had now reached forty kilometres on a front of seventy-five, and some five hundred fortified emplacements had fallen. The six days' offensive had used up the Finnish reserves, three divisions and one brigade, brought from the rear. On 18th June the Soviet troops overthrew the remains of the defeated units and broke through the third position towards Mouola and Soumma.

There was no slowing down of the advance and, on 20th June, the eleventh day of the offensive, the Soviet troops broke through the outer defences of Viborg, attacked the city and overran it.

So, in eleven days, the Leningrad front had broken the powerful Finnish positions, conquered Viborg and broken the last link of the blockade of Leningrad.

After taking Viborg the Soviet troops cleared the outskirts and destroyed the last resistance in the north and the north-east.

Confused by the speed of the Soviet advance, the Finnish Command had diverted a brigade from Kandalachka, two divisions from Medvejegorsk, three divisions and a brigade from the Svir front towards Viborg. To prevent any desertion on the part of the Finns the Germans had sent them the 122nd Infantry Division and the SS Motorized Division ' Niederland ', taken from the Narva front, but they had not entered the battle.

The Soviet Attack in Karelia. Taking advantage of the Finnish loss of strength in Karelia, General Meretskov's front of Karelia attacked south of Lake Onega and on the Svir. With the support of the Ladoga Flotilla these troops were to make an attack with their left along the coast line of the lake in the Olonets-Pitkiaranta direction. After taking Olonets they would turn north towards Lake Siam to cut the Petrozavodsk-Souoiabri railway. On the right, between Lake Onega and Svirstroi after mopping up the Finnish bridgehead on the south bank of the Svir, the troops would deliver two attacks : one along the coastline of Lake Onega, the other on the axis of the Podperojie-Petrozavodsk railway. The troops north of Lake Onega were to attack Medvejigorsk, then proceed north to south along the Petrozavodsk railway, while other units would press westward to cover the action towards Petrozavodsk from the north. The plan was to encircle and destroy the Finnish forces of Petrozavodsk and liberate Soviet Karelia.

On 21st June, after a short but powerful artillery and air bombardment, the Karelia front attacked. The very first day it broke through the defences, liberated Povienets, liquidated the bridgehead south of the Svir and crossed this river towards Lodeinoie Polie.

On the 23rd, pursuing its offensive, it forced a crossing of the Svir towards Podporojie. The next day, helped by the flotillas of the Ladoga and the Onega, it held the whole north bank of the Svir after penetrating twenty to thirty kilometres into the Finnish defences.

Meanwhile, north of Lake Onega, the Soviet troops had overrun Medvejigorsk. Then they launched concentric attacks towards Petrozavodsk, starting from Medvejigorsk, Voznecenie and Podporojie, while the Onega Flotilla effected a landing in the Petrozavodsk region. The Soviet troops were drawing near Petrozavodsk from the north-west and the south-east. No sooner had the marines landed than they rushed towards the city. The resistance of the Finnish troops, attacked on three sides, gave way and on 29th June, Petrozavodsk, the capital of the Karelo-Finnish Soviet Republic was occupied. Souoiarvi followed on the 13th July and Pitkiaranta on the 19th.

The capture of Kondepoga and that of Petrozavodsk-Kirovskaia, freed the whole length of the Murmansk railway. The occupation of Soviet Karelia progressed rapidly, all along the line the frontier was reached during the second half of the month.

The victory over the Finns removed any threat to Leningrad and the north-west borders of the U.S.S.R. Viborg, Petrozavodsk and the greater part of the Republic of Karelia had been recaptured and the Kirov railway and Baltic-White Sea canal, of major importance for liaison with the Allies via Murmansk, had been recovered. Finland was soon to give up the struggle.

5. THE GERMAN DEFEAT IN WHITE RUSSIA, JUNE–JULY, 1944

(Sketch No. 49)

The offensive by the 1st Baltic front and the 1st, 2nd and 3rd White Russian fronts in June-July, 1944, which was crowned by the defeat of the German forces of White Russia, appears as the most important of the ten operations carried out that year by the Red Army.

At the beginning of the summer, after the operations of the Leningrad and Volkhov fronts in the north and those of Ukraine in the south, the front ran through : Poustochka (fifty kilometres west of Veliki-Louki), Lake Nechedro (forty kilometres north-east of Polotsk), Stretinka (south-west of Vitebsk), Novka, Vasiouti Liozno, Lebedevo, Zaretchie, Novi Bikhov, Rogatchev, Strechine, Tchernik, Gorbovitchi. Towards the east it formed an immense salient of 250,000 square kilometres, barring the way to East Prussia and threatening the communications of the 1st Ukrainian front in the south. To the Germans it was, therefore, of the utmost importance.

The rivers running north to south, the Dnieper, Prout, Berezina, Svislotch and behind, the Niemen and the Vistula, facilitated the defence.

The salient was covered in the north by the Dvina and in the south by the Pripet and the Pinsk marshes. Vitebsk on the Dvina, Orcha, Mohilev, Rogatchev and Jlobine on the Dnieper, Bobruisk on the Berezina had been made into centres of resistance with trenches, fieldworks and concreted blockhouses. They formed a barrier to the lines of penetration towards the centre of White Russia. Moreover the Germans had a vast bridgehead on the Dnieper east of Orcha and Mohilev.

The main position ran through Vitebsk, Orcha, Mohilev, Rogatchev, Jlobine. Numerous lakes, marshes and large forests aided the establishing of defence zones where the towns themselves served as strong points. In addition to the Todt organization the Germans had pressed the local populace into building up defence works.

The defence of the salient fell to the Centre Group of armies comprising : the IIIrd Armoured Army, the IVth, IXth and IInd Armies, in all fifty divisions, thirty-five of which were in the first line, ten or twelve in reserve, that is about one million men, 15,000 guns and heavy mortars. Moreover, two armoured divisions and one motorized division made up the mobile reserves. Broadly speaking the dispositions were as follows :

Facing the 1st Baltic front (Bagramian) and the
   3rd White Russian front (Tcherniakovski) —IIIrd Armoured Army
Facing the 2nd White Russian front (Zakharov)—IVth Army
Facing the 1st White Russian front (Marshal
   Rokossovski)   —IXth Army and some
                                   units of the IInd

The strategic reserves—twenty armoured divisions—were mainly south of the Pripet opposite the expected offensive coming from Kovel and Tarnopol.

After the winter and spring victories the tactical situation called for an offensive aimed at the destruction of the German forces in White Russia and the liberation of this region in order that the Vistula and frontier of East Prussia could eventually be reached. This offensive was based on powerful concentric attacks coming from Vitebsk, Rogatchev and Mozir to encircle the centre group of armies from the north and from the south.

The fronts concerned were allocated their missions : the left of the 1st Baltic front, linking up with the right of the 3rd White Russian front, to break through north-east of Vitebsk, encircle and annihilate the German forces there and then proceed westward, while the 3rd White Russian front, moving towards the south-west, would encircle the Germans east of Minsk ; the 1st White Russian front to break through towards Rogatchev, Jlobine, Gorbovitsi to encircle and destroy the German forces of Bobruisk ; the 2nd White Russian front, coming from Lebedevo-Novi Bikhov, would hold up the enemy and, should the latter fall back, vigorously pursue him. Having accomplished these missions, the fronts would complete the liberation of White Russia in order to reach the frontiers of East Prussia as soon as possible. Photo reconnaissance enabled the Russians to study the system of defence in detail.

From 13th to 18th July and during the last few nights before the offensive began, long range bombers carried out mass attacks upon the airfields of the Orcha, Bobruisk, Minsk, Baranovitchi, Pinsk, Belostok and Brest regions.

The deployment for the attack was carried out in the greatest secrecy and on 23rd July, after a powerful artillery and air bombardment, the main forces of the 1st Baltic front and the 2nd and 3rd White Russian fronts rushed to the attack on the four axes, Vitebsk, Bogouchev, Orcha and Mohilev. They were followed the next day by the 1st White Russian front marching on Bobruisk. On a front six hundred kilometres wide, one of the greatest battles of the Second World War was about to take place.

FIRST PHASE—23RD TO 28TH JUNE

1. *The Vitebsk Operation* (Sketch No. 50). Vitebsk, the northern bastion of the centre group of armies, ensured communications with the northern group and barred one of the ways of access to the Baltic. The city was surrounded by a double line of defences, the inner covering the outskirts and the outer some twelve or fifteen kilometres away. After the 1943 and 1944 offensives the Soviet positions now formed an arc east and north of the city.

The defence was allotted to the 53rd Army Corps, comprising the 206th and 246th Infantry Divisions, the 4th and 6th Divisions of the Luftwaffe and the 197th Infantry Division of the 6th Army Corps with the 95th Infantry Division in reserve.

The Soviet Plan. The attack on Vitebsk was to be made by the 1st Baltic front and the 3rd White Russian front. General Beloborodov's troops were deployed north and north-west of the city and were to outflank it from the west. To effect this their right was to break through north of the Vitebsk-Poletsk railway in the Novaia, Igumenchina, Tochnik sector (thirty kilometres north-west of Vitebsk), to reach the Dvina near Gnezdilovitchi, as well as further west, then to establish a bridgehead south of the river.

At the same time, General Lioudnikov's troops, deployed east and south-east of the city, were to break through with their left south of Vitebsk in the Karpovitchi, Kouzmentsi sector (fifteen kilometres south of Vitebsk) to reach the south bank of the Dvina on the third day between Ostrovne and Lake Sarro, then, joining General Beloborodov's troops, close the circle round the German forces of Vitebsk.

The troops, tanks, infantry and artillery, specially trained for this attack had been carrying out combined exercises over similar ground. The infantry were trained to advance twelve to fourteen kilometres without a break, that is to reach the artillery positions. The neutralization of resistance pockets left behind was left to second echelon units. In order to cross the rivers, the units had been issued with individual lifebelts and rubber dinghies. Special groups were to take the bridges before destroying them. This precaution was later to make it possible to take two bridges intact south of Vitebsk and in the city itself.

The Attack. On 23rd June at 0700 hours, after a powerful artillery and air bombardment, the 1st Baltic front (General Beloborodov) attacked. The infantry, tanks and SP guns broke through the German positions, took immediate advantage and quickly pressed forward. They outflanked and captured from the rear the important Choumilino centre, thirty-six kilometres north-west of Vitebsk, thus cutting the Vitebsk-Polotsk railway.

The German counter-attacks, depending mostly on infantry and tanks, failed. By the evening the Soviets had advanced sixteen kilometres on a thirty kilometre front. The same day, at 0900 hours, General Lioudnikov attacked on a six kilometre front, broke through the lines south of Vitebsk, forced a crossing of the River Loutchesse, cut the Vitebsk-Orcha railway near Zamostotchie station and reaching the artillery positions captured all the guns of the 197th Division. By the evening he had advanced sixteen kilometres.

The remains of the 197th Infantry Division fell back towards the north-west as well as the 280th Regiment of the 95th Division which had come as a reinforcement.

On the 24th the advance went on at a fast pace. Beloborodov pressed toward the south-east and, repulsing all counter-attacks, reached the Dvina near Gnezdilovitchi and established bridgeheads. His left broke through north of Vitebsk and reached Kasalapinki.

Lioudnikov arrived with his left at Ostrovno where he fought some hard battles. His right, on a narrow front, overran the defences east of the city and reached its edge.

On the 25th Beloborodov and Lioudnikov met south of the Dvina encircling the 53rd Army Corps. The same day Lioudnikov's right entered Vitebsk and was engaged in violent street fighting.

His left attacked towards the north and reached the Dvina at Dorogo Koupovo and Kanichi, splitting the German forces in two—the 206th and 246th Divisions and two regiments of the 6th Division of the Luftwaffe south-west of Vitebsk and some units of the 4th Division and a regiment of the 6th Division of the Luftwaffe north of Ostrovno.

During the night of the 25th/26th Lioudnikov's right took the only bridge over the Dvina inside the city by surprise and forced the Germans to fall back towards the south-west. But they had no way out left and on the 27th by 0700 hours the mopping up of Vitebsk was finished.

In the south-west, on the 26th, the encircled forces undertook more than twenty counter-attacks in an endeavour to free themselves. Some units coming through the woods towards Lake Mechno were stopped by General Poplaveski's troops who, after operating south of Vitebsk towards Bogouchev, faced north and again encircled them.

During the evening and night of the 26th the circle tightened round the three groups on which the air force had inflicted heavy losses.

On the morning of the 27th Lioudnikov attacked on three sides of the most important group south-west of Vitebsk and split it into several groups the survivors of which gave themselves up. The group at Ostrovno suffered the same fate.

Thus ended the 206th, 246th, 197th Infantry Divisions, the 4th and 6th Divisions of the Luftwaffe. Two more divisions, the 56th and 96th, sustained heavy losses. The Germans had 20,000 killed, 10,000 taken prisoner amongst which were the General commanding the 53rd Army Corps and two major-generals. The equipment destroyed included 560 guns and heavy mortars, 54 tanks and SP guns, over 1,000 machine guns and 1,400 motor vehicles.

The centre group of armies now had its northern flank uncovered and its communications with the north broken. The advance towards the west could be resumed in the direction of Berezina and Minsk.

On 28th June the 1st Baltic front reached Orekhovno and cut the Polotsk-Molodetchno railway (Sketch 49). Other units of the same front were taking Lepel, an important centre, at the same time.

2. *The Bobruisk Operation* (Sketch No. 51). This operation, in the course of which the 1st Baltic front and the 1st, 2nd and 3rd White Russian fronts completely defeated thirty German divisions, stands out as one the most brilliant of those carried out by the Red Army during the Summer of 1944.

Situation—Preparing the Attack. On 23rd June the 1st Baltic front between Komaritchi and Chtchibrine comprised General Romanenko's troops with the main forces on their right towards Rogatchev, General Batov's troops between Zduditchi and Korma and General Loutchinski's troops between Korma and the Pripet. These last had come out of reserve and relieved Batov's troops south of Korma on 20th June. General Pliev's mobile units were behind the point where Loutchinski and Batov linked up.

The White Russian front also included major formations of artillery, air force and the Dnieper Flotilla assembled at Chatsilki on the Berezina.

The German dispositions and defences. The fortified region of Bobruisk was defended by the IXth German Army under General Jordan. The 35th Army Corps with six infantry divisions was operating on the main axis and defended the approach routes to Bobruisk in the east and south-east. Its sector extended from Loudtchitsa on the Dnieper to Zdouditchi on the Berezina. In the south-west as far as the Pripet, units of the 41st Armoured Corps were deployed. Both these corps were reinforced with artillery and tanks. In first reserve was the 20th Armoured Division. The German Command anticipated a Soviet attack between Rogatchev and Jlobine and immediately protected Bobruisk in the east at the expense of the north and south flanks.

In mid-June the 1st Baltic front was divided into two assault groups— one north of Rogatchev (left of General Gorbatov) and the other, and more important, south-west of Jlobine. Both groups were to play the main part in the attack on Bobruisk.

Two successive positions covered Bobruisk in the east, the distance between them varying from twelve to thirty kilometres, and their total depth reaching one hundred to one hundred and ten kilometres. The main position, the first one, eight kilometres deep, had five or six lines of trenches joined together by communication trenches acting at the same time as supporting trenches.

As fire positions the Germans had sunk numerous tank turrets equipped with a gun and a machine gun with all round fire. Every locality had been made into a strongpoint and the city of Bobruisk itself constituted a powerful centre of resistance with two defence belts covered with supporting defences and minefields. The work had been done by the local population and the refugees from Smolensk who had been mass-mobilized.

The Soviet plan. General Rokossovski, commanding the 1st White Russian front, decided to break the defences north of Rogatchev and south of Parichi, and by means of two powerful attacks on a narrow front in the direction of Bobruisk and Gloucha, to encircle and destroy the forces of Bobruisk, then to work in the direction of Ossipovitchi, Poulovitchi and Sloutsk.

The northern attack fell to General Gorbatov, who was to attack on the Ozerani, Tikkinitchi front in the direction of Bobruisk. Having reached the Olsa he would cover himself in the north from Svislotch.

On Gorbatov's left, Romanenko was to force the Drut between Tikkinitchi and Rogatchev with his right, and proceed afterwards towards Bobruisk and 'spread out' the German front on the west bank of the Dnieper.

The southern attack, allotted to the combined flanks of Generals Batov and Loutchinski, was to break the front on each side of Korma and press on towards Gloucha and Krinka, on one side, in order to cut the German communications west of Bobruisk (General Batov) and on the other towards Sloutsk (General Loutchinski).

After reaching the Sekeritchi, Liouban, Volosovitchi line, General Pliev's troops would enter the gap towards Viounichtchi, Zoubarevitchi, with the task of seizing the Ptitch crossings.

The preparation. Since May, air and land reconnaissance, methodically carried out, had revealed precisely the lines of defence and the means of fire. The troops had been trained in swimming across rivers, the use of lifebelts and rubber dinghies and building light footbridges quickly.

The regimental or divisional supporting artillery, already allotted to the battalions and companies, had supplied each gun with fascines and planks to cross over the trenches. The tanks were trained in setting up fascine roads across marshy areas. The small tank and SP units had infantrymen and sappers included and members of the supporting artillery were attached to ensure the tank-artillery liaison during the advance. Tank-air liaison was also ensured by the attachment of air force officers.

Whilst making its reconnaissances, the air force bombed the railway junctions of Brobruisk, Osipovitchi, Sloutsk, Baranovitchi, Slonine and Volkovitz. Two days before the attack the air force began to comb the advanced German defences and the battery positions.

In twenty days the sappers had neutralized nearly 35,000 anti-tank and anti-personnel mines and opened nearly 200 corridors through the minefields for the tanks and infantry.

The attack (Sketch No. 52). On 24th June at 0600 hours, after a powerful artillery bombardment, the infantry and tanks rushed to the attack. Unfavourable weather conditions prevented the air force from taking part in the preparation. Gorbatov met with sharp resistance but by 0800 hours, after repulsing violent counter-attacks, he seized the first trenches on the Ozerani, Veritchev line.

Romanenko did not meet with any better success on the first day. The Drut, both wide and marshy, impeded the advance of the infantry and, even more, of the tanks. Nevertheless, after two hours' fierce fighting his troops succeeded in seizing the first two trenches and keeping them.

The operations proceeded more favourably on General Batov's front. At 0700 hours, General Svanov broke through between Mikhailovka and Korma and pressed on towards the north-west. Towards the end of the morning the weather improved and the air force was able to carry out over 2,000 sorties.

By noon, five lines of trenches had been crossed and at 1300 hours the Russian advance had reached five to six kilometres, the resistance centres of Rakovitchi, Nikolaevka and Petrovitchi had been reduced. At 1800 hours Batov brought in Panov's tanks near Tchernine and Romaniche and by the end of the day they had taken Gomza and Sekeritchi where they were joined by the infantry.

Loutchinski had broken through between Tcherniavka and Rog and met with sharp resistance. He replused the 35th Division, however, and in the evening reached the Brodtsi, Opsino, Rog line.

During the day the German air force showed very little activity, fewer than 150 planes, mostly bombers, being identified.

To sum up, on 24th June, the German front had yielded south of Paritchi along a thirty kilometre front by five to ten kilometres deep. Elsewhere only small gains were reported.

On 25th June at 0700 hours, General Pliev's mobile forces, assembled near Kobilchina, received orders to pass through the participating troops and, proceeding in a north-westerly direction, to outflank the Bobruisk forces from the west and cut the Sloutsk and Minsk roads. At 1130 hours the armour and cavalry overtook Loutchinski's troops and rushed to the pursuit of the Germans who destroyed the bridges and mined the roads. On the 26th at 1500 hours they took Zastenok, Berezovka and Kholopenitchi, advancing thirty kilometres the first day and forty the second. The roads to Bobruisk in the south and south-west were now cut off.

This movement made possible the progress of Batov's troops who defeated the Germans at Paritchi and on the evening of the 26th reached the line Novaia Belitsa, Obolenki, Balachevitchi.

Despite a stiffening resistance, Panov's tanks drew near the Sloutsk road west of Bobruisk. After a night advance they cut the Bobruisk-Ossipovitchi railway at Miradino on the 27th and reached the Berezina further north.

The remains of the 35th and 26th Infantry Divisions and of the 141st Armoured Corps fled towards Bobruisk. The river flotilla caught them going up the right bank of the Berezina and annihilated them.

In four days Batov and Pliev had reached the rear of the German forces in Bobruisk, thus cutting off all roads for a withdrawal towards the west, the south-west and the north-west.

The break-through towards Rogatchev and the encircling of the German forces of Bobruisk. During the night of the 24th/25th June, north of Rogatchev, the Germans tried repeatedly, but in vain, to repulse the Soviet troops beyond the Drout.

On the 25th at 1900 hours, after a forty-five minutes bombardment, Gorbatov attacked the Germans and forced them towards the west. At 2000 hours his centre and left took Kruchinovka, Kalevitchi, Tikhintchi.

On the 26th Gorbatov joined forces with Zakharov's tanks beyond the Dobritsa in order to reach Startsi in the Germans' rear. At 0500 hours air reconnaissance reported endless columns of Russian artillery and vehicles moving from Dobisna towards the west. When nearing Bobruisk they turned partly to the north-west towards the east bank of the Berezina. They were joined by the tanks which spread panic in their path. Their progress was slowed only by the vehicles which the Germans had left burning along the roads. At 1100 hours they took Bartchitsa and after restoring the bridge over the Dobisna they resumed the pursuit. At 1700 hours they reached Startsi and at 1900 hours Titovka, two kilometres east of Bobruisk. Forming themselves into a circle between Dumanovchina, Titovka and Babin, they barred all ways of access to Bobruisk from the east.

Exploiting the success of the tanks, the infantry, in the early morning of the 27th, reached the Mohilev-Bobruisk road between Borovitsa and Startsi. During the night of the 26th/27th June other units forced the river Ola and during the morning reached Volosovitchi and the road junction of Bortniki.

In three days Gorbatov's troops had killed 3,000 Germans, destroyed 150 guns, 120 mortars, numerous tanks and vehicles and captured important material.

On the 26th Romanenko had taken Jlobine and reached the Ozeri, Krivka, Pristan, Chedrin line.

So, by the 27th June the 1st Baltic front had achieved the encirclement of two German army corps in the Bobruisk region. On that day the Germans made their first attempt to open a passage to the north and the north-west for themselves. It had now become a question of destroying them as soon as possible and continuing towards Sloutsk and Minsk.

Destruction of the surrounded forces. In an area some twenty to twenty-five kilometres long by twenty-five to thirty broad was contained the whole 35th Army Corps and the 41st Armoured Corps, that is six divisions, notably the 296th, 6th, 383rd, 45th, 36th Infantry Divisions and numerous units and services. The Soviet infantry was for the most part east, south and west of the circle while in the north two large armoured units completed it. Leaving it to Batov and Romanenko to destroy the surrounded forces, Rokossovski's intention was to continue towards Minsk and Sloutsk with the maximum amount of resources. Gorbatov was, therefore, to proceed from his left towards Lioubonitchi-Svislotch ; Zakharov's tanks would cross the Berezina north of Bobruisk and press towards Ossipovitchi.

When Bobruisk had been taken, Batov would thrust the main body of his forces towards Ossipovitchi, Daraganovo, Dorogui station, to work towards Sloutsk ; Panov's tanks were also making for Ossipovitchi. Finally Loutchinski would pursue the Germans in the Sloutsk, Liouban, Pogost direction.

On 27th June the General commanding the IXth German Army gave the 35th Corps the following order—' Release the encircled troops at all costs, either through Bobruisk, or from the north, linking up with the IVth Army. Act independently '.

General Lutzov, commanding the 35th Corps, decided to break through in a northerly direction towards the IVth Army on the night of 27th/28th. He ordered the destruction of all equipment keeping only the essential needs of the battle.

But Gorbatov was already solidly blocking the roads to the north. On the evening of the 27th the Germans, after destroying their equipment, used their crack troops in a counter-attack but all in vain. The circle continued to tighten while the Soviet artillery and air force continually harassed the Germans.

At 1600 hours the air force discovered near Teloucha, Stoupeni, Doubovka some major infantry units, some 150 tanks, 1,000 guns and 6,000 vehicles. During the evening mixed units amounting to a regiment, supported by groups of ten to fifteen tanks, tried as many as fifteen times to counter-attack the Soviet tanks near Titovka. The surrounded troops were at the mercy of the Soviet air force. At 1900 hours the Russians were all along the front line and five hundred bombers set off without any opposition from enemy fighters. For a whole hour they rained down bombs. Fires started, ammunition exploded and motor columns burned. Leaving behind both arms and equipment the Germans fled to the woods. A number tried to reach Bobruisk by swimming across the Berezina but were stopped by the bullets of the infantry. At 2015 hours, when the planes withdrew, the Soviet infantry and tanks, supported by the artillery, attacked some SS units who were still resisting. At 2200 hours Romanenko, pressing towards Babine from the east and Doubovka from the south-west, split the German forces. Giving up all hope of escape, groups of over a hundred, led by officers, began to give themselves up. Among them was General Lutzov, commanding the 35th Army Corps. Only a few survivors reached Bobruisk. On the 26th at 1300 hours the Soviet troops and air force finished annihilating the surrounded troops and moved towards the Berezina.

In two days, 27th and 28th June, 10,000 Germans had died, 6,000 mortars, over 1,000 machine guns and 4,000 vehicles had been destroyed.

Capture of Bobruisk. The garrison of Bobruisk was 10,000 men strong and was increased by the remains of the 35th Army Corps and the 41st Armoured Corps, detachments of the 6th, 45th, 134th, 36th, 83rd, 35th Infantry Divisions, the 20th Armoured Division, 18th A.A. Division, 511th Service Regiment and a few supporting battalions. General Hamann commanded the town which was surrounded by fortifications and organised for street fighting.

On the evening of the 27th the first attack by Panov's tanks failed. During the night, after violent fighting on the perimeter, the Germans suddenly withdrew towards the north and north-west districts to prepare an attack. This attack was delivered during the night 28th/29th. At 0130 hours, after a short artillery bombardment, some tanks, accompanied by detachments armed with machine pistols, tried to force a way towards the north. Assault battalions, composed of officers, followed. Roused, the Soviets pushed some artillery and mortars to the north of Bobruisk and under their fire the German columns fell back and broke up. At 0200 hours the attack was resumed. Drunken officers and soldiers rushed towards the Soviet trenches under the fire of artillery and machine guns. By 0230 hours some elements had filtered through as far as the artillery positions. At 0400 hours Batov attacked the city and street fighting began. At 0800 hours the Germans massed 8,000 men north of the city and launched a third and last attack which broke through the Soviet lines. Through this passage, exposed to the cross-fire of the Soviet troops, they rushed in the hope of escaping, but too late—Batov held Ossipovitchi and Sloutsk and firmly blocked all ways out.

On the 29th at 1000 hours, Batov and Romanenko finished mopping up the city.

A column of 5,000 men led by General Hofmeister commanding the 41st Armoured Corps, fell on the Ossipovitchi road. Other groups met with a similar fate. In six days of desperate battles the Germans had lost 50,000 killed, 23,700 taken prisoner, 1,300 guns, 215 tanks and SP guns, and 8,400 vehicles, the bulk of the IVth Army. The offensive could now continue, in the west towards Sloutsk-Baranovitchi and in the north-west towards Minsk.

3. *Offensive of the 3rd White Russian front against Orcha, Borissov and of the 2nd White Russian front against Mohilev* (Sketch No. 49). While the 1st Baltic front and the 1st White Russian front were scoring decisive successes on both flanks of the attack at Vitebsk and at Bobruisk, the 2nd and 3rd White Russian fronts in the centre had broken the German resistance and also progressed towards the west.

The very first day General Tcherniakhovski's 3rd front broke through the German lines in the direction of Bogouchev and advanced ten to twelve kilometres. The crack 78th Division barred the road north-east of Orcha. Its chief, General Traut who was made a prisoner after his units had been destroyed, wrote in his logbook :

" On 23rd June a hurricane of unprecedented violence swooped on the right of the division. The barrage continued without a break for five hours. After three hours the barrage moved from the first lines towards the interior of the position. At the same time infantry attacks were launched with equal violence. Shortly after the artillery had opened fire bombing began over the whole depth of the position ".

The next day, 24th June, the advance towards Bogouchev again reached ten to fourteen kilometres, outflanking Orcha from the north. Powerful tank and cavalry formations were thrust into the breach followed by infantry. The 3rd White Russian front defeated the German forces and advanced rapidly towards the Berezina having destroyed four divisions and severely punishing three more. In four days the advance had reached forty-five kilometres on a front of a hundred and fifty.

Further south, General Zakharov's 2nd White Russian front broke through towards Mohilev on 23rd June, gained thirty kilometres in three days, destroyed the German bridgehead east of the Dnieper, forced the river and by the evening of the 28th had taken three important centres—Chkhov Mohilev, Bikhov, which covered Minsk from the east.

In six days, the co-ordinated actions of the four fronts had secured the surrounding and destruction of the Germans at Vitebsk and Bobruisk, the break up of the front in the directions of Bogouchev, Orcha and Mohilev and had advanced one hundred and twenty to one hundred and fifty kilometres on a front of six hundred kilometres. Between the 23rd and 28th June German losses reached 100,000 killed, 38,000 prisoners. Ten divisions, taken from other fronts to reinforce the IVth Army, had sustained heavy losses. Having split up the enemy forces the Soviet troops, especially the 1st and 3rd White Russian fronts, were in a position to exploit their success towards the west without giving the Germans time to recover. Also, the German defeats on the north and south flanks of the salient of White Russia allowed concentric attacks against the main forces withdrawing in the direction of Minsk in front of the 2nd White Russian front. The reserves sent in one after the other to stop the Soviet advance did not even succeed in slowing down its rhythm of twenty to twenty-five kilometres a day.

It was now only a question of destroying the remains of the IVth German Army.

Having failed to establish a front on the Berezina, the German Command wished to prevent the Red Army from reaching East Prussia and organised a new position on the Vilna, Lida, Baranovitchi line which was held by reserve units or units removed from other fronts.

SECOND PHASE—28TH JUNE TO 3RD JULY

Surrounding and destruction of the German forces East of Minsk (Sketch No. 53).   On the 29th and 30th June, the 2nd and 3rd White Russian fronts resisted sharp German attempts to push them back beyond the Berezina. After repulsing these counter-attacks they crossed the river at numerous points. On 1st July they defeated the forces of Borissov and freed the town. The 5th Armoured Division rushed from Kovel by the Borissov road, began

94

to check the Soviet advances, but finding itself attacked on both its flanks beyond the Berezina, particularly at Stoudienka, the very place where Napoleon crossed the river in 1812, it was defeated and pushed back. In order to give air cover to the crossing, the Soviet air forces made as many as 2,000 sorties a day. The Germans lost 22,500 killed and 13,000 taken prisoner.

The 3rd White Russian front entered the big wooded masses which were intersected by marshes, west of the Berezina. The right flank marched towards Lake Narotch, the centre towards Molodetchno and the left flank towards Minsk, outflanking and destroying sporadic resistance as they met it.

On 2nd July armour and cavalry overran Krasnoie and Vileika, attacked Molodetchno and cut off communications with Vilna and Lida.

To the east and south-east of Minsk the offensive went equally well. The 1st White Russian front did not wait for the destruction of the surrounded troops at Bobruisk before thrusting its weight of armour upon Minsk. Other units, preceded by Pliev's forces, made for Sloutsk which the cavalry outflanked and captured on 30th June. The infantry followed by forced marching. On this day, 30th June, the 1st front alone took 12,000 prisoners.

On 2nd July after covering eighty kilometres over difficult ground, the mobile forces occupied Stolbtsi, Gorodeia, Nesvitch and cut off Minsk from the south-west, threatening to surround the main elements of the IVth Army lingering east of the city.

The IVth Army, energetically pursued by the 2nd front and outflanked north and south, fell back on the Mohilev-Minsk general axis with the remains of the IXth Army and watched the situation deteriorate daily.

On 3rd July Tcherniakhovski attacked Minsk from the north-east. His armoured forces, followed by the infantry, advanced through Smolevitchi and Logoisk, broke the German resistance on the outskirts of Minsk and swept upon the city. Soon the capital of White Russia, a most important communications centre, was freed.

The 2nd front, however, continued to meet with strong resistance on the river Svislotch between Pukhovitchi and Ossipovitchi. The 12th Armoured Division halted it for two days on the Pukhovitvhi-Minsk road but was driven back by vigorous air action while a Soviet armoured unit outflanked it in the south from the Sloutsk-Minsk road.

On 3rd July the tanks of the 1st front reached the southern edge of Minsk and joined the 3rd front within the city itself. The infantry immediately strengthened the encircling movement started by the armour which now included the remains of the 12th and 27th Army Corps and of the 39th Armoured Corps, i.e., some 100,000 men, within the vast region east of Minsk between Volma, Pekalin and the Berezina. In this mass, into which the Soviet forces gradually infiltrated, there was no longer any general command. Groups of major or lesser importance tried to break the stranglehold in the north-east and the south-west. On the 7th and 8th July the air force pounded one of these groups and, in collaboration with the infantry, it methodically completed the reduction of the surrounded portions. By the evening of the 11th all resistance had ceased. In three weeks the Soviet forces had advanced five hundred kilometres and opened a gap of four hundred kilometres into the German front.

THIRD PHASE—5TH TO 23RD JULY

The exploitation (Sketch No. 49). After the heavy defeats of Vitebsk, Bobruisk, and Minsk, the German Command no longer had the means to check the pressure of the 1st Baltic front and the three White Russian fronts.

The 1st Baltic front, marching towards the north-west, reached the outskirts of Dvinsk with its right. The centre took Novie Sventzani and Outena, the left drew near Oukmerg.

The 3rd White Russian front pursued the Germans towards the west. Vilna, the gateway to East Prussia and consequently fortified and well defended, resisted for several days but fell on 13th July. After a two hundred kilometres bound the 3rd front reached the Niemen, crossed it and on 15th July established several bridgeheads south and north of Alitous, towards Meretch and south of Drouskenki.

The 2nd front pressed on to Novogroudok and beyond it towards Grodno and Volkovisk which it reached after covering two hundred and fifty kilometres. On 16th July, linking up with the left flank of the 3rd front, it captured Grodno.

The 1st White Russian front operated north of the Pripet. Its main direction was to the south-west. On the 8th, after two days' fighting, it took Baranovitchi, continued towards Slonim, Prujani and Bereza-Kartouzskaia. Kobrine overran Pinsk on the 14th after covering one hundred and fifty to one hundred and seventy kilometres ; he marched upon Brest-Litovsk, an important communications centre and a covering position on the Warsaw axis.

In one month, from 23rd June to 23rd July, the 1st Baltic front and the three White Russian fronts had killed over 380,000 Germans and taken 150,000 prisoners including 22 generals, amongst whom were 5 army corps generals and 13 major-generals. The material losses reached 630 planes, 2,400 tanks and SP guns, 8,700 guns, 7,000 mortars, 23,000 machine guns and 57,000 vehicles.

White Russia, most of Lithuania and part of Poland had been liberated. Three roads were opened to the Red Army ; west, towards East Prussia, north-west towards the Baltic, south-west towards Poland. By the end of the month it had occupied Chaouliai and Bielostok, on 27th July, Brest on the 28th, Pelgave (Mitau) on the 31st, Kovno (Kaunas) on 1st August. The Red Army was drawing near the frontier of East Prussia.

The first attack against East Prussia (Sketch No. 62). On 16th October the 3rd White Russian front, having crossed the Niemen on all its length upstream of Tilsit, launched its first attack against East Prussia. It met an organized force. On 20th October an armoured corps with 220 medium T.34 tanks and brigades of tankborne infantry, attacked south of the Stalluponen Gumbinnen road and, in the evening, forced the crossing of the river Pissa south of Gumbinnen. The next day the Germans counter-attacked on the flanks of the pocket, in the north with the ' Hermann Goering ' Armoured Division, coming from Stalluponen, in the south with the ' Gross Deutschland ' Division coming from Goldap. The attacking Soviet troops, some 20,000 strong, were surrounded and General Tcherniakhovski ordered a withdrawal. With the aid of the ' Stormoviks ' they managed to extricate themselves though they lost two-thirds of their tanks. The offensive had been halted.

The Soviet Command estimated that the Germans had massed opposite the Niemen nearly 130,000 men, 440 tanks, 2,000 guns and 400 planes including 150 fighters. Three lines of fortifications covered the river Angerapp. The attack was to be resumed when the ratio of forces had reached three to one and the frost had removed the obstacle made by the lakes of Mazuria.

During these battles on the frontier of East Prussia, the French Regiment of fighter planes, engaged in 1943 north of Orel and in 1944 in White Russia, won its finest victories. Equipped with the new planes YAK 3 it carried out one hundred and twenty missions on 16th October, the day of the launching of the offensive, and during the day brought down twenty-nine planes.

6. THE GERMAN DEFEAT IN WESTERN UKRAINE, JULY-AUGUST, 1944

(Sketch No. 54)

The offensive of the 1st Ukrainian front upon Lwov followed those of the 1st, 2nd and 3rd Ukrainian fronts in February-March which released the right bank of the Dnieper.

At the beginning of April the 1st Ukrainian front held the line Kovel, Brodi, Kolomia, its left resting upon the spurs of the Carpathians. Towards the west it occupied an advanced position of 200,000 square kilometres between two German salients—that of White Russia in the north and of Jassy, Kichinev in the south.

With the reduction of the White Russia salient in June, the threat from the north disappeared. The 1st front was now able to attack towards Lwov.

Organization of the German defence. Complicated ground features, wooded masses, marshy areas and numerous rivers made the organization of their defence easier for the Germans. In three and a half months' work, calling largely on mobilized local labour, they had set up three positions blocking the road to Lwov : the first consisted of three to four lines of trenches, all interconnected ; the second, named " Prince Eugene Line ', ten to twelve kilometres further, consisted also of several lines of trenches and numerous pockets of resistance ; twenty to thirty kilometres further back, the third position followed along the west Boug and the Gnilaia Lipa. Further west, the Dniestr, the San and the Vistula formed as many obstacles, as did also some towns made into centres of resistance : Kovel, Vladimir, Volynsk, Sokol, Broni, Zalotchev, Rava Rouska, Jolkov, Lwov, Khofdorov, Stanislav, Drogobitch and finally the fortress of Przemysl, modernized in 1939. German defence in western Ukraine rested on the triangle Brodi, Rava Rouska, Lwov.

The German Command had decided to fight on the second position, leaving only covering troops on the advanced position. It hoped that then the artillery preliminary bombardment would fall on empty ground and spare the concentrated resources of the second position. The Soviet Command having discovered this, organized its attack accordingly. The defence fell to the Northern Ukraine group of armies which held the Kovel, Stanislav front and included the Ist and IVth German Armoured Armies and the Ist and IInd Hungarian Armies.

The Soviet plan (Sketch No. 55). The task of destroying this group of armies and liberating Western Ukraine was given to Marshal Koniev's 1st Ukrainian front. He prepared five simultaneous attacks on a two hundred and seventy kilometres front, from Vladimir Volynsk to Stanislav, which would paralyze the use of reserves. If he succeeded the whole German system east of the Ukraine would collapse at once.

The two main attacks, given to the centre of the front, aimed at Jaroslav : the first, in the Gorokhov Zavidtche sector, in the direction of Rava Rouska and Jaroslav, was to outflank the main German forces of Brodi from the north ; the second, coming from between Podkamen and Ozenra towards

Lwov-Przemysl, was to outflank these same forces from the south. In this way the Soviet attacks aimed directly at the triangle Brodi, Rava Rouska, Lwov.

To carry out this plan the Russians formed groups of all arms including the armoured forces of Generals Ribalko, Leliouchenko, Katukov, and a large artillery force (200 guns per kilometre), all of which were supported by a strong air force.

The three secondary battles were to be : the first from the west of Loutsk towards Vladimir Volynsk, Zamoustie (cover of the right flank) ; the second from the west of Tarnopol towards Khoderov ; the third from Tchetkov towards Stanislav.

A methodical training of staff and men on ground organized in the same way as the sectors to be attacked, had, amongst other things, catered for the crossing of rivers. Air and land reconnaissance had multiplied. Finally staff officers supervised the deployment of the troops most carefully camouflaged, while the artillery maintained its normal rate of fire.

The German Command endeavoured to discover the layout of the Soviet attack, particularly to pinpoint tank formations and, to this end, paratroops were dropped behind the lines but were captured. On 14th July Hitler sent the following Order of the Day to the group of armies of Western Ukraine :

' The enemy is ready to take the offensive, hard battles are to be expected in your sector.

' Any division which, in the event of a break-through, does not immediately counter-attack to fill the gap and maintain its position and which, with this aim in view, does not fight to the last man, will expose numerous units to the gravest danger. The whole of Germany will watch you during these difficult days and weeks.

' If you do your duty, the Bolshevist offensive will be broken and drowned in its own blood.'

The Attack (Sketches Nos. 54 and 55). *Breakdown of the German defence.* On the right flank on 13th July, and on the rest of the front on 14th July, thousands of guns and mortars prepared the way for an attack by advance detachments which, thanks to the effect of the bombardment, penetrated two or three kilometres into the first position before noon. The German Command thought it was dealing with the main effort of the enemy.

On the right flank on the very first day, Generals Gordov's and Pukhov's troops broke through near Vladimir-Volynski and Sokol on a sixty kilometre front and advanced ten to fifteen kilometres. The unrelenting defence of Gorokhov, the garrison of which had been reinforced by an infantry regiment and some forty tanks, finally yielded before massive artillery fire co-ordinated with air bombing and dive-bombing attacks. Prisoners said that they had received the order to withdraw to the main positions the next day.

On 14th July a new advance of four to five kilometres allowed an attack to be made on the Prince Eugene line. Surprised by the speed of the advances the Germans sent in the 16th and 17th Armoured Divisions. Using their main forces the Russians broke through the Prince Eugene line on 15th July and on the evening of the 17th they took Stoianov, Radzekhov and made contact with the rear position which, in turn, they overran. In the direction of Sokol the advance units reached the Boug. Others in the south-west forced the crossing of the river near Kristinopol, Kamenka at the end of the day. The gap on the right flank of the front was now seventy kilometres in depth by one hundred in width. General Katukov's and Baranev's troops consolidated it.

On the left of the front Generals Moskalenko and Gretchko completed the planned break-through.

But the most violent battles took place in the centre of the front south of Brodi. In this sector General Kourotckhine attacked on 14th July at 1430 hours between Podkamen and Ozerna. The Germans, supported by a thick network of trenches, forest masses and river sections defended themselves fiercely. At the end of the day, thanks to their fire power, the Soviet troops broke through the first position and advanced six or seven kilometres.

On 16th July the infantry gained ten to fifteen kilometres through wooded country and reached the Zolotchev-Sasov road, thus opening a breach into the ' Kotli Corridor ', only three or four kilometres wide, into which Ribalko's tanks rushed on 17th July. These tanks routed the 14th Division, widened the breach, swung towards the north-west on the Zolotchev-Bousk road, destroying on the way a German strong-point, and captured Krasnoie, where they cut the Brodi-Lwov railway. The same evening they reached the Peltev, restored the bridges by night and on the morning of the 18th pressed towards the west in the direction of Lwov and to the north-west to meet General Baranov's cavalry. Towards noon they took the town of Bousk, on the west bank of the Boug, thus cutting the last Brodi-Lwov road.

In their rear, however, a fierce battle was raging as the Germans tried to break the Kotli corridor with five divisions, two armoured, deploying 300 tanks round Zolotchev. These forces attacked from south to north on their way to meet the Brodi group which was proceeding north to south from Olesno.

These attacks were launched on 16th July supported by important artillery and air formations, and in certain sectors were renewed as many as ten times. The Germans had 300 bombers in the air and, above the battlefield violent fighting also took place. On several occasions it appeared that the corridor was about to give way, but the Soviet forces continued to reinforce the flanks with second echelon of infantry and with artillery. Leliouchenko's tanks also came into action and set up an impassable barrage to the north and south.

On the 17th, 18th and 19th July fighting went on with the same violence. On the 18th the Russians took Zolotchev and on the 20th Leliouchenko's tanks rushed towards Peremichliani.

Destruction of the surrounded forces west of Brodi. The Germans had lost their last hope of re-establishing contact with the surrounded forces which comprised : the staff of the 13th Army Corps, the 316th and 340th Infantry Divisions, the 454th Protective Division, the 14th SS Division ' Galicia ', the remains of the 349th Infantry Division and the 505th and 507th Tank Battalions.

During the night of the 21st/22nd July, the Germans in column formation attempted a last break-through but sustained heavy losses and rolled back, dislocated and demoralized by the artillery and the air force, and repulsed by the infantry fire. On the morning of the 22nd they began to surrender and by the evening the move became general, some units telephoning Soviet Command for instructions on how to reach the points of assembly of prisoners. On the 23rd all resistance had ceased. Amongst the 17,000 men thus captured were General Hauffe, commanding the 13th Army Corps, and all his staff and two major-generals.

Over 30,000 dead lay on the battlefields, amongst which was the General Commanding the 340th Infantry Division. Moreover, in the Zolotchev region, the 357th and 75th Infantry Divisions and the 1st and 8th Armoured Divisions had also sustained heavy losses. The general commanding the 13th Army Corps stated : ' Knowing that the Soviet air force was engaged in White Russia, we never could have imagined that it could intervene against us with such resources. It has ceaselessly bombed us so that we could not even raise our heads. Even the old officers who had fought in the 1914-18 war were morally shaken.'

Without waiting for the destruction of the surrounded forces at Brodi the offensive continued towards Rava Rouska and Lwov. On 20th July, Gordov stormed Vladimir-Volynski ; on the 21st he forced the passage of the Boug ; on the 23rd he liberated Groubechov. General Poukhov broke through the third position on the 19th, crossed the Boug south of Sokol and the next day overran Rava Rouska and cut the Lwov-Lublin railway. On the 23rd he reached the San in the Siniava-Jareslav sector and widely outflanked Lwov in the north-west. The tanks which were daringly pushed through the Kotli Corridor reached the outskirts of the city on the 20th, defeated the 367th Infantry Division and the 509th Independent Armoured Battalion which lost sixty tanks.

On the left flank the troops which took Boutchatch on the 21st liberated Golitch on the 23rd and outflanked Stanislav.

North of the 1st Ukrainian front, the 1st White Russian front which had captured Kovel on 6th July, advanced fifty kilometres on a one hundred and fifty kilometres front in three days, reaching the Boug without giving the Germans time to destroy the bridges. It now protected the action against Lwov from the north.

In ten days the 1st Ukrainian front had broken the front from Kovel to Stanislav, split up and partly destroyed the group of armies of Northern Ukraine. The whole German front fell back and on the main axes the Soviet advance gained one hundred and eight kilometres. The battle for Lwov had begun.

Liberation of Lwov (Sketches Nos. 55 and 56).   The Germans were determined to defend Lwov and had sent in four divisions, one armoured and one motorized. Having been informed of this Soviet Command decided upon an encircling movement by large armoured units. Containing the Germans north and north-west of Lwov, Ribalko's tanks were to outflank them widely in the north-west and west in order to take them in the rear and prevent any withdrawal towards the San.

Leliouchenko's tanks were to outflank them from the south, enter Lwov and cut off the roads leading south-west. At the same time the infantry would attack the Vinniko heights east of the city.

On 20th July a brigade of tanks from the Ural, on a narrow front in the south-east, broke through the outer belt of the city which it entered at 0400 hours by an only road pounded by the German artillery. After violent street fighting the tanks reached the central districts towards noon. Other tanks entering Lwov from the south-west overcame resistance and advanced towards the centre.

At the same time the assault upon Vinnikov by the infantry was taking place. Ribalko's tanks were secretly removed from the battle and following a round about route via Koulikov, Maguerov, Nemirov, Javorov arrived the next morning in the Javorov, Soudevaia-Vichnia region and cut off the Lwov-Jaroslav and Lwov-Przemysl roads. The only road left to the Germans was the Sambor road in the south-west.

The infantry had advanced one hundred and twenty kilometres in thirty-five hours and caught up with the tanks. On 25th July, while pushing some units towards Przemysl, Ribalko linked up with Leliouchenko and near Roudki cut off the Jaroslav road, the very last one. The circle was closing.

The destruction of the forces thus netted was to occupy two days.

The infantry captured the Vinnikov heights and entered the city from the east. All resistance ceased on the 27th, the Germans leaving 8,000 dead on the field. The Soviet troops took 3,500 prisoners and besides 35 tanks, 800 guns and mortars and 500 machine guns, they captured twenty trainloads of material. The group of armies of Northern Ukraine was now either destroyed or dislocated. As early as 23rd July the 2nd Ukrainian front reached the San near Jaroslav with its advance units.

Battles of the San and the Vistula (Sketch Nos. 56 and 57). The San remained the chief obstacle in the Cracow direction. The Germans had therefore fortified the west bank and turned all localities, both large and small, into centres of resistance. To defend the San, the 23rd and 24th Armoured Divisions, from Rumania, were reinforced by the 7th Hungarian Division, units of the Ist and IInd Armoured Armies, provisional battalions and even by NCOs training schools and convalescent units.

On 24th July Katukov and Pukhov together with the Baranov cavalry, overthrew the German covering troops, forced a crossing of the river at several points and within twenty-four hours had set up a bridgehead north of Jaroslav.

On the 25th Ribalko's tanks reached the San near Przemysl. Violent fighting began over one hundred kilometres between Niske and Przemysl. The bridgehead north of Jaroslav was widened and the Germans brought up reinforcements. The tanks crossed the San between Jaroslav and Przemysl, threatening both these cities from the south. Other units marching directly from the south-east towards Przemysl, caught the Germans by surprise and gave them no time to destroy the bridges across the Viar. The tanks of Colonel Arkhipov and Lieutenant-Colonel Tchougounkov crossed the river and began street fighting on the west bank. By noon they held half the town on this bank. Some tanks had crossed the San near Radino, captured Jaroslav from the south, taking numerous prisoners, then entered Przemysl from the west bank.

Thus on the 28th July, the same day that Lwov fell, Jaroslav and Przemysl also fell. The defence on the San had collapsed.

The Soviet plan had provided for the crossing of the Vistula at Baranov and Jousefouv. The aim was to reach it before the armoured and motorized forces which the Germans were rushing there under the protection of delaying troops. On 30th July the advanced guard of the 1st White Russian front reached the Vistula, leapfrogged the retreating Germans and began to cross the river.

North of Sandomir, in the sector between Jousefouv and the junction with the San, General Gordov established small bridgeheads. South of Sandomir, from Tarmovjec to Baranov, Katoukov's tanks and Poukhov's infantry also scored successes. General Vekhin's division, the first to arrive on 31st July, built emergency rafts, crossed the river and dug in on the west bank.

For four days running the Germans counter-attacked with a fresh armoured division and a fresh infantry division but to no avail. The Soviet troops finished mopping up the east bank and widened their bridgehead which reached twenty-five kilometres by thirty kilometres wide on 3rd August.

From the 1st to the 10th August the failure of the counter-attacks which tried in vain to prevent the Russians from doubling their bridgehead, forced German Command to form three groups with troops coming from other sectors and from Rumania. Containing, amongst others, six armoured divisions, they were to destroy the bridgehead by attacking in three different directions.

For four days there was extremely violent fighting. In one sector alone the Germans used two infantry regiments and seventy tanks supported by successive waves of thirty to forty planes. They penetrated the Soviet positions but were repulsed. One Soviet artillery unit destroyed twenty-two tanks alone.

Elsewhere the armour repulsed the attack of two divisions and fifty tanks which left 1,000 dead and 18 tanks on the field. Further similar attempts of the same kind failed and cost the Germans enormous losses.

Finally, having collected together its resources, Soviet Command launched two simultaneous attacks ; one from the bridgehead north of Sandomir towards the west, the other from the southern bridgehead towards the north-west, encircling three divisions reinforced with special formations. Upon their refusal to capitulate they were annihilated. 12,000 dead Germans lay on the field and 1,500 were taken prisoner.

The appearance of the Soviet advance guard on the Vistula caused the insurrection of Warsaw on 31st July long before it had been arranged. On 4th August General Bor's volunteer army, some 50,000 strong, conquered the city but when the Soviet offensive stopped they were doomed. For two months, while waiting for the Soviet army, it heroically resisted the attacks of the SS divisions and of Hitler's air force but eventually the 10,000 survivors had to capitulate on 2nd October.

Battles to the south of Western Ukraine (Sketch No. 54). After breaking through the German defences left of the 1st Ukrainian front in the direction of Khodoru and Stanislav, Generals Moskalenko's and Gretchko's troops took advantage of the pressure on Peremichliani by Leliouchenko's tanks and crossed the Stripa, the Koropets, the Zolotaia Lipa and, on the 24th, the Gnilaya Lipa, they occupied Regatin and Galitch.

Avoiding a frontal attack upon Stanislav, which was protected by several rivers and firmly held, Gretchko outflanked the city from the north and south. The units coming from Galitch cut the communications in the north and north-west, others those of the south and south-west. Having completed the circle the city was attacked from the east and fell on 27th July. The remains of the German troops fled in disorder and scattered in the woods. The next day the fighting was resumed forty kilometres beyond Stanislav and, by the end of the month, after crossing the Dniestr near Drogobitch, the Soviet troops entered the mountains south and west of Stanislav.

It now remained to liberate the important industrial area and oil-basin of Drogobitch, Borislav on the north spurs of the Carpathians. The very tortuous nature of the country aided the defence. The roads were mined, demolitions prepared and the important points firmly held. Coming from Kaluch, Gretchko advanced while fighting and reached Stryi, a railway and road junction. Attacked from the front and outflanked from the south, the town fell on 5th August.

Gretchko, now attached to the 4th Ukrainian front, also broke the German resistance north-east of Drogobitch which he overran on the 6th.

An attempt was made by the Germans to resist at Borislav, a big oil centre, but the Soviet troops, making use of the mountain paths, came upon them from the rear. On the 7th they took the town and, after a brilliant night attack on the same day, Mosalenko (1st Ukrainian front) captured Sambor, an important railway junction.

Western Ukraine being completely lost, the Germans transferred their resistance to the approaches to the passes in the Carpathians where it was later to be broken in September.

The victory of Western Ukraine opened two new roads to the Red Army —one towards Cracow, the other towards Czechoslovakia.

The huge bridgehead beyond the Vistula in the Sandomir region considerably reduced the value of the river as an obstacle. It was now possible to consider new operations upon Lodz and Cracow.

The crossing of the Carpathians and, in November 1944, the entry of the troops of the 4th Ukrainian front into Czechoslovakia, was to be the consequence and the crowning of the victory gained by the 1st Ukrainian front.

Between the 13th June and 12th August the figures for the German losses were : 172,000 killed or taken prisoner, 690 planes, nearly 2,000 tanks and SP guns, 3,600 guns, 3,000 mortars, 5,700 machine guns and 11,700 vehicles.

The Germans saw themselves deprived,not only of rich agricultural regions, but also of the Drogobitch oil.

7. THE JASSY-KICHINEV OPERATION (AUGUST, 1944)

(Sketch No. 58)

The Jassy-Kichinev operation carried out in August, 1944 by the 2nd and 3rd Ukrainian fronts under General Malinovski and General Tolbukhin respectively appears as one of the most brilliant of the war. In a fortnight, an advance carried out at a surprising pace, brought the Red Army to Bucharest and separated Rumania from Germany.

This operation had two phases—from the 20th to 25th August the breakthrough of the front and the encircling of the Kichinev forces ; from the 26th August the liquidation of these forces.

The situation. Since its spring victories in the Ukraine and the entry into Rumania, the Red Army had been holding a front running south of Pascani, north of Jassy, north of Ungueni, north of Mechti, then along the Dniestr. It had repulsed the counter-attacks launched against the bridgehead at Bender, west of the Dniestr.

For the Germans the Jassy-Kichinev salient constituted the strategic right flank of the front, barring access to Rumania, her oils and the Balkans.

The defence organization was set up at the beginning of the summer and on the north flank, at Jassy and Targu-Frumos, were two fortified areas with concrete works. The defence of the salient fell to the group of armies of Southern Ukraine, comprising the VIth and VIIIth German Armies and the IIIrd and IVth Rumanian Armies, sixty divisions in all, twenty of which were German and placed at the most important points and ten in reserve. Of these one was armoured and one motorized.

Before the summer the German Command had massed nearly the whole of its armour on its right. Now it pushed it towards the north to face the

Soviet offensive in White Russia and Western Ukraine. It estimated that these two offensives had used up the Red Army's capabilities and had no further anxiety for its right. The attack of the 20th August was therefore to come as a surprise.

The Soviet plan. The Soviet Command wished to reduce the Jassy-Kichinev salient in order to destroy the Germano-Rumanian forces defending it, to invade Rumania and separate her from Germany. The operation consisted of two concentric attacks—one between the Prut and the Seret in the direction of the south and south-west, the other from Tiraspol in a westerly direction. The link-up was to be made near Leova on the Prut. Subsidiary attacks would contain the enemy north-east of Jassy and near Cherpeni.

The main attack in the north was given to the 2nd Ukrainian front between Pascani and Jassy. Over a distance of twenty-five kilometres, the sector aimed at had no fewer than 350 concreted works and ten to twelve batteries per kilometre. The attack was to be carried out in the direction of Vaslui and Huci (Khuchi) then towards Falcin (Feltchin) and would thus prevent any withdrawal towards the west. The attack group of the 2nd front combined power with mobility; it deployed 200 guns per kilometre of front not counting the small calibre artillery; it comprised two large tank units under Generals Kravtchenko and Alexeiev and enjoyed strong air support.

Mixed units of cavalry and tanks were to cover the operation in the west by attacking along the Seret, from Belcesti towards Targu-Frumos and Roman. In the Bender sector, spread over thirty-five kilometres, the assault group of the 3rd front consisted of two strong armoured units, a strong air force and 224 guns per kilometre. The break-through was to start from the bridgehead south of Bender and the advance would follow the Trajan wall in order to link up with the 2nd front on the Prut.

A secondary covering action was to destroy the forces of the Bielgorod Dniestrovski (Akherman) region in the south.

The 3rd front was to work ultimately towards Galatz, Braila Ismail, with the Black Sea fleet making landings at Vilkov, Sulina, Constanza and Tulcea on the Danube.

These preparations were completely missed by the Germans whose reserves were held up by apparent activity north-east of Jassy and near Cherpeni. Both fronts attacked simultaneously on 22nd August.

The attack by the 2nd front. The artillery bombardment, with several thousand guns, lasted one and a half hours while the air force made 1,600 sorties during the day. At first the infantry and tanks did not meet with any resistance and, having broken through the first position, Kravtchenko and Alexeiev entered the gap that same evening. On the 21st and 22nd they broke through the second and third positions. The tanks and the air force, the latter making 2,500 further sorties, cut short the counter-attack of four divisions, one of them armoured.

On the 22nd Targu-Frumos, Jassy and Ungueni fell. The advance reached sixty kilometres. On the 23rd Kravtchenko overran Vaslui and the infantry destroyed the strong-points left behind. The air force took by surprise and dispersed three divisions, one of them armoured, on their way to counter-attack.

On 24th August Kravtchenko occupied Barlad, and Alexeiev occupied Huci. The advance units reached the Prut at Leova and Liucheni. At the same time, mixed cavalry and armoured units occupied Roman and Bacau on the right flank thereby preventing any withdrawal from Jassy-Kichinev towards the west and south-west.

In five days the 2nd front had advanced one hundred and twenty kilometres at an average speed of twenty-five kilometres a day.

The attack by the 3rd Ukrainian front. The 3rd front attacked after an artillery bombardment of one and three quarter hours. During the day the air force made 1,600 sorties. After breaking through the main position on a front of forty kilometres by thirty in depth, Generals Karkov's and Jdanov's armour rushed forward. On the 22nd they broke the intermediary lines, moved along the Trajan wall and on the 23rd reached Komrat which had been hurriedly evacuated by the staff of the VIth Army. They surrounded and destroyed 5,000 Germans.

Finally the left flank units occupied Bielgorod-Dniestrovski (Akherman) on 23rd August and outflanked the defenders of the region from the west who either surrendered or died.

The right flank reached the Jatmana, Djamana, Kainari line. On 24th August Kichinev, the capital of the Soviet Republic of Moldavia, was liberated and the link up between the 2nd and 3rd fronts achieved. The latter lined the Prut from Leova to Cahul.

On 25th August the circle closed round the twenty-two divisions, the backbone of the south-east front to which numerous units had been added. Six days had been sufficient to achieve this. It now remained to destroy these forces and prevent the Germans from organizing a new front.

Destruction of the surrounded forces and penetration into the centre of Rumania. Up to 3rd September the 2nd and 3rd fronts, acting independently of each other, destroyed the troops surrounded in the Lopouchna, Kotovskoie Minjir region and annihilated five divisions north of Huci. Only one group of 7,000 men, filtering through the woods, reached the Seret near Bacau (Bakeou). They too were overtaken and destroyed. At the same time the Soviet troops pressed on without a break towards the south and south-west, the 2nd front towards Tecuciu (Tekoutchi) and Fecsani, the 3rd towards Ismail and Galatz. The armoured forces covered forty to fifty kilometres per day. On the 25th the 2nd front occupied Tecuciu and, on the 27th, Fescani and Ramnicu-Sarat.

The ' Gates of Fescani ', the key to Rumania's oil, fell into the hands of the Red Army. For its part, the 3rd front took Ismail, Galatz and on 28th August Braila (Brailov).

At the end of August, in conjunction with the 3rd front and the air force, the Black Sea Fleet made successful landings on the coast and occupied the ports of Vilkov, Soulino, Tulcea and Constanza on the 29th. On the 30th the 2nd front took Ploesti, the centre of the oilfields, and on the 31st it entered Bucharest from the south.

The results. The balance sheet is as follows : the German group of armies of Southern Ukraine with the VIth and VIIIth Armies had been defeated, twenty-two German divisions had been destroyed, not to mention the Rumanian divisions, eight brigades of SP guns (Ferdinands), eleven artillery regiments, fourteen independent artillery groups, twenty-five special units ; 106,000 prisoners including 13 generals, enormous losses of equipment, 340 planes, 830 tanks and SP guns, 3,500 guns of all calibres and 33,000 vehicles. Among the dead left on the field were two army corps generals and five major generals.

The spectacular success of these operations had been facilitated by the air attacks against the German headquarters which, for the most part, had been disorganized since the first day. On the second day all army corps and division command posts had had to fall back. On 23rd August General Friessner, commanding the group of armies of Southern Ukraine, lost all contact with his major units ; on the 26th his staff fled from Galatz behind the Carpathians where it was followed by the staff of the VIIIth Army. The German Command lost all control of the operations.

The German defeat of Jassy, Kichinev had a decisive influence in South East Europe. Rumania gave up the struggle and Bulgaria soon followed her example. Both turned against their former ally.

The Red Army was to offer a helping hand to Tito's supporters and invade Hungary. A new manoeuvre to encircle the south flank of the German armies became possible.

8. THE GERMAN DEFEAT IN THE BALTIC STATES (SEPTEMBER TO OCTOBER, 1944)

(Sketch No. 59)

The situation. The victories of the Leningrad and Volkhov fronts in January and February and of the Baltic and White Russian front during the summer, provided the Red Army with excellent bases for an operation from the east, the south-east and the south against the German armies of the Baltic.

At the beginning of September the Leningrad front crossed the Narva, established a bridgehead west of the river, captured the isthmus between Lake Tchoud (Peipous) and Lake Bistr-Jary, liberated Tartu and reached the river Erna. As a result of previous operations the 2nd and 3rd Baltic fronts held the line Lake Bistr-Jary, Anoudi, Goulbene, Madena, Gostini. After its victory in White Russia, the 1st Baltic front reached the following line by the end of July—Kroustpils, Tervidani, Pelgava (Mitau), Berzoupe Station, Raoudoniani (on the Niemen).

The advance of the 1st Baltic front towards Riga threatened to cut off the Estonian and Latvian forces from East Prussia. To ward off this danger, the German Command thrust major armoured units into the Mitava and Cholau (Chaulai) region, but all attempts to widen the narrow corridor remained unsuccessful.

North of Lake Tchoud, and then between this and Lake Bistr-Jary, the Narva group was operating. In Southern Estonia and in Latvia, facing the Baltic front, the northern group of armies, consisting of the reconstituted XVIth and XVIIIth Armies, was fighting. The Germans were anxious to retain this salient, however exposed it may have been, in order to hold up important forces and threaten the rear of the 1st Baltic front from the north. The country, everywhere wooded, marshy and furrowed with lakes and rivers, was favourable to the defence.

The mission of the fronts. The operations of the Leningrad front and of the three Baltic fronts in September and October, 1944, aimed at the destruction of the German forces of the Baltic and the occupation of the Baltic States. The Leningrad front under Marshal Gororov was to attack from the Narva towards Kadrina and from Tartu towards Kaike-Maria in order to eliminate the German forces from the Narva and occupy the north of Estonia; the 3rd Baltic front, under General Maslennikov, was to attack south of

106

Bistr-Jary in the direction of Valmera, and north of Anouchi in the direction of Smiltene, in order to destroy the XVIIIth German Army and arrive on the Bay of Riga ; the 2nd Baltic front, under General Eremenko, linking up with the 3rd front, was to attack between Goulbene and Gostini in order to take Riga ; finally, the 1st Baltic front, under General Bagramian, was to push its right into the Nausedjai, Tervidiani, Berzomouija region towards Riga in order to isolate East Prussia from the northern German armies.

Powerful attack formations with a large proportion of artillery and tanks were built up and brought to a position of readiness during the first fortnight in September.

The attack—Leningrad front. Between the 17th and 21st September the troops in the Narva sector broke the German defences, advanced one hundred kilometres in five days and reached Kadrina. With equal success, the main forces of the front forced the Tartu positions and reached Viaike-Maria.

From the 22nd to the 27th September the Leningrad front exploited its success with surprising speed in the west and south-west directions.

On the 22nd the units starting from Kadrina covered ninety kilometres during the day and occupied Tallin, the capital of Estonia, and a large port on the Baltic. On the 23rd they marched upon Khapsour (Hapsal). On the 24th the Baltic Fleet landed at Paldiski (Port Baltique). On the 27th the Baltic coast was liberated from Tallin to the Bay of Matsulu-Lakht.

Other units starting from Viaike-Maria on 23rd September in the south-west direction arrived the same day on the Bay of Piarnu (Pernau) and liberated the Port of Piarnu, having covered one hundred and forty kilometres in twenty-four hours. Units coming from Tiouri (Turi) reached Virstu and Karouze on the 27th. Other groups from the same region marching south arrived at Viliandi on the 23rd. The German group of the Narva, disrupted and without its ports, was liquidated during the following days. The Soviet Republic of Estonia was occupied with the exception of the islands of Dago (Khiuma) and Oesel (Sarema).

The Germans had lost 46,000 killed or taken prisoner, 175 tanks and SP guns, nearly 600 guns, 750 mortars and 1,500 vehicles.

The Baltic fronts. The 3rd Baltic front attacked with its right towards Valmera (Wolmar) and with its left towards Smiltene. In spite of a stubborn German defence, especially at Balga, the break-through succeeded in both places.

Other units attacked from the Rouiena, Valmera front in a south-west direction, that is to say, towards Riga. On the 24th, after hard fighting over difficult ground, they reached the region of Mieleni after clearing the coastline from Salasgriva to Skoulte, but north of Riga they came up against the fortifications.

The 2nd Baltic front, covering the south flank of the 3rd, reached the Kartouji, Ioumprava line on 29th September.

On the 15th, the 1st Baltic front attacked in the Naoisedjai, Berzomouija region. It broke the German positions and took Baouska, an important strong-point. On the 19th it reached Tekava on the south bank of the Dvina.

With the XVIIIth Army defeated in this way, the Red Army reached the gates of Riga. It only remained to take the city and cut off the communications with East Prussia.

From 19th September to 4th October the Soviet troops made the necessary adjustments. On 4th October the 2nd and 3rd Baltic fronts broke through the fortifications north and north-east of Riga. On 23rd October, while pursuing the retreating Germans towards the west, the Soviet forces crossed the river Lieiloup along its whole course and reached the Toukoum-Mitava (Pelgava) railway.

At the same time the offensive of the 1st Baltic front was taking place on a wide front, from Krouolei to Raoudeniani. Its right had been reinforced in order to defeat the XVIth Army, reach the Baltic and cut off from East Prussia the Germans of the north-west of Latvia. Breaking through north-west and south-west of Cholau, the Soviet troops advanced one hundred kilometres in four days, having put out of action two infantry divisions, one armoured division, four supporting regiments and one SS brigade. Having been obliged to withdraw some forces from the Riga region German Command, by so doing, facilitated the conquest of this city by the 2nd and 3rd Baltic fronts.

On 8th October the 1st Baltic front took Telchia (Telchi) from which it split towards the north-west, the west and the south-west. On the 10th the west units reached the Baltic at Palanga (Polangen) and cut off the communications between Latvia and East Prussia. Oh the 23rd the south-east columns also reached the cost north of Chilouta thus isolating the Germans remaining at Memel (Klaipeda). The same day the left reached Tilsit on the Niemen and cleaned up the north bank of the river from its mouth to Raudoniani. The remains of thirty German divisions were isolated in the north-west of Latvia.

From 30th September to 26th October the Baltic Fleet and the troops of the Leningrad front took the Estonian islands. Moukhou (Mohn) was taken on 30th September, Dago (Khiouma) on 30th October and Œsel (Sarema) on 24th November.

The offensive of the Leningrad front and of the three Baltic fronts made it possible to occupy Estonia and the greater part of Latvia, to destroy the German forces of the Narva, to defeat the northern group of armies, the remains of which were isolated between Toukoum and Libau (Libava). Finally Finland ceased hostilities and declared war on Germany.

9. THE DEFEAT OF THE GERMANO-HUNGARIAN ARMIES IN HUNGARY (SEPTEMBER TO DECEMBER, 1944)

(Sketch No. 60)

The situation at the end of September. After the Germano-Rumanian disaster of Jassy-Kichinev which brought about the desertion of Rumania and Bulgaria, the troops of the 2nd and 3rd Ukrainian fronts finished driving the German troops from both these countries. At the same time the 4th Ukrainian front, taking advantage of the success of the 1st front at Lwov, conquered the spurs of the Carpathians.

During the second fortnight of September, the 2nd Ukrainian front, under Marshal Malinovski, attacked towards Cluj and to the north-west of this city. The Germano-Hungarian forces tried to stop the Soviet advance in the Transylvanian Alps but gradually the Red Army neared the Hungarian plain. By the end of September Malinovski held the line Tirgoumouriech, Turda, Arad, Timisoara (Temesvar). At the same time the 3rd Ukrainian front, advancing westward, reached the Rumanian-Yugoslavian frontier in the Timisoara, Turnu Severin region. The 4th Ukrainian front, under General Petrov, reached the frontiers of Czechoslovakia from the north and east. All efforts were now used to compel Hungary, the last ally of Germany, to give up the war, and bring help to Yugoslavia and Czechoslovakia.

By the end of September the 2nd and 4th fronts were facing the South Ukraine group of armies, which in October were to become the southern group of armies, with the VIth and VIIIth German armies and the Ist and IInd Hungarian Armies. Moreover, facing the right flank of the 4th Ukrainian front were some units of the Ist Armoured Army, attached to the Northern Ukraine group. Against the 3rd front and blocking the roads which gave access to Yugoslavia from Rumania and Bulgaria was the Army ' F ', later in October to become the Group of Armies ' F '.

The German-Hungarian Command, perturbed by the Soviet advance, brought up major reinforcements with all possible speed. During the second fortnight of September, the Southern Ukraine group of armies received fourteen divisions, two from Poland, four removed from opposite the right of the 4th Ukrainian front and the others from the rear. The Army ' F ' received five divisions from Greece and Yugoslavia. Despite these reinforcements the situation of the Germans and Rumanians, threatened on their north and south fronts, remained precarious. In the north the 4th Ukrainian front under Marshal Tolboukhine was to cross the Rumanian-Yugoslavian and Bulgarian-Yugoslavian frontiers and march straight upon Belgrade and Kroujevats. Fearing above all an invasion of the Hungarian plains from the north, the German Command pushed its main reserves and most of its tanks towards Cluj.

The Offensive. First Phase (6th October to 1st November). On 6th October the 2nd front made a surprise attack with its left. Starting from Arad, it crossed the Hungarian frontier and the same day took Dioula (Gyula) and Macca (Mako). Cavalry and tanks rushed into the gap ; in the north, on the 9th, they neared Dbreczen and on the 12th they reached the Tisza on a wide front ; towards the west they also reached the Tisza as early as the 8th. They forced a crossing on the 11th and took Szeged and Kis-Kun-Halas (Kichkounkalach). Overcoming all resistance the 2nd front attacked Debreczen from the south-east and the south-west while the cavalry and tanks outflanked the city. This was stormed on the 20th and by the end of the month the cavalry and tanks had reached the Tisza to the north of Debreczen. They met with a strongly organized resistance which necessitated a well-prepared attack. ·

On 11th October the right flank of the 2nd front captured Cluj, the capital of Transylvania. Mopping up this province the Soviet forces crossed the Hungarian frontier north-west of Satou-Mare (Satmar) and reached the Tisza near Csap.

With the combined German and Hungarian resistance broken on a wide front by the offensive of the 2nd front the Soviet troops penetrated deeply into Hungary. Being compelled to move its reserves from one direction to another, the German-Hungarian Command found it impossible to organize an effective defence. For instance, during October, seventeen divisions coming from other fronts or from the rear, reinforced the south group in the Cluj and Budapest directions, but these reinforcements, which included the IIIrd Hungarian Army, proved insufficient to stop the Red Army whose new attacks brought about the collapse of the whole front.

On 18th October the 4th Ukrainian front crossed the Carpathians and entered Czechoslovakia ; the same day the advance from the south along the Carpathians caused the fall of Siguet, Sichetul. On the 26th, Moukatchevo (Munkacevo), in Czechoslavakian territory, fell, and the next day Ujgorod (Uzhorod), the capital of Sub-Carpathian Ukraine and an important communications centre.

On 24th September the 3rd front, following its reconnaissance units, crossed the Rumanian-Yugoslavian and Bulgarian-Yugoslavian frontiers south of Turnu-Severin and towards Vrachats (Vrzac). It swept aside all resistance and outflanked Belgrade from the north and south and cut the Belgrade-Nich railway at several points.

At the same time other units were attacking north-west, starting from Veliki-Kikinda. They forced a crossing of the Tisza on 9th October and three days later captured Soubotitsa (Szabadka) where they cut off the direct link between Belgrade and Budapest. By the end of October they reached the Danube from Baja to Novisad and crossed the river downstream of Monsad.

The offensive of the Red Army in Yugoslavia also progressed with some speed in liaison with the Yugoslav army of liberation and then with the Bulgarian army. The German Command realized the danger which threatened its troops remaining in Greece and hurriedly reinforced its right flank with nine divisions from Greece and Yugoslavia and created the Army of Serbia. The Army 'F', the IInd Armoured Army and the Army of Serbia, made up the new Group of Armies ' F '.

On 16th October the troops of the 3rd front, in conjunction with some Yugoslav units, began the battle for Belgrade which was grimly defended by the Germans. The city, encircled and attacked by the Soviet forces from the east, south-east and south, and by the 1st Yugoslav Army Corps coming from the south-west along the Save, and by the Danube Flotilla, held for five days and fell on the 20th. The garrison was annihilated. On the left of the 3rd front the Bulgarian Army took Nich, Lescovac and Vranis in the middle of October and penetrated deeply into Yugoslavia. By the end of October the front of the attack stretched from the Carpathians to the edge of the Greek-Yugoslav frontier.

The first phase of the operations in Hungary ended with the arrival of the advance on the Tisza from Tchop to the confluence, the crossing of the river on its lower reaches, the occupation of Transylvania, the conquest of a bridgehead on the Tisza from which to reach Budapest, the liberation of a large part of Sub-Carpathian Ukraine, of Belgrade and of several Yugoslav provinces.

In one month, from 6th October to 6th November, the Germans and Hungarians had lost 100,000 killed, 42,000 prisoners, 800 planes, over 1,000 tanks and SP guns and several thousand guns and machine guns, in their battles with the 2nd front.

Second Phase (November to December, 1944). The 2nd Ukrainian front concentrated on its right a powerful assault group and on 31st October attacked between the Tisza and the Danube towards Budapest. The next day it took Kecskemet. Other units widened the breach towards the north, advanced up the Tisza, took Szolnok, crossed the river between this town and Polgar and pressed towards Miskolez and Eger. On 11th November they cut the Budapest-Miskolez railway.

To protect Budapest, the German Command directed twelve reserve divisions towards the gap. They made perfect use of the ground and, moving in to the villages, offered a relentless resistance during the whole first half of

November. When the 2nd front had drained the enemy's reserves, the 3rd front made a surprise attack, forced a crossing of the Danube on a wide front and took Pecs on 29th November. The mobile forces thrust deeply into the enemy's defences and the main forces followed them up reducing the strongpoints and mopping up the gaps.

Towards the west, Kaposvar was taken on 2nd December and the units advancing up the right bank of the Danube overran Paks. On 7th December the south banks of Lake Balaton were cleared up. In the north the Soviet troops reached Szakes-Fehervar and in the west Nagy-Kanizsa. Despite some resistance at Beske (Bicske) they outflanked Budapest from the west.

The German-Hungarian Command were frightened by the advance of the 3rd front and during the second fortnight of November and the beginning of December they deployed ten divisions (two coming from Italy) south of Lake Balaton and south-west of Budapest, but to no avail.

In the north the 4th front took Setchovtse on 2nd December, Chatoralia-Vihely the next day and pressed towards Kochitse. Being attacked on all sides and not knowing where the main Soviet effort was to be applied, the German-Hungarian Command dispersed its forces from one sector to another. For instance, as the defences covering Budapest in the north-east were not being attacked, it withdrew its divisions at the beginning of December and sent three south-west of the city and one towards Miskolez. However, the Soviet Command concentrated major forces north-east of Budapest. Fog and rain helped to keep this move secret and, on 9th December, the attack, launched by surprise over one hundred and twenty kilometres, overthrew the German-Hungarian positions. The tanks and cavalry pressed north and north-west, occupied Miskolez (an important industrial centre), Balassagiar-mat and Vacz, crossing the Danube south of Budapest and took Erd.

By the end of December, north of Budapest, the 2nd front reached the river Ipel (Ipoly), and in the north-west Levice in Czechoslovakia.

With Yugoslavia and Czechoslovakia rescued, the Carpathians crossed and considerable losses inflicted upon the German-Hungarian armies, it only remained for Budapest, the last enemy bastion in Hungary, to be reduced.

10. THE GERMAN DEFEAT AT PETCHENGA (PETSAMO), OCTOBER 1944

(Sketch No. 61)

The situation on the eve of operations. While the Red Army was drawing near to Riga, entering Transylvania, Hungary and Yugoslavia, the Karelia front, with General Meretskov, launched a decisive attack against the German left flank in the Petchenga (Petsamo) region.

At the very beginning of the war the Germans had seized this region, rich in nickel and copper, and above all a naval and air base against the Arctic routes to Murmansk, the chief Soviet port in the far north.

In the course of three years, they had covered the Petchenga region, and also their naval bases in northern Norway, with the very latest fortifications with concreted works, scarps, anti-tank ditches and minefields. Moreover the ground lent itself to defence ; everywhere one found lakes, streams, marshes, steep cliffs and no roads. Then as a last obstacle, the Arctic climate.

The German Command anticipated that the XXth Army of Lapland would be sufficient to break any attack and even believed that the Red Army would never be able to undertake any major offensive in this sector.

The Soviet plan. With the help of the naval and air forces of the North Fleet, the right of the Karelia front was to break the German defences, defeat the XXth Army, seize the town and harbour of Petchenga, continue in the north-west, west and south-west directions, take the Norwegian town and harbour of Kirkenes and mop up the Petchenga district. To begin with the main effort had to be applied to the region of Lake Tchapr in the direction of Luostari, in order to cut the Petchenga-Rovaniemi road, the only practicable road from Petchenga to South Finland and North Norway. Then the attack would outflank Petchenga from the south-west and the west, linking up with the landing units in operation along the Petchenga Fjord and putting out of action the 19th Mountain Corps. Other units, cutting the Petchenga-Rovaniemi road west of Luostari and marching towards Salmiarvi, would prevent the arrival of reinforcements. Ultimately two actions would start from Salmiarvi, one towards Kirkenes and the other towards the south-west.

Two secondary attacks, one coming from the Sredni peninsula and the other from Bolchaia Zapadnaia Litsa, were to hold up the German forces to help the main attack, which, after the break-up, would press on towards Petchenga from the north-east and the south-east.

The Baltic Fleet was to blockade Petchenga from the sea, to effect landings on the flanks and rear, to disorganize the coastal artillery, help in the capture of Petchenga and finally of Kirkenes and support the movement of the troops along the coastline.

The attack—Capture of Petchenga. The regrouping and disposition of the troops went unnoticed by the Germans. The artillery and air bombardment literally knocked over the enemy's positions and in two days the Soviet troops had broken the first position, pressed north-west across a country without roads, reached the second position on the river Titovka and broken through.

The troops met with incredible difficulties. The columns pushed their way through places where no human foot had ever trodden. The Germans had hoped that this ground would stop the tanks, artillery and even infantry. During the offensive an abnormal rise in temperature followed the frost and the men sank up to their knees in the icy water dragging their equipment behind them. Even the amphibian vehicles were bogged down, and to enable them to cross the lakes it was necessary to break a thin layer of ice. Eventually they were dragged by hand across the mud to the next lake. Supplies came by air and the wounded were evacuated on reindeer or by sleighs. In three days the tundra was crossed and the Petchenga-Rovaniemi road was reached in two places. The German air force tried to intervene but the Soviet air force, with its mastery of the air, attacked it in the air and on the ground.

On 14th October the Soviet forces crossed the river Petchenga towards Luostari, outflanking Petchenga from the west. Other units marching straight northwards from Lake Tchapr cut the Petchenga-Titovka road. At the same time, groups starting from the Sredni peninsula and from Bolchaia Zapadnaia Litsa broke the resistance east of Petchenga, while units landing each side of the Petsamo Fjord attacked south and south-west.

These co-ordinated attacks, constantly supported by the air force and the navy, disrupted the German forces and enabled Petchenga to be surrounded.

Reinforcements vainly tried to break the circle but were dispersed by the air force.

On 15th October the town and the harbour of Petchenga were cleared up.

The garrison was almost entirely destroyed and the pursuit of the 19th Mountain Corps began.

Capture of Kirkenes and the nickel mines. In order to save Kirkenes, its last advanced naval base against Murmansk, the German Command brought the Brigade ' Norway' from Norway, some units of the 210th Infantry Division from the Varanger Peninsular and the 163rd Division, some units of the 18th Mountain Corps and of the 36th Army Corps from Finland and Norway. So the German resistance grew in the region of the nickel mines and in front of Kirkenes.

The Soviet forces attacked in two directions : in the north-west, towards Kirkenes, from Luostari towards Salmiarvi outflanking the Lake of Kuets-Jarv in the north and south. Dealing with the pockets of resistance across the tundra they encircled and overran Nikel on 22nd October. The next day they marched upon Salmiarvi and cut the Kirkenes-Rovaniemi road. The troops attacking from Petchenga towards Kirkenes, in conjunction with other units landed north and north-east of Kirkenes, reached the Norwegian frontier on a wide front and pressed on towards Kirkenes.

Access to the city was barred by three fjords with sheer cliffs, and by deep defensive positions. Soviet Command launched concentric attacks. Ships and naval air force blockaded the Varanger fjord and energetically bombarded the German fleet and coastal defences. The troops of the Karelia front, coming from Petchenga, forced a crossing of the Iarfjordien which they also outflanked from the south across steep mountains. The landing parties destroyed a series of coastal batteries and proceeded east and north-east. The units which had taken Nikel and Salmiarvi arrived from the south. The city being thus isolated, the Soviet troops attacked from the south, helped by secondary attacks launched from the east and north-east. Finally the city was stormed.

On 1st November the troops advancing from Salmiarvi towards the south-west completed the liberation of the Petchenga district.

After the capture of Kirkenes, the right flank troops overthrew a group of German forces and seized Neiden (Neiken).

The offensive carried out by the Karelia front and the Northern Fleet resulted in the destruction of the XXth German Army of Lapland, the occupation of the Petchenga district and of the Norwegian region of Kirkenes. The Germans lost two naval bases, Petchenga and Kirkenes, and rich nickel and copper mines. The Soviet troops had overcome unprecedented difficulties and displayed prodigious energy in crossing the hitherto untrodden tundra with their tanks and vehicles.

Comments

The year 1944, which was one of great Soviet offensives, was also that of great victories.

Whilst in 1943, after halting the Kursk offensive, the Red Army began to take the initiative in the operations and scored big successes in the Ukraine, in 1944 the Germany army found itself doomed to receive, without ever returning them, terrible blows dealt either simultaneously or in succession from the Black Sea to the Sea of Barents.

The Soviet strategy of 1944 can only compare with that of Marshal Foch in 1918, when after resuming the initiative of the operations on 18th July, he heavily attacked the vulnerable points of the front, the collapse of which he gradually achieved.

In winter in the snows of Leningrad, in spring in the mud of the Ukraine, in summer in the plains of White Russia and Rumania or facing the Mannerheim Line, in autumn in the Carpathians and the Hungarian plains, and finally in the icy waters of the Petsamo Tundra, everywhere and all the time the superiority of the Red Army over the German army proved unquestionable. Not that the latter showed less energy in adverse circumstances than it did in the lightning offensives of the early years of the war. Just as in 1943, the German Command resolutely faced up to all attacks. Its reserves, constantly moving from one sector to another, indefatigably tried to stop up the gaps opened by unexpected and ever renewed attacks. But the balance of forces, broken a year previously during the battle of the Ukraine, could not be restored. With each new Soviet offensive whole divisions were trapped and destroyed. Men and equipment seemed to melt away in the gigantic crucible of the eastern front.

After the Leningrad defeat both the Ukraine and White Russia saw the famous panzer divisions, on which Hitler had staked all his hopes, wear themselves down one after the other in vain counter-attacks.

At the same time, the German air force, another factor of primary importance in the Fuhrer's strategy, saw itself definitely outclassed by the Soviet air force. In the end, concentrating upon the defence of German soil which was being devastated by Allied squadrons, it left the surrounded troops to the mercy of the Red bombers, and certain extinction. Each new success tipped the scales a little more on the Soviet side. By the end of 1944 what was left of the 257 German divisions which, at the beginning of the year, were still resisting the Red Army ? As to the fifty divisions of the satellite countries, they were destroyed or else had gone over to the enemy. Out of 136 divisions decimated during the course of the year, some were able to re-form up to a point. Out of 32 divisions fetched from other fronts as reinforcements, several from Italy, 16 had completely disappeared.

At the same time the Red Army, all the time kept up to strength both in men and equipment was, according to German data, concentrating 400 divisions of various composition and value, but all perfectly trained and fired with the certainty of victory.

The Soviet advance towards the west reached 550 to 1,100 kilometres. By the end of 1944 not a single German, apart from hundreds of thousands of prisoners, remained in the U.S.S.R. The Red soldiers were already treading the soil of East Prussia.

One after the other, Rumania, Bulgaria, Finland, Hungary, in the face of the Allied victory and fearing just reprisals, left Germany to her fate. Germany, the cause of so many useless sacrifices, now stood alone.

Defeated in the east, driven back as far as the Apennines in Italy, she saw in France the collapse of the ' Westwall ' and of the ' Southwall ', held to be impregnable, and the Western Allies cross her frontiers. She saw a resurrected French Army make up for its weak numbers by its heroism.

Against this Germany held in a vice-like grip, the Red Army was preparing the decisive effort which was, in a few months, to take it to Berlin and on to the Elbe.

PART FOUR

The Collapse
1945

THE SITUATION AT THE END OF 1944

(Sketch No. 62)

THE EASTERN FRONT, which formerly extended from the Black Sea to the White Sea, was now considerably shortened but, in December 1944, still measured 2,000 kilometres, that is three times the length of the Western front, from Basle to the mouth of the Meuse. Its northern part, from the Baltic to the Carpathians, followed the lower Niemen, the Narov, the Vistula and the San, a line which was very favourable to a concentric attack starting from the Niemen and the Narov, against East Prussia. On the middle Vistula, between Warsaw and Sandomir, it also lent itself to an east to west offensive aimed at splitting it in two.

The difficulty was to force the river lines on which the German defence was resting, but the Red Army had the advantage of the very great experience it acquired when crossing such rivers as the Dnieper, the Dniestr, the Prut, the Berezina and others. Moreover, it had established bridgeheads on the main axes, particularly on the west bank of the Vistula in the Sandomir region. Heitz, the German Army Corps General, called this Sandomir bridgehead a ' pistol levelled at the back of Germany's head '. This explains the violence of the counter-attacks which it carried out for over a month with five armoured divisions and several infantry divisions, and which cost the Germans 400 tanks.

In December, 1944 two hundred and twenty divisions, two hundred of which were German, were facing the Soviet Army, whereas there were only seventy-five on the western front. The majority covered the Reich from the Baltic to the Carpathians but sixty divisions remained allocated to the south flank.

Between East Prussia and Hungary the Soviet troops had had to pause to re-establish their communications and re-deploy. The Germans made use of this respite to reinforce the three lines of defence on which they counted to prevent the Red Army from entering the Reich.

The first line was from the Kuriches Haff through Insterburg, the Lakes of Mazuria, the Narev, Modlin, Warsaw and the Vistula. On its northern flank East Prussia formed a huge fortress which was covered by a complicated system of permanent defences as far as the fortified town of Koenigsberg. On the Vistula, especially in front of the Sandomir bridgehead, the Germans had organized three successive positions covering twenty kilometres. In the main sectors there were as many as five to ten concreted works per kilometre.

The second line started from the Lower Vistula, through the towns of Graudenz, Chelmno, Bydgoszez (Bromberg), then past the fortified region of Posen, on the Oder, as far as Oppeln.

The third line ran across Pomerania from Stolp to Neustettin, taking in the towns of Schneidemuhl and Kustrin and running along the left bank of the Oder with the towns of Glogau and Breslau. This last line was intended to catch any troops that might march upon Berlin via Posen in a pincer movement.

The East Prussian and Oder fortifications had been established for years and were linked up by a network of field works supported by the rivers Pilitsa, Nida and Warta.

On the whole, from the point of view of power and especially of depth, this organization was in no way inferior to the Siegfried line. Apart from the positions on the Mannerheim line, the Red Army had never met any stronger.

Field Marshal Guderian was appointed Supreme Commander and given the task of preventing the Red Army from entering Germany.

On the Soviet side, seven fronts succeeded one another from the Baltic to Lake Balaton : on the Niemen, the 3rd White Russian front (Tcherniak-hovski), on the Narev, the 2nd White Russian front (Rokossovski, who had succeeded Zakharov), on the Vistula, the 1st White Russian front (Zkuhov, who had succeeded Rokossovski) and the 1st Ukrainian from (Malinovski) and the 3rd Ukrainean front (Tolbukhin).

The Soviet plan. Above all, the Red Army wanted to destroy the main forces concentrated on the Berlin axis. To effect this, two fronts were to march from the Vistula to the Oder—the 1st White Russian front on the Warsaw-Posen-Kustrin axis, the 1st Ukrainian front on the Sandomir-Breslau axis. Having reached the Oder, Zhukov was to march upon Berlin with Koniev covering him on his left.

In the north this main effort depended upon the conquest of East Prussia which was to be attacked from east to west by the 3rd White Russian front starting from the Niemen, and from south to north by the 2nd White Russian front starting from the Narev.

In the south, the 2nd Ukrainian front was to liquidate the Budapest defences and push straight on to Vienna which the 3rd Ukrainian front would outflank from the south.

The new ' Stalin' tanks[1], which were superior to the ' Tigers', had been added to the Red Army's equipment, and its units had been reinforced. The Germany Army had endeavoured to fill its gaps with ' Kampfgruppen' made up of recalled invalided soldiers and scarcely trained young recruits. It was to put up a fierce resistance for another four months nevertheless.

THE OPERATIONS

The Offensive on the Danube (December, 1944-January, 1945). The con-tinuous rain of December had turned the Hungarian plain into a sea of mud where traffic was impossible except on the roads which were easily defended. Moreover, the Germans had organized numerous places as centres of resistance.

On 26th December, the 2nd Ukrainian front attacked north of Budapest, crossed the Danube, entered both this city and Komarno and linked up with the 3rd Ukrainian front. In this way some important forces were surrounded in Budapest and split in two—one part, in the north, was annihilated on the 29th in the Danube bend and the other, and more important, was beseiged in the capital. To avoid unnecessary losses and the destruction of the city, the Soviet Command sent truce flags forward. In violation of the laws of war the bearers were killed as soon as they reached the enemy lines.

---

[1]Characteristics : 56 tons, 122 mm gun, 105 mm armour.

Without waiting for Budapest to fall, the Soviet Command started the march upon Vienna. The German Command brought up its reserves—the 44th and 71st Divisions from Italy and the 271st from the Western front. Counter-attacks at the rate of twenty a day only succeeded at the cost of heavy losses. District by district and house by house the conquest of Budapest progressed, the relentlessness of the fighting rivalling that of Stalingrad.

Further north, the 4th Ukrainian front and the right flank of the 2nd advanced along the southern spurs of the Carpathians through hilly and difficult country and liberated a major part of Czechoslavakia.

Operations in Western Poland and Silesia. During the whole of December and the first fortnight in January the Germans anxiously awaited the Soviet attack. In order to hinder its preparation they launched an unsuccessful preventive attack on the boundaries of East Prussia.

During the first fortnight in January, the Soviet Command concentrated considerable forces in the bridgeheads of the Vistula, while along the whole east bank of the river other and more numerous troops were preparing to cross it. The artillery was placed very much forward and the reserves, made up mostly of large armoured units, were spread out in depth.

On 12th January at dawn, with thick fog covering the Vistula, the 1st Ukrainian front attacked. Its artillery opened fire and the infantry drew near the German lines. Thinking this was the main attack the Germans opened up with their artillery thus revealing their dispositions. The Soviet artillery ceased firing and the infantry halted. The attack appeared to have been checked and the German infantry came out from cover. Then suddenly over the bridgheads of the Vistula the fire of thousands of guns shook the ground. The whole Soviet artillery had come into action. This bombardment went on for nearly two hours over the whole depth of the defence and, indeed, with such effect that the officer in command curtailed it by fifteen minutes and thus saved thousands of shells. Owing to weather conditions the air force was not able to go into action throughout the whole day.

In the Sandomir bridgehead, which extended forty kilometres, the infantry, supported as closely as possible by tanks and accompanied by light artillery and mortars, moved forward behind a creeping barrage.

In the first German defence line it saw the terrifying effectiveness of the artillery on the shelters, including the armoured ones, machine gun nests and trenches completely wrecked. Thousands of dead were strewn on the ground. One by one the three lines of the first position were conquered and in a few hours whole regiments and divisions destroyed.

As early as the first day, Generals Poluboiarov's and Kuznetsov's tanks caught up with the infantry, overtook it and disrupted the German communications. In only two days the advance of the 1st Ukrainian front had reached forty kilometres over a front of sixty kilometres.

To counter-attack in the direction of Kieloe, the German Command concentrated two armoured divisions and one motorized division. Information of this reached the Soviet forces and they were able to disorganize the armoured divisions by means of a preventive attack. The Germans failed to cling to either of the rivers Nida and Pilitsa, or even to the Wartha. On 18th January the Soviet forces outflanked the defences east of Czestochowa and entered the city. The 1st Ukrainian front crossed the Silesian frontier and the German reserves thrust into its path were unable even to slow down its progress.

On 14th January the 1st Ukrainian front also attacked from the bridgeheads of Mniszev and the Pulawy, thousands of guns taking part in the preliminary bombardment. The four German divisions concerned lost 70 per cent of their numbers while the Soviet infantry, supported by tanks and self-propelled guns advanced without a break both by day and by night in the direction of Radom. On the third day it had linked up both bridgeheads and advanced sixty kilometres breaking through the German positions one after the other. The attacking front had now advanced one hundred and twenty kilometres. The Soviet armour and motorized infantry rushed into the gaps while the infantry mopped up the pockets of resistance left in the rear. The Warsaw-Lodz railway was cut off.

At the same time the 1st White Russian front attacked north of Warsaw, cleaned up the region between the Vistula and the Boug and crossed the Vistula on the heels of the Germans.

On 17th January, the fourth day of the offensive, a combined attack coming from the west, north and south, liberated Warsaw. The 1st White Russian front carried straight on towards the west capturing Kutno, an important junction, on the 19th. Without stopping it swept upon Bydgoszez (Bromberg), widely outflanking the German forces of East Prussia from the south, and those of Kalisz from the north.

Further south the 1st Ukrainian front, which had reached the advanced positions of Breslau on 21st January, after advancing towards the north-west, suddenly thrust its armour on the left in the opposite direction towards the south-east, making a surprise rush into the coal and industrial basin of Silesia. At the same time attacks were started towards Chrzanow and Katowice, via Cracow, and in a few days the whole Silesia basin fell to this pincer attack. The huge factories were intact and still working, in fact their electricity supply had not even been turned off.

In the north the 1st White Russian front made equally good progress. On 23rd January it took Bydgoszez (Bromberg) and part of its forces went northwards reaching the mouth of the Vistula on the west bank. The left of the front encircled the strong-point of Posen. At the end of January it thrust its left and centre in the direction of Berlin, crossed the frontier and entered Brandenburg, whilst its right, which had forced a crossing of the Netze, encircled Schneidemuhl and entered Pomerania. On 14th February Schneidemuhl fell.

In Silesia the capture of the fortress of Oppeln on 24th February by the 1st Ukrainian front heralded the start of the battle for the crossing of the Oder. Between Oppeln and Breslau the river is up to five hundred metres wide, the west bank was heavily fortified and its approaches covered with ice. The motorized infantry were the first to arrive and hastily gathered together makeshift material to build pontoons and rafts. The infantrymen collected reeds and stuffed clothes with straw on which they could float their arms, equipment and rations while swimming the icy river. So without waiting for normal means of crossing the advanced elements occupied small bridgeheads on the other side of the river. Shortly afterwards a shuttle service was organized by the sappers under enemy fire. As soon as the crossing was complete the Germans gave up their positions on a twenty kilometre front and retreated to the south and south-west. Almost simultaneously other units had forced the Oder downstream from Breslau and in four days' fighting advanced sixty kilometres on a front of one hundred and sixty kilometres. On the 13th they surrounded the strong-point at Glogau and on the 16th, approaching from the north, west and south, Breslau.

In March the left of the 1st Ukrainian front destroyed a strong German group south-west of Oppeln. This completed the collapse of the Oder line, the last bastion set up in south-west Germany.

Operations in East Prussia. It was in East Prussia that the Soviet troops were to meet with their greatest difficulties. This province, which was the traditional bastion of the Germans, was defended by crack troops, the IInd, IIIrd and IVth Armoured Armies with some forty infantry divisions.

Gumbinnen and Insterburg, which had become powerful fortresses, barred the way to Koenigsberg. Every important locality was a centre of resistance with concrete works.

The Soviet plan was to cut off East Prussia from Germany, to surround its defenders and split them up with a general attack towards Koenigsberg before defeating them separately. To this effect the 2nd White Russian front (Rokossovski) was to press with all speed from the south to north along the lower Narev in the direction of Marienburg and the Frischeshaff, while the 3rd White Russian front (Tchernaikhovski) would attack from east to west north of the Lakes of Mazuria.

The 2nd front launched its attack from its bridgehead on the right bank of the Narev on 14th January. The German defences comprised very powerful positions consisting mostly of large works with six embrasures commanding the surrounding country. Special assault detachments were formed consisting of fifteen to twenty machine pistols, two heavy machine guns, one or two 45 mm guns, one or two tanks or self propelled guns, six or seven sappers. The tanks and self-propelled guns moved forward and from one hundred to one hundred and fifty metres opened fire directly upon the embrasures. Protected by them the machine-pistol men crept forward, followed by the sappers armed with explosives. When the group was sufficiently close to the objective a signal was given to the tanks to stop firing and the blockhouse attacked, the explosives placed and the obstacle blown up. An attack company was then ready to enter the breach to consolidate. Whenever possible heavy tanks would outflank the blockhouses and with their fire neutralize the embrasures. By this method the first position was overrun completely in four hours. German Command counter-attacked immediately with the SS Armoured Division ' Gross Deutschland ', the 7th Armoured Division, a number of infantry units and some artillery attack groups but in a few hours the Soviet forces' fire had stemmed the attack. Beating fresh counter-attacks all the time the troops of the 2nd White Russian front covered forty kilometres in four days. But nowhere did they have a clear field, concreted positions, barbed wire entanglements and minefields delayed their advance. Nevertheless they reached Mlava on 19th January and on the 26th, that is twelve days after beginning the attack, Rokossovski had overrun five positions in succession, advanced two hundred and fifty kilometres and reached the Baltic.

For its part the 3rd White Russian front, coming from the lower Niemen, encountered a series of positions before reaching the river Deime. The strongest of these was centred on the river Angerapp and the fortified town of Insterburg. In spite of these obstacles, the 3rd front advanced forty-five kilometres over a front of sixty kilometres in five days. On 22nd January, as a result of a daring manoeuvre, it outflanked the fortifications of Insterburg on both sides and took the town. The crossing of the Angerapp made the situation of the Germans in East Prussia critical. Hundreds of tanks and self propelled guns were rushed up to counter-attack but without success and by 27th January the Soviet forces had broken through the German defences on the Lakes of Mazuria and reached the positions which immediately covered Koenigsberg.

The German forces were now separated in three distinct groups. In the north, in the Samland peninsula ; in the centre round Koenigsberg ; in the south towards Heilsburg. Soviet Command destroyed them successively, beginning with Heilsberg. The result was a slowing down of operations, but the concentration of resources, especially artillery and air, on these three objectives, enabled them to bring to bear the maximum possible fire power on each one. As soon as the Heilsberg pocket was reduced, reinforcements rejoined General Bagramian in charge of the assault on Koenigsberg. General Vassilevski co-ordinated the operations in East Prussia in place of General Tchernaikhovski who had been killed in action.

Since 1938 the Germans had been modernizing the fortifications of Koenigsberg. The twenty-four old forts of the double belt which were protected only by bricks two and a half to three metres thick and covered with three to five metres of earth, had been given concrete casings and modern armament. Work was continued all through the war and intensified in 1944 when the threat became more definite. The result was a network of field fortifications round the city. The outer belt was fifty kilometres long and the inner belt fifteen kilometres. On the outskirts of the city stone buildings were also used for the defence. The new arrangements included works and shelters protected by concrete one and a half metres thick. A large number of guns on the flanks were sheltered in concreted casemates. Finally the defences had several anti-tank ditches covered with minefields and barbed wire entanglements.

For a whole month Soviet Command worked hard to find out the precise layout of the defence. Numerous aerial photographs supplied an accurate plan and a large scale model was used for briefing units. The Soviet plan aimed at outflanking the city both from the north and the south while covering itself in the north against the forces of the Samland peninsula. In order to ensure perfect co-ordination between arms, the tanks, infantry and artillery trained together over ground prepared to resemble that of the attack.

General Bieloborodov was to attack from the north-west and General Galitzki, with the armour of the 2nd front, being the first to arrive on the Baltic west of Koenigsberg, was to attack from the south. They would meet in the centre of the city.

On 6th April at 1000 hours thousands of guns and some two thousand planes launched a bombardment which lasted five hours. The effect of the heavy artillery upon the forts proved devastating. Fort number 4 alone received ninety-six direct hits. Out of thirty-seven batteries in the northern sector six were completely destroyed and twenty-five partly so. Out of thirty-two batteries in the south only one remained intact.

At 1200 hours the infantry attacked behind a creeping barrage and accompanied by self-propelled guns and light artillery. Under cover of a smoke screen they threw assault ladders across the ditches, captured Fort No. 4 and took thirty officers and one hundred and fifty-four men prisoners. In the same way they overran the forts ' Frederic III ', ' Reine Louise ' and ' Penart '. In the evening the garrisons of Forts No. 5 and ' Gneisenau ' laid down their arms. The penetrations into the first belt were now ten kilometres wide and four kilometres deep in the north, and eight kilometres by three kilometres in the south.

On 8th April the Soviet forces reached the outer belt and completed the circle round the garrison which was now completely cut off from the Samland peninsula. On 9th April, after half an hour's preparation, they broke through the inner belt and street fighting began. Whole groups of Germans surrendered and in the evening the remainder of the garrison capitulated. The prisoners number 1,819 officers, including four generals, and 91,000 men. The arms captured included over 2,000 guns of all calibres, 1,600 mortars, over 4,600 machine guns and about 100 tanks and self-propelled guns.

In the Samland peninsula the Germans continued to resist, but on 25th April a fresh attack overran Pillau, the last Baltic base in German hands. Some surrounded elements still remained in East Prussia between Elbing and Danzig and their resistance was not to cease until 8th May.

Operations in Pomerania. In February, when Zhukov's troops having crossed the Netze entered Brandenberg and took Schneidemuhl, the German Command launched a counter-attack from north-west to south-east against the right flank and the rear of the 1st White Russian front. This counter-attack was decisively stopped at once by the artillery.

The Soviet Command then carried out an operation on an unprecedented scale to cut off Pomerania from the rest of Germany. The 1st White Russian front made a surprise attack from Scheidemuhl towards Kolberg, while at the same time, west of the Vistula, the 2nd White Russian front attacked in a parallel direction from north of Bydgeszcz towards Kosling. Both these attacks were successful and isolated the Pomeranian armies, which in turn were divided into several ' pockets ' which the Soviet troops destroyed one after the other. At the end of March the 2nd front took Gdynia and Danzig, the last German bases in Pomerania.

The February-March Battle on the Danube. At the beginning of February, while the Red Army was carrying out operations in East Prussia, Poland and Pomerania, the German-Hungarian forces of Budapest continued to resist desperately. German Command tried for a second time to release the besieged troops. The panzer divisions withdrawn from the Western front after von Rundstedt's counter-offensive arrived in Hungary. Five armoured divisions, several motorized divisions and infantry divisions, reinforced by self-propelled guns and supported by bomber squadrons, launched a strong attack on a twenty-five kilometre front north-east of Lake Balaton, with the intention of reaching the Danube and then moving towards Budapest from the south. Their superiority in numbers allowed the Germans to create a salient in the Soviet front but the artillery prevented any further advance and the salient was reduced by counter-attacks from both south and north.

At the same time the Soviet troops were gradually destroying the Budapest resistance. Buildings had been made into fortresses and barricades and minefields blocked all roads. The Red Army, which Stalingrad had taught defensive street fighting, were now learning the art of offensive street fighting, but it was only on 15th February, after one and a half months' uninterrupted fighting, that the garrison finally surrendered. The 2nd Ukrainian front captured over 110,000 prisoners and an enormous amount of material.

The capture of Budapest released the 2nd front and enabled it to launch its offensive against Vienna. In the face of this threat the Germans counter-attacked for the last time on 5th March in three directions :—

From the south, starting from the Drave, against the flanks and rear of the 3rd Ukrainian front ;

From the west, between the Drave and Lake Balaton ;

From the north-west, between Lake Balaton and the Danube, at the junction of the 2nd and 3rd Ukrainian fronts.

The German Command expected to encircle the Russians on the west bank of the Danube with these attacks. Seven SS armoured divisions, withdrawn from the western front, were added to those already engaged in Hungary. The main assault group north-west of Lake Balaton had no fewer than eleven armoured divisions. But once more the Soviet artillery got the better of the German armour and broke the last counter-offensive of the war. General Nidelin's artillery alone destroyed 745 tanks. And not only did their barrage stop the assailants, but it prepared the way for an immediate Soviet counter-offensive. The battle of the Danube, which had been going on for four months, entered a new phase. With the attack group put out of action and the German positions north-east of Lake Balaton broken over a large area, the Soviet tanks rushed towards Austria. West of Lake Balaton the left of the 3rd Ukrainian front crossed the two hundred kilometres to Vienna in ten days.

At the same time the 2nd Ukrainian front attacked from the north bank of the Danube towards Barislava. On 29th March, the 3rd front took Szombathely, entered Austria and reached Vienna from the south via Neustadt and the Semring pass. Simultaneously the 2nd front, having taken Bratislava on 7th April, after some street fighting, the Austrian capital was occupied, and the armour of the 3rd front pressed on towards Linz to meet the Americans. The fall of Vienna, the sixth capital liberated by the Red Army, dislocated the whole south flank of the German front.

Three fronts had now reached Moravia : in the south, the right of the 2nd Ukrainian front ; in the centre, the 4th Ukrainian front under Eremenko who had succeeded Petrov ; in the north the left of the 1st Ukrainian front having come from Oppeln.

The capture of Berlin. By mid April, that is three months after the launching of the Soviet general offensive, the fighting everywhere was on German soil. The separate pockets were being liquidated—100,000 prisoners were taken at Koenigsberg, 100,000 at Danzig, 50,000 at Posen—and only the surrounded forces at Kurland and Breslau were still resisting.

The final Soviet offensive was launched on 16th April. The 1st White Russian front attacked Berlin directly from the east, while the 1st Ukrainian front made a detour round the city from the south and moved towards the Elbe where it later joined the Americans on 26th April. Zhukov had 22,000 guns of all calibres to support his attack and he deployed this mass of artillery in the small bridgeheads established on the other side of the Oder. On the main axes the density was more than 280 guns per kilometre. The deployment and dumping programme was carried out entirely by night and escaped the attention of the Germans. During the last few nights over seven million shells were brought up.

The first German position, strongly organized and covered by barbed wire entanglements and very dense minefields, had three lines of trenches with numerous resistance centres over a depth of eight to ten kilometres. Some fifteen kilometres behind this lay another similar position. Woods and ponds aided the defenders.

For the first time the artillery preparation and the infantry attack was to be carried out entirely by night. The preparation began on 16th April at

0500 hours and lasted only twenty-five minutes. At 0525 hours by the light of 143 searchlights, the infantry rushed forward protected by a creeping barrage. At dawn the advance had covered from one and a half to three kilometres and by 1200 hours, due mainly to the fire directed upon the centres of resistance, General Zhukov had broken through the first position. The next day, the 17th, the attack was resumed after a 30 minute preparation and at the end of the day the advance had covered sixteen kilometres on a front of one hundred and twenty. The second position had been broken.

On 21st April at 1120 hours, Commandant Zioukine's artillery group opened fire upon Berlin and a battle of unusual violence began for the conquest of that city. Eleven thousand pieces of artillery and heavy mortars supported the advance of the infantry and the density of the artillery, including the heavy mortars, reached the hitherto unequalled figure of 610 ' barrels ' per kilometre. Heavy guns of 203 mm particularly had been placed in the front line to destroy the buildings used as strong-points. Whilst the advance continued through the city a pincer movement was also being carried out with the 1st White Russian front in the north and the 1st Ukrainian front in the south. On 25th April the circle closed tighter upon Berlin but the fighting continued for several more days.

Hitler had decided to organize a redoubt in the Bavarian Alps, round Berchtesgarten, with himself as commander. He had despatched Goering there with the task of regrouping the western armies pushed back by the French and Americans, but these, badly disorganized, saw their last units cut to pieces and the Allies break into Bavaria. Goering, who had expressed his intention of negotiating, was relieved of his command.

Despite the advice of his ministers Hitler had decided to remain in Berlin. He still had a few divisions grouped south of Hamburg under command of General Wenck and intended to counter-attack the Americans on their north flank. At the last minute Hitler thought to direct these reserves towards Berlin to break the Red Army's grip and Keitel was detailed to organize this eleventh hour manoeuvre, but it was too late. The last few German fighting units were everywhere being broken. Rokossovski had taken Stettin and the Soviet armies, having completed the occupation of Brandenburg, now thrust their armour towards the Elbe across Mecklenburg.

In Berlin itself the fighting drew near to the centre. There was fighting in the Tiergarten and Soviet troops stormed the Reichstag and hoisted the red flag. It was the end. The last radio message sent on 30th April by the Fuhrer's ministers stated ' Hitler is dead '. On 2nd May the remnants of the Berlin garrison laid down their arms. On the 8th, Admiral Doenitz, whom Hitler had entrusted with the command of the troops in the north zone and whom he had appointed as his successor, signed the capitulation in the presence of representatives of the Soviet, American, British and French armies.

In his speech of 1st May 1945, Stalin read out the balance sheet of the losses sustained by the Germans on the east front during the last three months of the war : 1 million killed, 800,000 prisoners, 6,000 planes, 12,000 tanks and self-propelled guns, over 23,000 field guns. He recalled that side by side with the Soviet forces there had been Polish, Yugoslav, Czech, Bulgarian and Rumanian divisions and that the German Command had had to with-draw several dozen divisions from the western front in order to reinforce the east.

The Liberation of Prague (Sketch No. 63).   The surrender of Berlin followed by the official capitulation of the German armies, marked the end of the operations in North Germany and the divisions which, since October, had been encircled in Kurland laid down their arms. On the other hand, south of the Dresden-Breslau line and in Bohemia, the troops under Field-Marshal Schoerner continued to resist. They numbered twenty divisions (fourteen infantry, three mountain, two armoured and one motorized) and the Soviet Command anticipated a counter-attack in the direction of Breslau in order to relieve its garrison. In any case Schoerner, supported by mountainous and wooded country, could prolong the struggle and it was therefore desirable that this last resistance should be wiped out as soon as possible. General Patton's 3rd American Army had entered Czechoslovakia but it had stopped at Pilsen. Soviet Command therefore decided to surround the Schoerner group and to this end sent two armoured formations towards Prague, one coming from the north across the Erzgebirge and the other from the south-east (Brno region).

The armoured forces of the north came from the 1st Ukrainian front (Marshal Koniev) and had just taken part in the conquest of Berlin. They formed two groups under Generals Ribalko and Leliouchenko who were given orders to enter Prague on 12th May.

From Berlin to Prague was three hundred and fifty kilometres. The plan was to outflank the German forces concentrated in the region of Dresden from the west and to cross the Erzgebirge by surprise.

On the morning of the 6th both groups crossed the Elbe downstream from Dresden and advanced beyond the Dresden-Leipzig road despite violent German counter-attacks supported by ' Tigers ' and self-propelled guns.

During the night of the 7th/8th, taking advantage of an attack upon the east bank of the Elbe towards Dresden by General Poluboiarov's tanks, General Ribalko's and General Leliouchenko's armoured columns rushed towards the Erzgebirge passes in pitch darkness. The vanguards with detachments of sappers removed the obstacles and hastily prepared the routes. On 8th May the tanks arrived in the Eger valley and the Verava Valley (upper Elbe). The same day General Mitrofanov's units cut the roads north-west and north-east of Prague.

On 9th May at daybreak, while Czech insurgents were fighting inside the city, to their great surprise they saw the first tanks of Ribalko arrive commanded by General Ziberov. Soon after, Leliouchenko's advance guard ranks reached the city from the north-west and finally the armoured troops of Generals Kravtchenko and Kuznetsov, coming from Brno, reached the south-east outskirts of Prague after overcoming strong resistance. Field Marshal Schoerner managed to escape and his troops, disheartened by the appearance of the Soviet armour, gave up all further resistance. From the 9th to the 13th May thirty generals and 672,000 men surrendered. The material taken included over 1,200 tanks and self-propelled guns, about 4,500 guns and 46,000 vehicles.

Thus a brilliant manoeuvre by the tanks put an end to the war on the Germano-Soviet front.

Comments

At the beginning of 1945, four years after the onslaught of the panzer divisions upon the east, the situation was reversed. Hitler's army, pushed back towards the Reich, had sustained a series of disasters in 1944 comparable with those of the Red Army in 1941. In its turn the latter was to learn the difficulties of a winter battle taking place several thousand kilometres away from its bases and with the rear areas completely ruined. Nevertheless the situation remained favourable to the Russians. Hitler's armies drew nearer to Germany but they found it devastated by the Allies' bombing. The destruction of the factories paralysed war production and that of railways paralysed transport. In 1941 the Urals remained out of Germany's reach and in 1945 Silesia and the Ruhr were the first to be invaded. East and west the grip tightened on a country without allies, with recruiting run dry, with devastated cities and shaky morale. In contrast the Red Army had never had so many men or so much material. The wartime output had reached its peak while Allied supplies flowed in via the Persian Gulf and Murmansk. Without wasting a single day the U.S.S.R. pursued the reconstruction of its industrial centres in the south. Yugoslavia was liberated and the frontiers of Czechoslovakia reached. Bulgaria, Rumania and Hungary, which yesterday were Germany's allies, were now placing their resources at the disposal of the Red Army. On this front operations had proceeded at so quick a pace that destruction comparable with that piling up in White Russia had been avoided. Moreover communications were better and the offensive upon Budapest could proceed uninterrupted. On the other hand, in the north, General Tcherniakhovski's foray in East Prussia in October had reminded the Soviet Command of the risks of a hurried attack against an opponent established on sound defence lines. The attack was to be resumed when communications had been re-established and re-deployment completed. All this caused delay but, in contrast to the Hitler Command in 1941, the Soviet Command accepted this. It preferred to attack in winter with all available resources rather in autumn with insufficient resources. It is true that winter operations held no fear for an army which since 1941 had never retreated because of the cold and snow. Another factor was that the ice on the Lakes of Mazuria would help the advance to Koenigsberg.

In East Prussia the operations took on the character of siege warfare, but on the Polish plain the rush of tanks recalled, in reverse, the best days of the Blitzkrieg. Hitler had expected that the Red Army would hesitate to drive deeply between the bulwarks of the defence—East Prussia in the north and Budapest in the south. Trusting to Prussian fortifications, he sent his last armoured divisions towards Budapest to take part in the final counter-attacks, but the Red Army's superiority enabled it to launch an attack of unprecedented violence over the whole front in January. Everything collapsed. Against the armies which swept straight down upon Berlin, after the loss of Silesia, there was but one last effort to be made, an attack from Pomerania against their north flank. A classic effort it was but doomed to failure through want of resources.

The battle of Berlin was nothing but a last act of despair, the last convulsion before death but a supreme opportunity for the Red Army to proclaim the onmipotence of its weapons. The abundance of its resources and the mastery acquired since the Stalingrad days by the Soviet Command enabled it to effect concentrations of artillery, tanks and planes of hitherto unequalled effectiveness, on narrow fronts, which crushed the last remaining German forces.

The gigantic effort which the U.S.S.R. had been making since 1941 found there its crowning glory. The Blitzkrieg ended with Leningrad, Moscow and Stalingrad ; the war of attrition ended in the ruins of Berlin.

Conclusion

Hitler gained easy and spectacular victories both in 1939 and 1941 owing to the fact that he had forestalled his opponents by a few years in the construction of mass produced tanks and planes and was able, thanks to their wholesale use, to co-ordinate both speed and power on his lines of attack.

In 1939 four armoured divisions and five infantry divisions were sufficient to crush Poland in three weeks. In 1940 ten armoured divisions (3,000 tanks) and ten motorized divisions put the French and British armies out of action in six weeks,[1] and in the spring of 1941 both the Yugoslav and Greek armies. The Blitzkrieg had triumphed.

On 22nd June 1941 it was the turn of the U.S.S.R. Since the Civil War the latter had continuously been reinforcing her means of defence. The Red Army had a permanent strength far superior to that of the Reichswehr. Her trained reserves numbered over ten million fighting men. The Germans put the strength of her armoured weapons of all categories at 21,000 and fighter planes at 8,000.[2] The Society for Military Training ' Osseaviakhim ' had trained several hundreds of thousands of specialists, amongst which were 30,000 pilots. Finally, since 1929, five-year plans had created new industries in gigantic factories provided with the latest equipment. But what was the use of this strength and power if, as everywhere else, the rush of armour was going to disrupt and overpower the active formations of the army in a few days, to reach at one sweep the vital centres (Leningrad, Moscow, the Donetz) and, before winter, reach the strategic objective of Arkhangel-Volga-Astrakhan ? Such was Hitler's plan.

On the other hand, since the publication of ' Mein Kampf ' the U.S.S.R. could not remain unaware that the extension of Germany's ' lebensraum ' at her expense remained the Fuhrer's main objective. But being absorbed in the execution of five-year plans which were to make her a great industrial power, she hesitated to switch over to war production at the expense of already established programmes.

In 1939 she refused to join Great Britain and France. Her neutrality, rightly called complicity by the Western Powers, enabled her to incorporate within her territory, in the west, the Baltic States and the Polish provinces claimed in the name of White Russia and the Ukraine, in the south, Bessarabia and in the north, part of Karelia. She improved her strategic frontiers but at the same time drove new allies straight into Germany's arms—Rumania, Hungary and Finland. The defeat inflicted upon the latter did not prevent her taking up arms again when the time came.

After putting the British and French armies out of action and preventing any threat from the Balkans, Hitler deployed on the eastern side of a starting line stretching from the Black Sea to the White Sea. On 22nd June 1941, the U.S.S.R. found herself alone, facing a victorious Germany intoxicated with her successes and deploying the immense human and material resources of the satellite or subjugated countries.

Since 1939 she had been feverishly speeding up her armament production but had not been able to avoid the delay caused by a complete switch-over of her factories. The removal of the southern factories to the Urals had not been completed and her new armaments were only just leaving the factories. The two-year reprieve gained by concluding the 1939 pact had not been

[1]Figures given by Guderian in 1947.
[2]Figures given by Jodl in a lecture in November, 1943.

sufficient to compensate for the initial delay in the production of tanks and planes.

The success of the panzers during the first weeks of the war recalled the lightning victories won in Poland, France and the Balkans. The whole world expected a new Hitler triumph and weighed the consequences, but Hitler had underestimated the Red Army and scattered his forces between the White Sea and the Black Sea. At Leningrad they were stopped and at Moscow they were defeated, just as they were within reach of their goal. This defeat, the first one sustained by Hitler's armies since 1939, came as a surprise. If one is to believe the author of ' I chose Freedom ', Russian patriotism had broken the rush of the panzers towards Moscow. Had there been a ' Moscow miracle ' similar to that of the Marne in 1914? The fact is that the thirteen German armoured divisions which attacked Moscow were stopped and cut to pieces by new equipment and new units. Out of fifteen hundred German tanks which were destroyed at Moscow, eleven hundred fell under artillery fire, chiefly that of the anti-tank 76 mm guns, Mark 36, which had been used, not in sections or companies but in whole regiments, on the lines of march of the panzer divisions. Four hundred others fell, victims of the ' Stormoviks ' protected by ' Yak ' fighter planes which were superior to the Messerschmidts. While on the roads German armour gave way to the artillery and the Stormoviks, in the woods the German infantry had to face reserve formations coming from the depths of the U.S.S.R. which had been prevented from taking part in earlier battles by the slowness of mobilization and transport difficulties in so vast a country.

From that moment the war of attrition began. It is true that in 1942 Hitler's armies had made up their losses and were again rolling on towards the Volga and the Caucasus, but similar causes produce similar results, and the battle of Stalingrad was a replica of that of Moscow. Whilst the Red Army was still unable to oppose the panzer divisions with an equivalent armoured force, the artillery which the Urals factories were producing at a very high rate ensured victory for it at Stalingrad both in the defensive as well as the offensive. Sixteen hundred tanks were destroyed and with them von Paulus' army. The Blitzkrieg was over.

The summer battle in the Ukraine proved to be the climax of the war, even more than Moscow in 1941 and Stalingrad in 1942. German industry, devastated by the Allies' bombing, was never able to replace the six thousand tanks lost at Kursk, Orel and Kharkov.

From 1943 onwards, the Germany army was never again able to take the initiative on the eastern front. The Red Army, taking full advantage of its superiority in men and material, continued to renew its powerful attacks until such time as Hitler's war machine collapsed under its blows and those of the Western Allies.

Germany, whose losses during the war were put at less than three million, only managed with difficulty to maintain the number of her divisions despite the total mobilization called for by Hitler in January 1943. On the other hand, the U.S.S.R., in spite of seven and a half million killed, three million disabled and eleven million civilian casualties, had nearly five hundred divisions and a total of ten million mobilized men in 1945. In the U.S.S.R. mobilization was even more complete than in Germany. In the collective farms as well as the factories Soviet women had taken men's places and carried out even the hardest tasks. Soviet women also supplied 80 per cent of the labour required for the maintenance of the armed forces and of the country and played a determined part in the victory. It was thanks to the women that war production survived the mass exodus of the male population to the front. The yearly production from 1943 was : 30,000 tanks, 40,000 planes, 120,000 artillery pieces (including heavy mortars). On the German side, according to Guderian, the production of tanks which reached 250 per month in 1939, 500 in 1942 and 1,000 in 1943, decreased from then on until the end of the war. While German factories crumbled under the bombs of the Allies the U.S.S.R. increased her industrial output in the Urals and then, without wasting a day, undertook the reconstruction of her industrial installations in the liberated regions. From the spring of 1943 onwards the mass delivery of Allied material further helped to tip the scales.

So, in the war of attrition which followed the Blitzkrieg, the U.S.S.R. won both on the strength of her resources and on her numbers. This statement in no way detracts from the merit of the Red Army Command. Without allowing itself to be discouraged by the early disasters, it learnt its lessons from them. As soon as it could resume the initiative it skilfully applied all the principles which at all times have won great men victory—seeking surprise, heavily concentrating its resources upon the directions of attack, close co-ordination of all its arms, destroying enemy forces by powerful enveloping manoeuvres, immediately consolidating its successes by means of numerous mobile units spread out in depth.

Hitler's strategy and tactics with armoured forces and planes were returned to their author in full measure, but the Soviet Command never allowed success to go to its head and, unlike the German Command, knew right to the end how to adapt its manoeuvres to suit conditions.

The General Staff and the troops equalled the Command in the carrying out of their tasks. Let us for a moment try to visualize the difficulty of feeding and directing the masses of the Red Army, ceaselessly engaged in all seasons, in advances of hundreds of kilometres through ruined areas, with very few lines of communication behind them.

As to the Soviet soldier who had overcome with such constant success the combined obstacles of enemy, ground and climate, he must have preserved the legendary endurance and hardiness of the Russian soldier of long ago besides acquiring his skill in the use of modern weapons. When called on by the heads of a new ideology he must have felt that patriotism, which once fired Suvorov's and Koutuzov's men, revive within him.

CROQUIS N° 1

LE PLAN BARBAROSSA

| 0 | 150 | 300 | 450 | 600 | 750 K. |

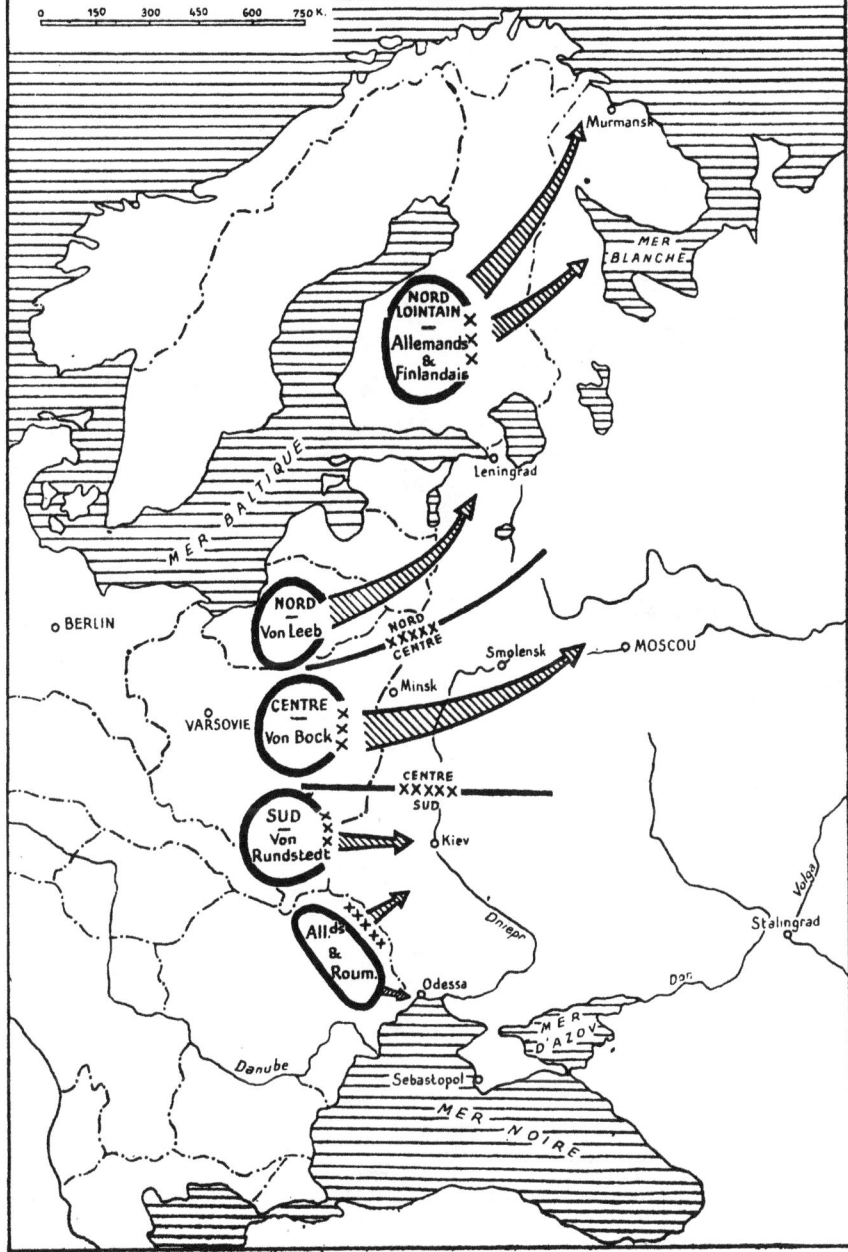

NORD
LOINTAIN
—
Allemands
&
Finlandais

Murmansk

MER
BLANCHE

Leningrad

o BERLIN

NORD
—
Von Leeb

NORD
XXXX
CENTRE

Smolensk

o MOSCOU

o Minsk

VARSOVIE

CENTRE
—
Von Bock

CENTRE
XXXX
SUD

Volga

SUD
—
Von
Rundstedt

o Kiev

Stalingrad

Dniepr

Don

Alld
&
Roum.

Odessa

MER
D'AZOV

Danube

Sebastopol

MER
NOIRE

MER BALTIQUE

CROQUIS N° 2

L'OFFENSIVE ALLEMANDE 1941

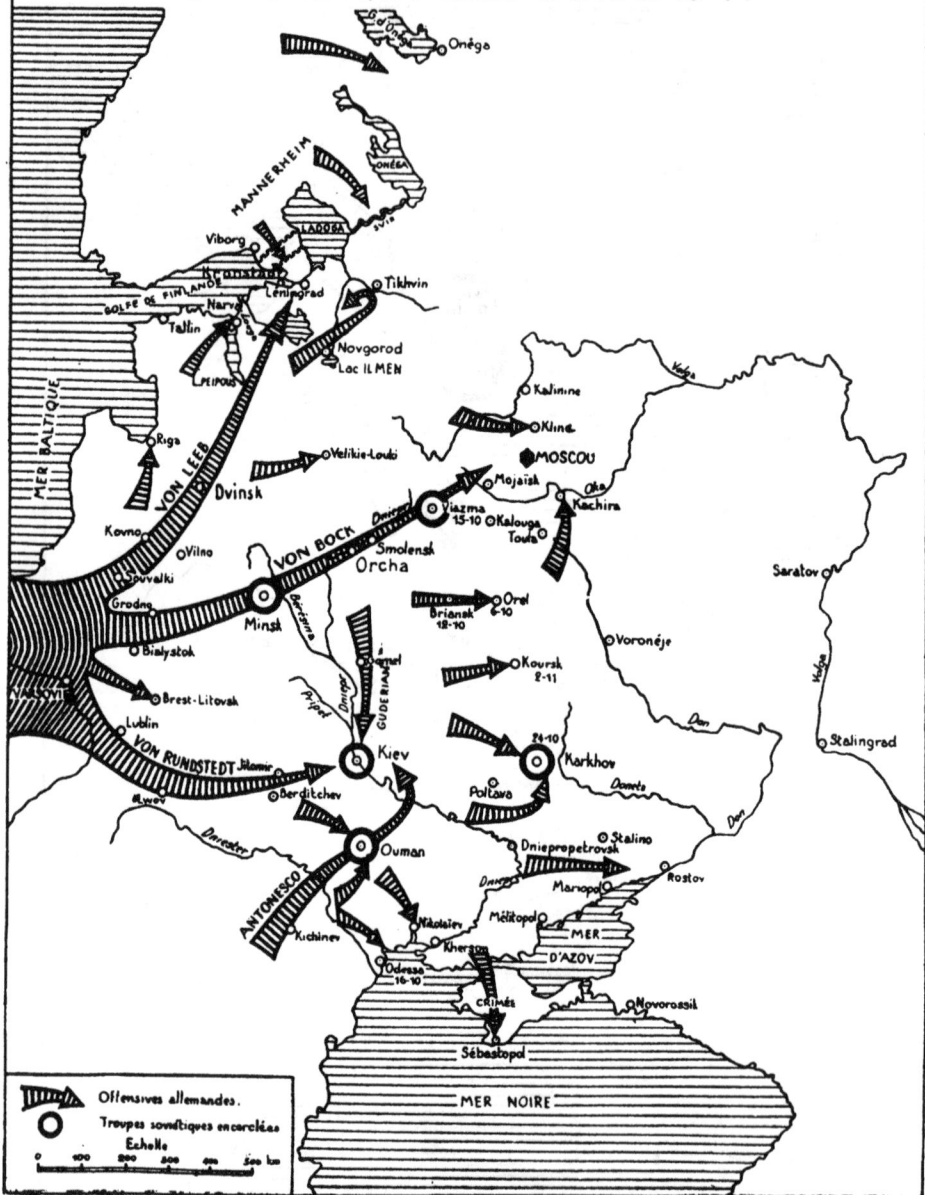

Onéga

MANNERHEIM

ONÉGA

LADOGA

Viborg

Tikhvin

GOLFE DE FINLANDE

Narva

Tallin

Léningrad

Novgorod

Lac ILMEN

PEIPOUS

MER BALTIQUE

Riga

VON LEEB

Dvinsk

Velikie-Louki

Kalinine

Kline

MOSCOU

Mojaïsk

Kachira

Kovno

Vilna

VON BOCK

Smolensk

Orcha

Viazma

15-10

Kalouga

Toula

Oka

Saratov

Souvalki

Grodno

Bérésina

Orel

6-10

Voronéje

Volga

Minsk

Briansk

12-10

Bialystok

Gomel

Koursk

2-11

Dniepr

Brest-Litovsk

Pripet

24-10

Karkhov

Don

Stalingrad

Lublin

VON RUNDSTEDT

Jitomir

GUDERIAN

Kiev

Poltava

Donets

Lwow

Berditchev

Dniester

Ouman

Dniepr

Stalino

Dniepropetrovsk

Rostov

Don

ANTONESCO

Kichinev

Nikolaïev

Mélitopol

Mariopol

MER

D'AZOV

Odessa

16-10

Kherson

CRIMÉE

Novorossik

Sébastopol

MER NOIRE

Offensives allemandes.

Troupes soviétiques encerclées

Echelle

0   100   200   300   400   500 km

CROQUIS N° 3
LE PLAN ALLEMAND

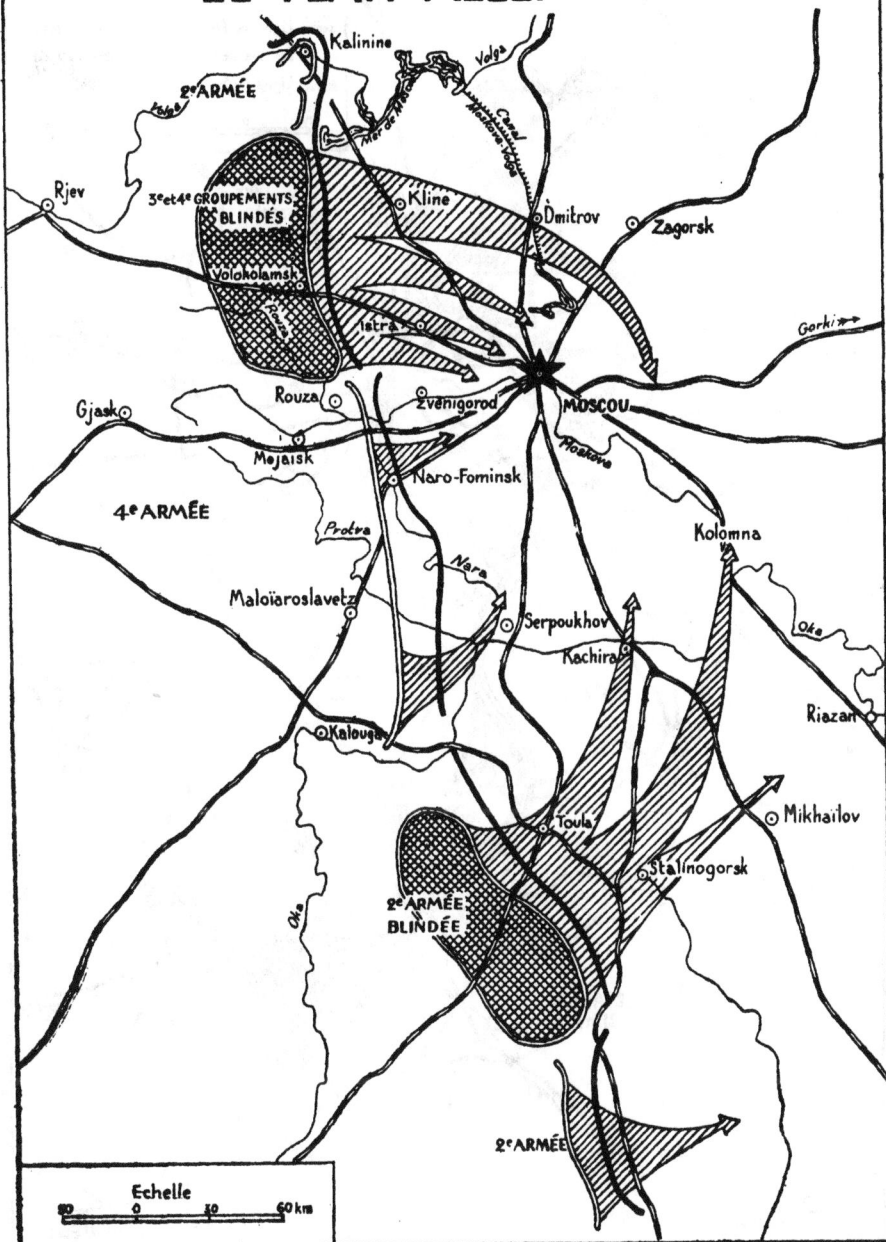

Kalinine

Volga

2ᵉ ARMÉE

Rjev

3ᵉ et 4ᵉ GROUPEMENTS BLINDÉS

Kline

Dmitrov

Zagorsk

Volokolamsk

Istra

Gorki

Rouza

Zvénigorod

MOSCOU

Gjask

Mejaïsk

Moskova

Naro-Fominsk

4ᵉ ARMÉE

Kolomna

Protva

Oka

Nara

Maloïaroslavetz

Serpoukhov

Kachira

Riazan

Kalouga

Mikhaïlov

Toula

Stalinogorsk

2ᵉ ARMÉE BLINDÉE

Oka

2ᵉ ARMÉE

Echelle

0   30   60 km

CROQUIS N°4

L'OFFENSIVE ALLEMANDE DE NOVEMBRE 1941

CROQUIS N°5

LA CONTRE OFFENSIVE SOVIÉTIQUE DE DÉCEMBRE 1941 JANVIER 1942

Front le 6 décembre 1941
Axes d'effort de l'Armée Rouge
Front le 20 décembre 1941
25   0   25   50   75

KALININE

Volga

Staritsa
9° ARMÉE
Rogatchevo
Vyssokovski
Kline
Dmitrov
Yakhroma
Zagorsk
IAROSLAV
Chakhovskaia
Solnetchnogorsk
Volokolamsk
Rouza
Krasnaia Poliana
GORKI
Krioukovo
3° ET 4° GROUPES DE CHARS
Istra
Dedovski
Gjaïsk
Rouza
Mostova
Lokofhito
Zvenigorod
Koliubakino
Golitsino
MOSCOU
Mojaïsk
Dorokhov
Koubinka
Aprelevka
Miakichevo
Iouchkovo
Bourtsevo
Novinskaia
Podolsk
Egorievsk
Moscova
Véréia
Naro-Fominsk
Ateptsevo
Stiznevo
4° ARMÉE
Protva
Borovsk
FRONT OUEST
Kolomna
Maloiaroslavetz
Nara
Médine
Serpoukhov
Oka
Kachira
Ozery
Krioukovo
Pianitsa
Boudevo
Barabanevo
Maslovo
Zaraïsk
Ioukhnov
Riazan
Mossalsk
Kalouga
Alexine
Laptevo
Mordves
Mechtchevsk
Veney
Reviakino
Mikhaïlov
Likhvine
Soukhinitchi
Toula
Chatt
Stalinogorsk
Kozelsk
Oupa
Didilovo
Ouzlovaia
RIAJSK
Osoévo
Plava
Belov
Logoroditsk
Plavsk
Epifane
2° ARMÉE DE CHARS
Volovo
Tcherne
Don
Kourkino
Mtsensk
Oka
Efremov
Orel
FRONT SUD-OUEST

CROQUIS N°6

L'OFFENSIVE GERMANO-FINLANDAISE CONTRE LENINGRAD : 1941

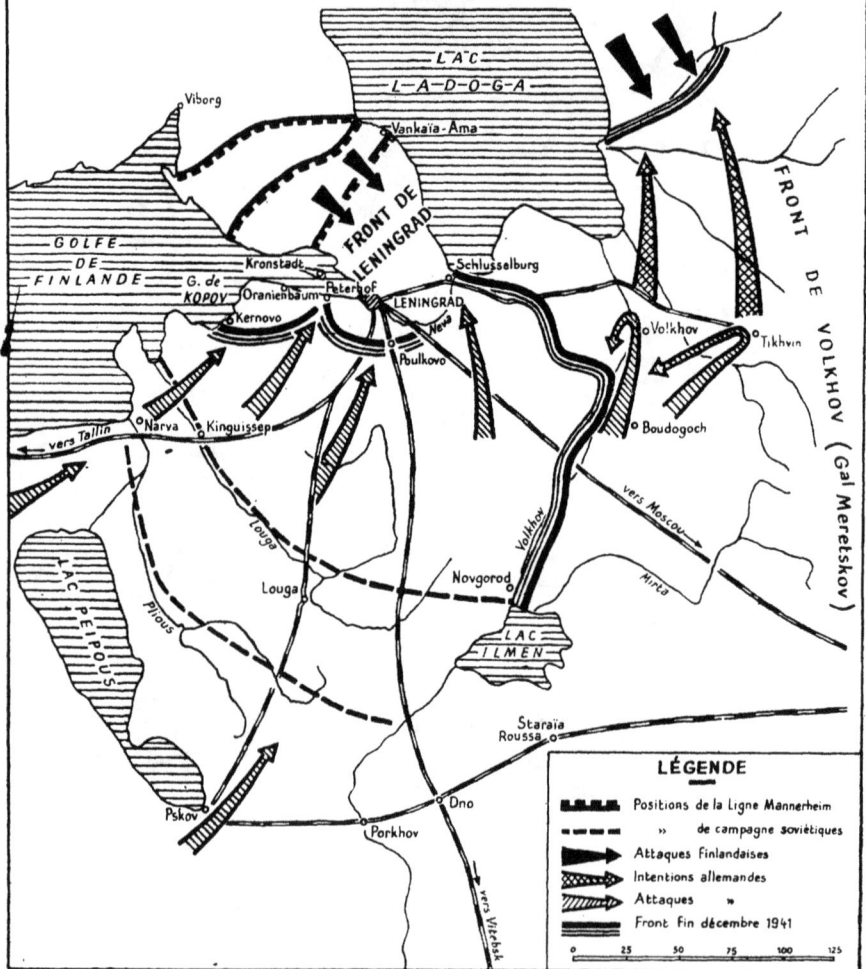

LÉGENDE

▄▟▄▟	Positions de la Ligne Mannerheim
▬ ▬ ▬	» de campagne soviétiques
◥	Attaques finlandaises
⬚	Intentions allemandes
⬧	Attaques »
━━	Front fin décembre 1941

0   25   50   75   100   125

CROQUIS N° 7

LE PLAN ALLEMAND

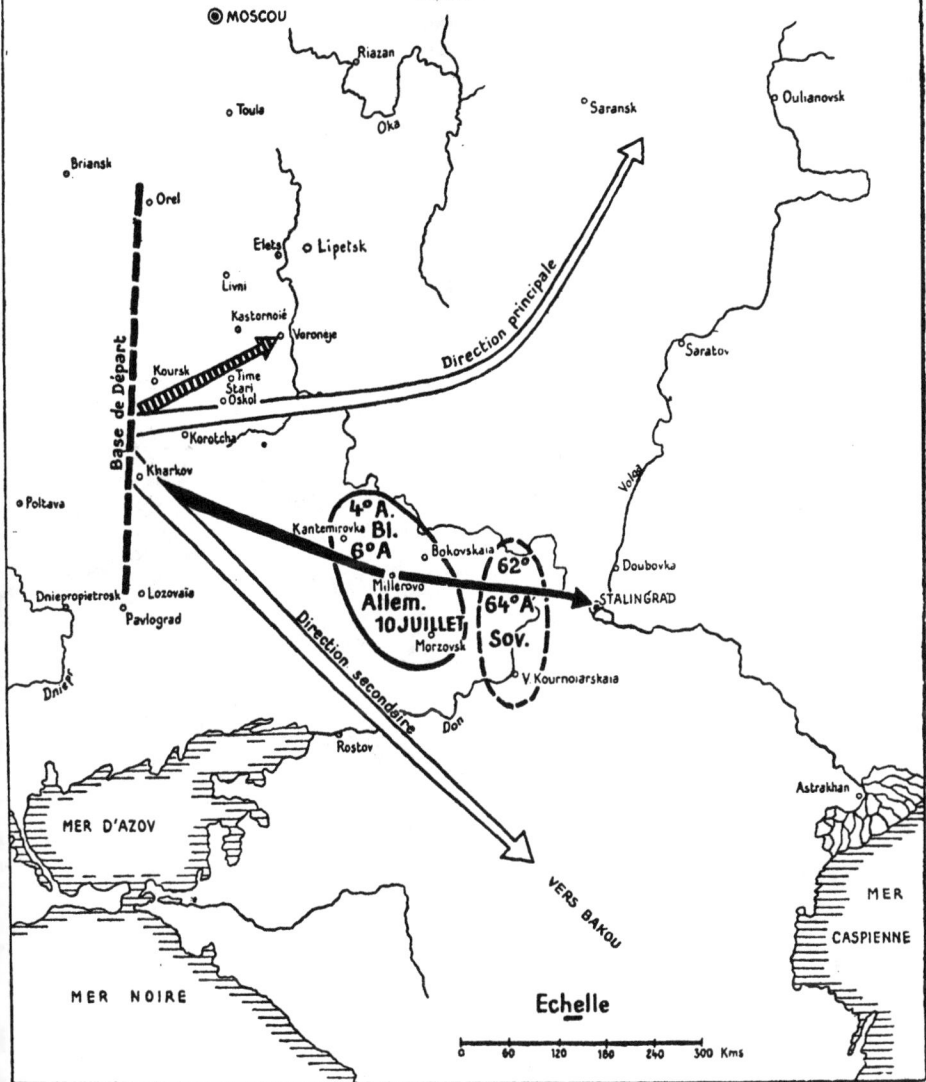

Échelle

CROQUIS N°8

L'OFFENSIVE ALLEMANDE ᴇɴ DIRECTION ᴅᴇ STALINGRAD
JUILLET-SEPTEMBRE 1942

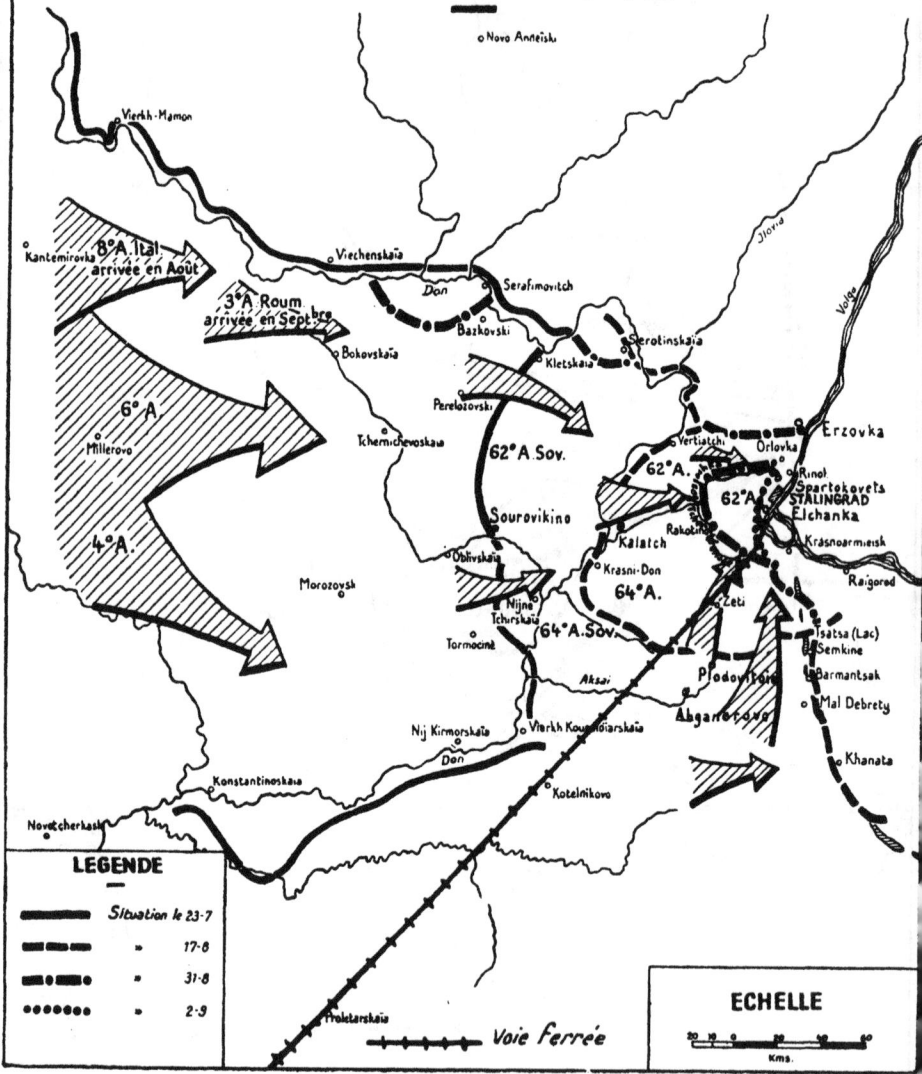

o Novo Anneiski

Vierkh-Mamon

o Kantemirovka

8°A. Ital. arrivée en Août

o Viechenskaïa

Don

Serafimovitch

3°A. Roum. arrivée en Sept.

Bazkovski

o Bokovskaïa

Kletskaïa

Serotinskaïa

6° A.

Perelozovski

o Tchernichevoskaïa

62° A. Sov.

o Vertiatchi

Orlovka

Erzovka

o Milierovo

62° A.

o Rinol

Spartakovets

STALINGRAD

62° A.

Elchanka

Sourovikino

Rakotin

Kalatch

4° A.

o Morozovsk

o Oblivskaïa

Krasni-Don

Krasnoarmensk

64° A.

Raigorod

Nijne Tchirskaïa

Zeti

Isatsa (Lac)

o Tormocine

64° A. Sov.

Semkine

Aksai

Barmantsak

Plodovitoïe

o Mal Debrety

Abganerovo

Nij Kirmorskaïa

o Vierkh Koumoïarskaïa

Don

o Khanata

o Konstantinoskaïa

o Kotelnikovo

o Novetcherkask

LEGENDE

──────	Situation le 23-7
▬ ▬ ▬	» 17-8
▬•▬•▬	» 31-8
••••••	» 2-9

Proletarskaïa

+–+–+–+ Voie Ferrée

ECHELLE

20 10 0   20   40   60

Kms.

CROQUIS N°9

LA DÉFENSE DE STALINGRAD
13 SEPTEMBRE 1942

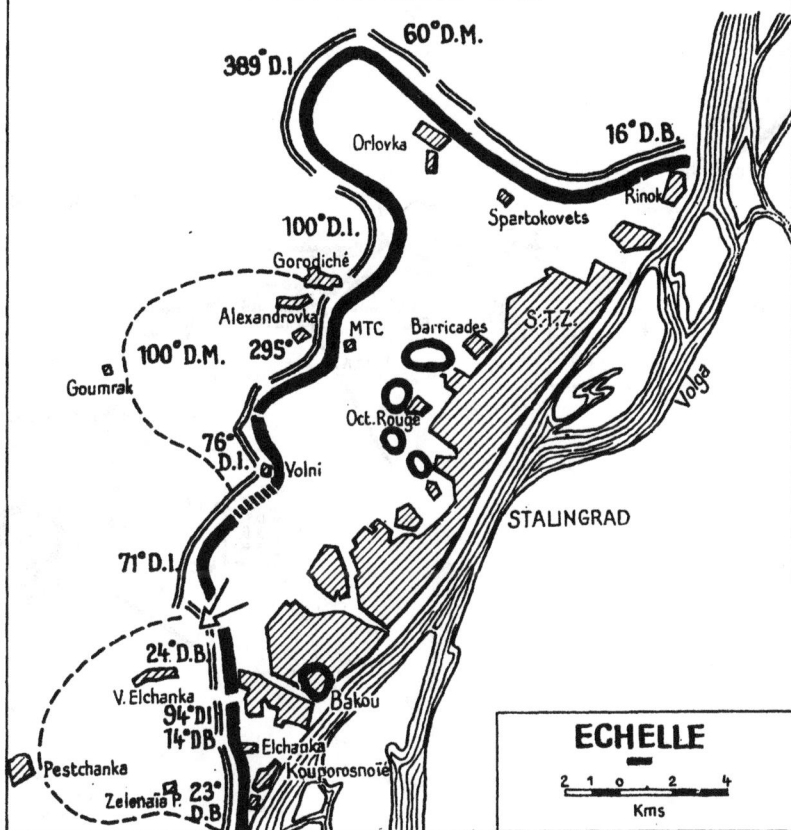

60° D.M.

389° D.I.

Orlovka

16° D.B.

Spartokovets

Rinok

100° D.I.

Gorodiché

Alexandrovka

MTC

Barricades

S.T.Z.

100° D.M.

295°

Goumrak

Oct. Rouge

Volga

76°
D.I.

Volni

STALINGRAD

71° D.I.

24° D.B.

V. Elchanka

Bakou

94° D.I.

14° D.B.

Elchanka

Pestchanka

Kouporosnoïé

Zelenaïa P.

23°
D.B.

ECHELLE

2 1 0 2 4

Kms

CROQUIS N°10

DISPOSITIF ALLEMAND

LE 11 NOVEMBRE 1942

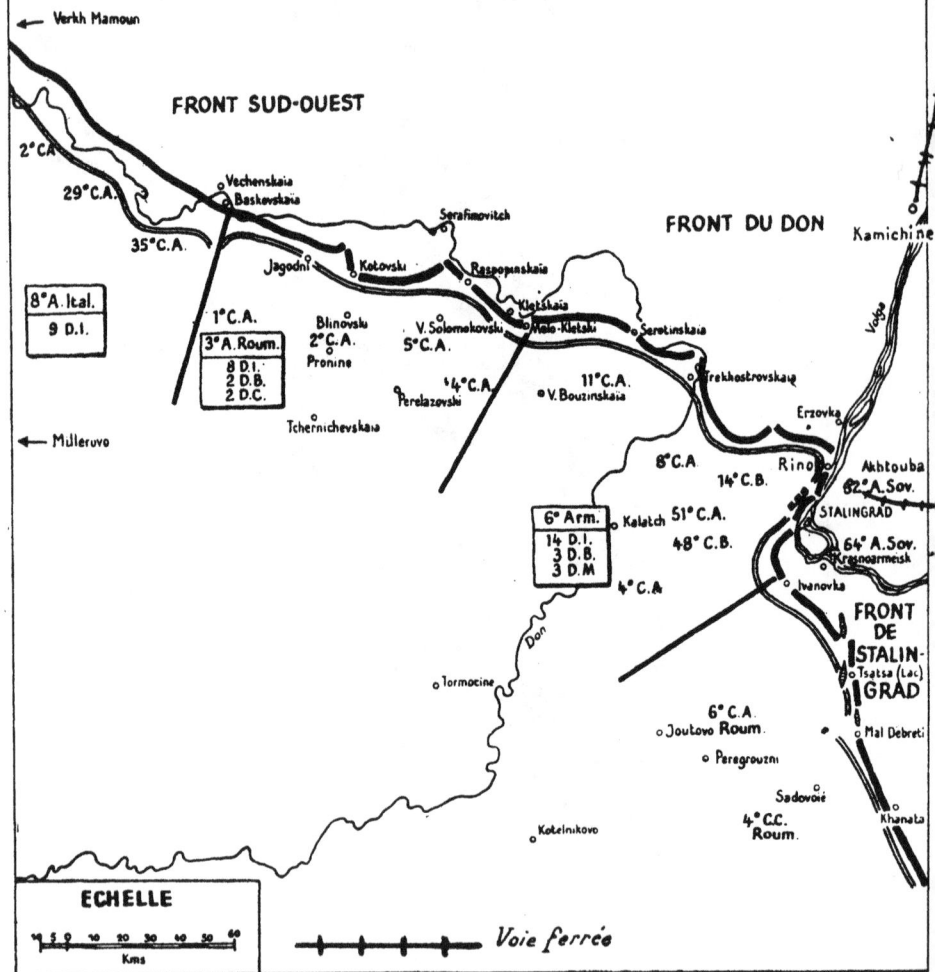

← Verkh Mamoun

FRONT SUD-OUEST

2° C.A.

29° C.A.

35° C.A.

Vechenskaia
Baskovskaia

Serafimovitch

FRONT DU DON

Kamichine

Jagodni   Kotovski   Raspopinskaia

8° A. Ital.
9 D.I.

1° C.A.

Blinovski
2° C.A.
Pronine

Kletskaia

V. Solomakovski   Malo-Kletski   Serotinskaia

3° A. Roum.
8 D.I.
2 D.B.
2 D.C.

5° C.A.

Trekhostrovskaia

Erzovka

← Milleruvo

14° C.A.

11° C.A.

Perelazovski   • V. Bouzinskaia

8° C.A.

Tchernichevskaia

14° C.B.

Rino

Akhtouba
62° A. Sov.

STALINGRAD

6° Arm.
14 D.I.
3 D.B.
3 D.M

Kalatch   51° C.A.
48° C.B.

64° A. Sov.
Krasnoarmeisk

4° C.A.

Ivanovka

**FRONT
DE
STALIN-
GRAD**

Don

Tsatsa (Lac)

Tormacine

6° C.A.

• Joutovo **Roum.**

• Peregrouzni

• Mal Debreti

Sadovoié

Kotelnikovo

4° C.C.
Roum.

Khanata

ECHELLE
0 5 0 10 20 30 40 50 60
Kms

╫──╫──╫──╫──╫ *Voie ferrée*

CROQUIS N°11

OFFENSIVE DE NOVEMBRE 1942
LE PLAN SOVIÉTIQUE

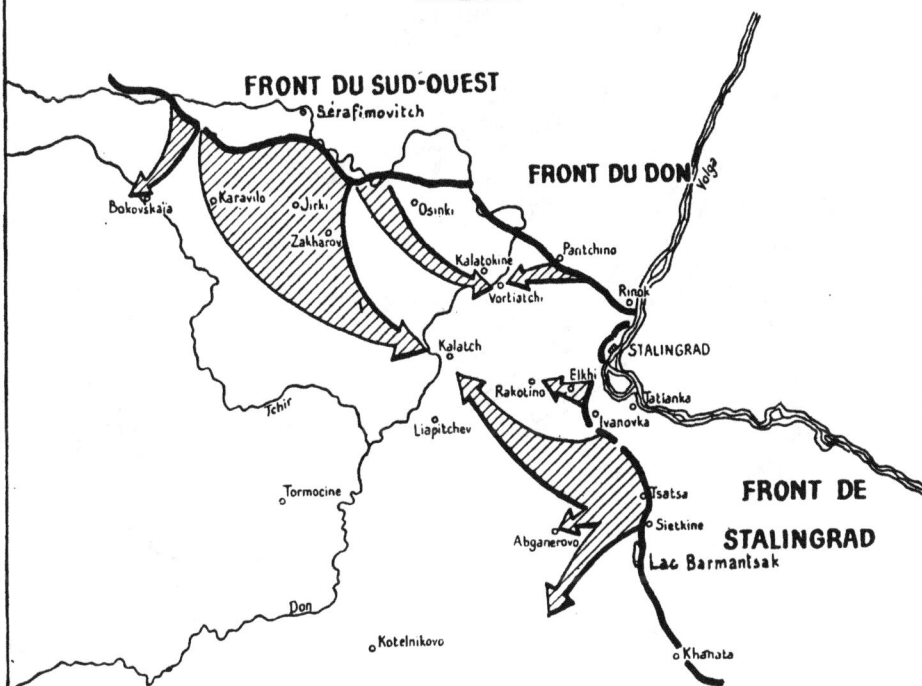

FRONT DU SUD-OUEST

Sérafimovitch

FRONT DU DON

Bokovskaia

Karavilo

Jirki

Osinki

Zakharov

Kalatokine

Pantchino

Vortiatchi

Rinok

Kalatch

STALINGRAD

Elkhi

Rakolino

Tatianka

Tchir

Ivanovka

Liapitchev

Tormocine

Tsatsa

FRONT DE

Sietkine

STALINGRAD

Abganerovo

Lac Barmantsak

Don

Kotelnikovo

Khamata

ÉCHELLE

20 10 0 20 40 60

Kms

CROQUIS N° 12

LA PERCÉE ET LA MANŒUVRE D'ENCERCLEMENT
19-30 NOVEMBRE 1942

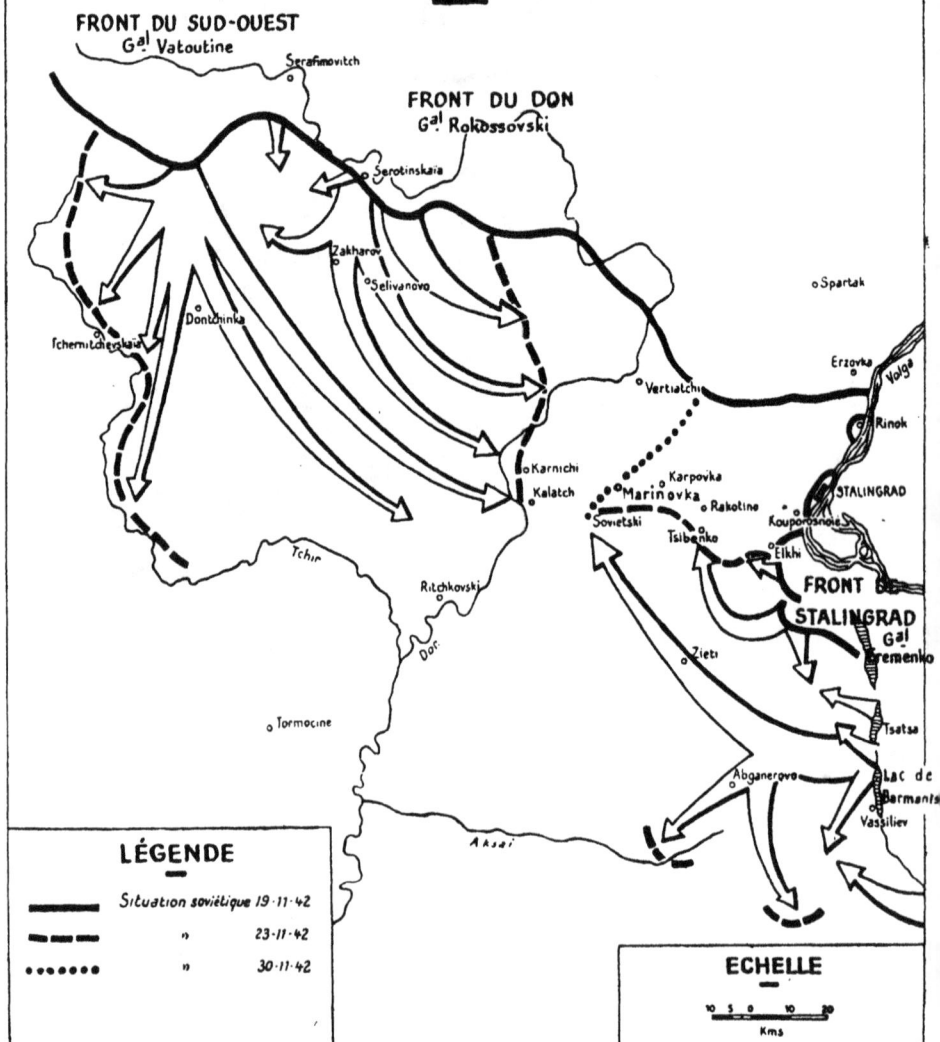

FRONT DU SUD-OUEST
Gal Vatoutine

Serafimovitch

FRONT DU DON
Gal Rokossovski

Serotinskaia

Zakharov

Selivanovo

Spartak

Dontchinka

Tchernitchievskaia

Erzovka

Volga

Vertiatchi

Rinok

Karnichi

Karpovka

Marinovka

Rakotine

STALINGRAD

Kalatch

Sovietski

Tsibenko

Kouporosnoie

Tchir

Elkhi

FRONT DE STALINGRAD
Gal Eremenko

Ritchkovski

Don

Zieti

Tsatsa

Tormocine

Abganerovo

Lac de Barmantsi

Vassiliev

Aksai

LÉGENDE

▬▬▬	Situation soviétique 19·11·42
▬ ▬ ▬	" 23·11·42
••••••	" 30·11·42

ECHELLE

10 5 0 10 20
Kms

CROQUIS N° 13

CONCENTRATION DES GROUPEMENTS ALLEMANDS DE KOTELNIKOVO ET DE TORMOCINE — INTENTIONS DU COMMANDEMENT ALLEMAND POUR DÉGAGER LES GROUPEMENTS ENCERCLÉS

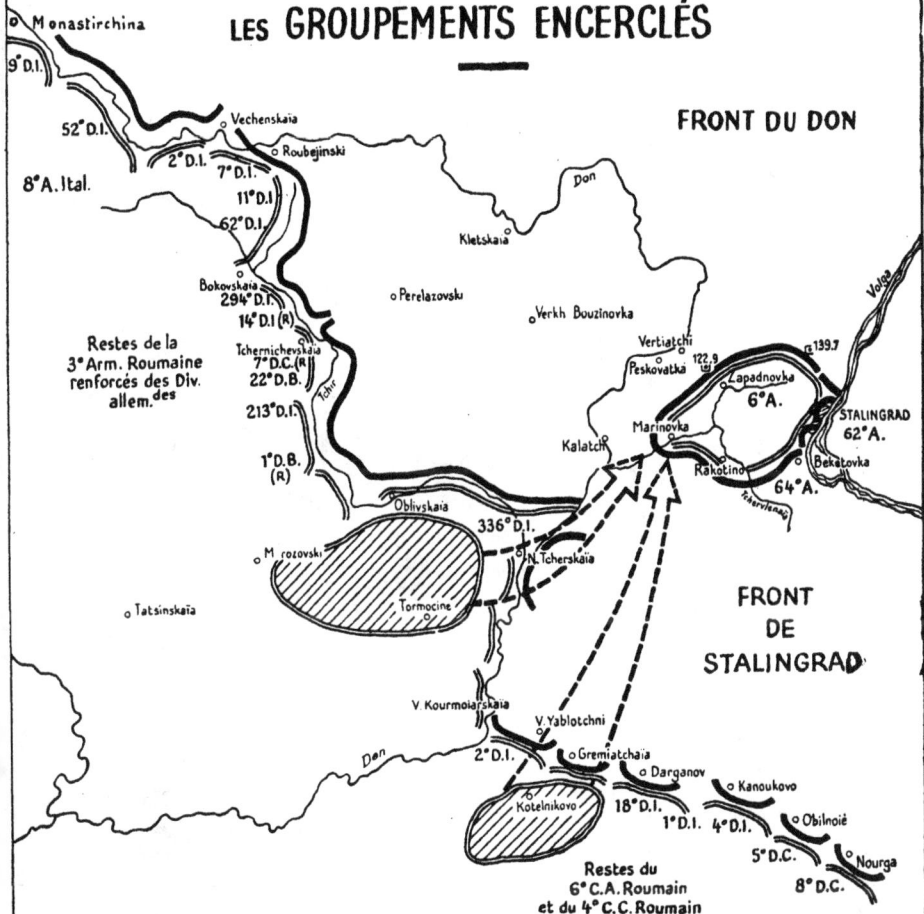

o Monastirchina

9° D.I.

52° D.I.

8° A. Ital.

o Vechenskaia

o Roubejinski

2° D.I.

7° D.I.

11° D.I

62° D.I.

FRONT DU DON

Don

o Kletskaia

o Perelazovski

o Verkh Bouzinovka

Bokovskaia

294° D.I.

14° D.I (R)

Restes de la
3° Arm. Roumaine
renforcés des Div.
allem.des

Tchernichevskaia

7° D.C.(R)

22° D.B.

213° D.I.

Vertiatchi

Peskovatka

122.9

139.7

Zapadnovka

6° A.

Volga

STALINGRAD

62° A.

Marinovka

Kalatch

Rakotino

Bekatovka

64° A.

1° D.B.
(R)

Oblivskaia

336° D.I.

o M rozovski

N. Tcherskaia

o Tatsinskaia

o Tormocine

**FRONT
DE
STALINGRAD**

V. Kourmoïarskaia

V. Yablotchni

2° D.I.

o Gremiatchaia

o Darganov

o Kanoukovo

Kotelnikovo

18° D.I.

1° D.I. 4° D.I.

o Obilnoié

5° D.C.

o Nourga

8° D.C.

Restes du
6° C.A. Roumain
et du 4° C.C. Roumain

Don

ECHELLE

10 5 0   10   20   30   40 50
Kms.

CROQUIS N° 14

ECHEC des TENTATIVES ALLEMANDES VISANT a DÉGAGER LES FORCES ENCERCLÉES devant STALINGRAD

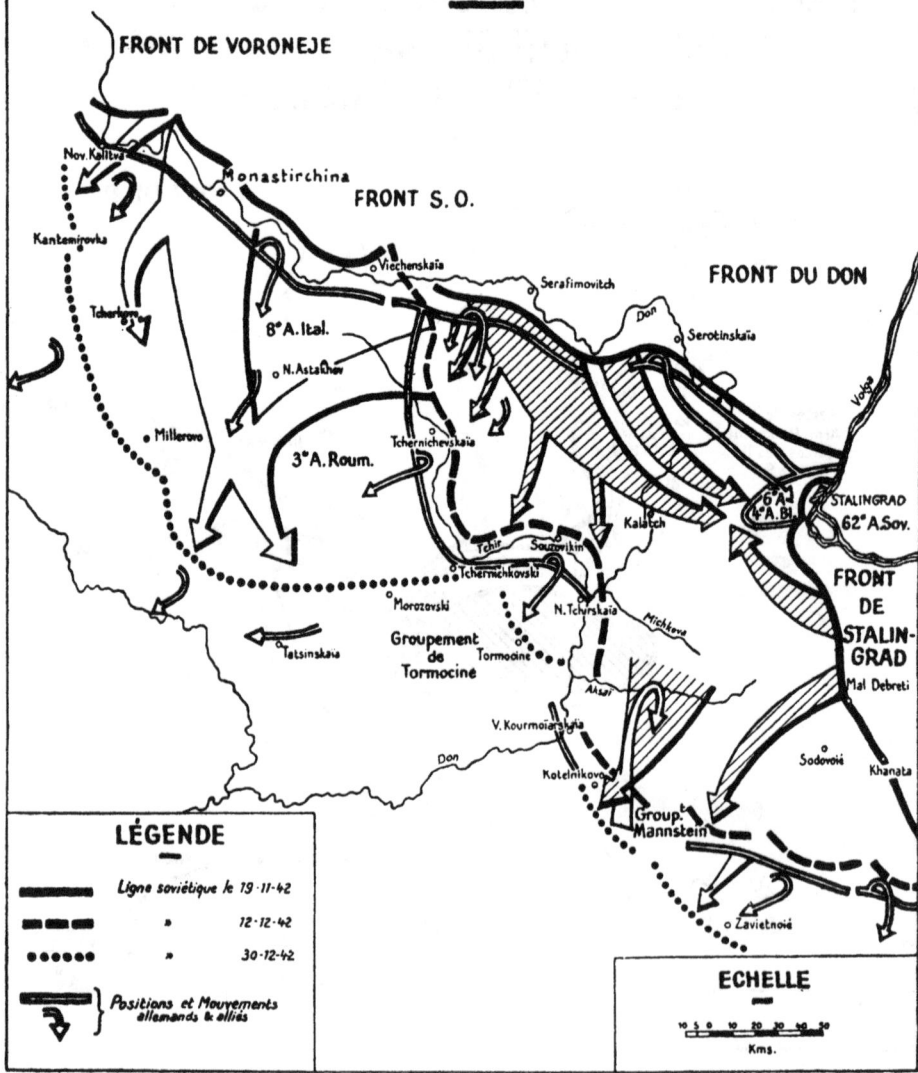

FRONT DE VORONEJE

Nov. Kalitva

Monastirchina

Kantemirovka

FRONT S.O.

Viechenskaïa

Serafimovitch

FRONT DU DON

Don

Serotinskaïa

Tcherkesy

8ᵉ A. Ital.

N. Astakhov

Millerovo

Tchernichevskaïa

3ᵉ A. Roum.

Tchir

Kalatch

Volga

6ᵉ A¹
4ᵉ A. Bl.

STALINGRAD

62ᵉ A. Sov.

Souzovikin

Tchernichevkovski

Morozovski

N. Tchirskaïa

Nijkovo

FRONT DE STALINGRAD

Mal Debreti

Groupement de Tormocine

Tormocine

Tatsinskaïa

Aksaï

Don

V. Kourmoiarskaïa

Sodovoié

Khanata

Kotelnikovo

Groupᵗ Mannstein

Zavietnoié

LÉGENDE

▬▬▬	Ligne soviétique le 19·11·42
▬ ▬ ▬	» 12·12·42
••••••	» 30·12·42
⟳	Positions et Mouvements allemands & alliés

ECHELLE

10 5 0 10 20 30 40 50

Kms.

CROQUIS N° 15

DISPOSITIF ALLEMAND LE 10-1-43 ET PLAN OFFENSIF DU COMMANDEMENT SOVIÉTIQUE POUR LA 1ère PHASE —

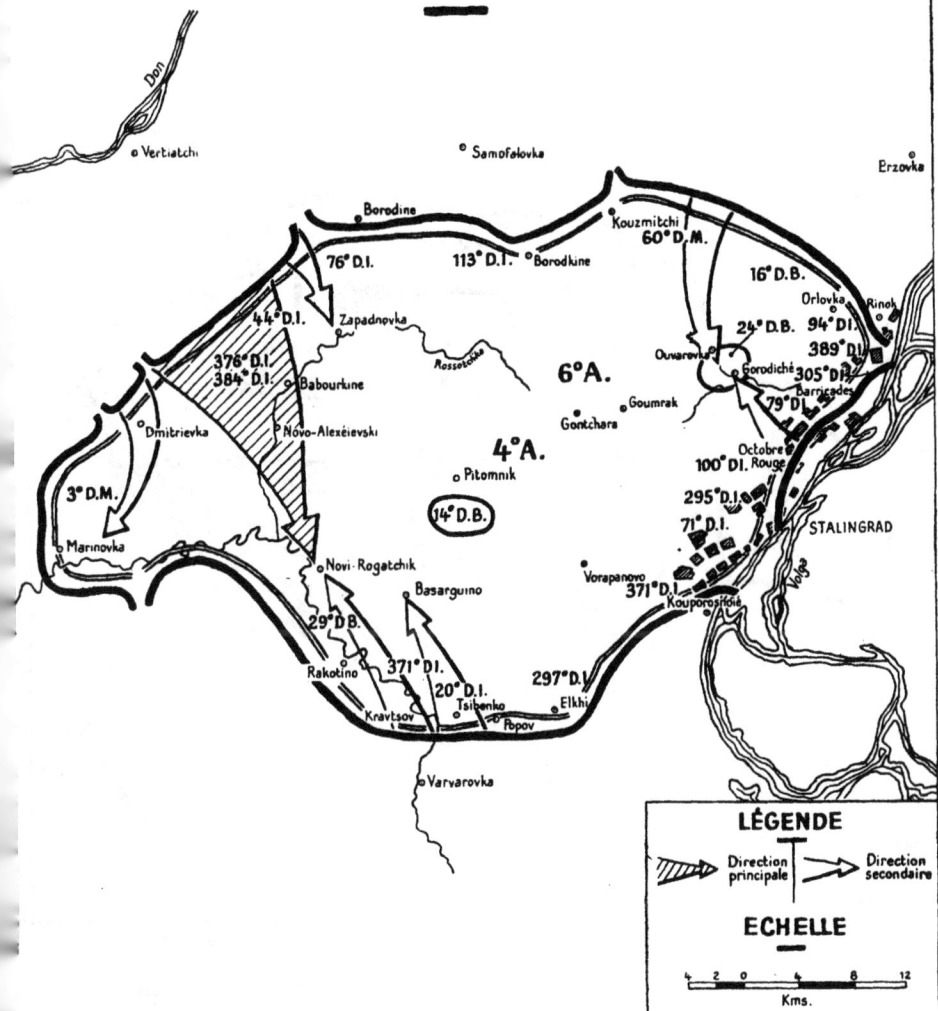

Don

Vertiatchi

Samofalovka

Erzovka

Borodine

Kouzmitchi
60° D.M.

76° D.I.

113° D.I. Borodkine

16° D.B.

Zapadnovka

Orlovka Rinok

44° D.I.

24° D.B. 94° D.I.

Rossochka

Ouvarovka

389° D.I.

376° D.I.
384° D.I. Babourkine

Gorodiché 305° D.I.

6° A.

79° D.I. Barricades

Goumrak

Dmitrievka

Novo-Alexéievski

Gontchara

4° A.

Octobre
100° D.I. Rouge

Pitomnik

3° D.M.

14° D.B.

295° D.I.

71° D.I.

STALINGRAD

Marinovka

Novi-Rogatchik

Vorapanovo

371° D.I.

Basarguino

Kouporosnoié

29° D.B.

Rakotino

371° D.I.

20° D.I.

297° D.I.

Kravtsov

Tsibenko Elkhi

Popov

Varvarovka

LÉGENDE

Direction
principale

Direction
secondaire

ECHELLE

4 2 0   4   8   12

Kms.

CROQUIS N°16

DESTRUCTION DES FORCES ALLEMANDES ENCERCLÉES
10 JANVIER   2 FÉVRIER 1943

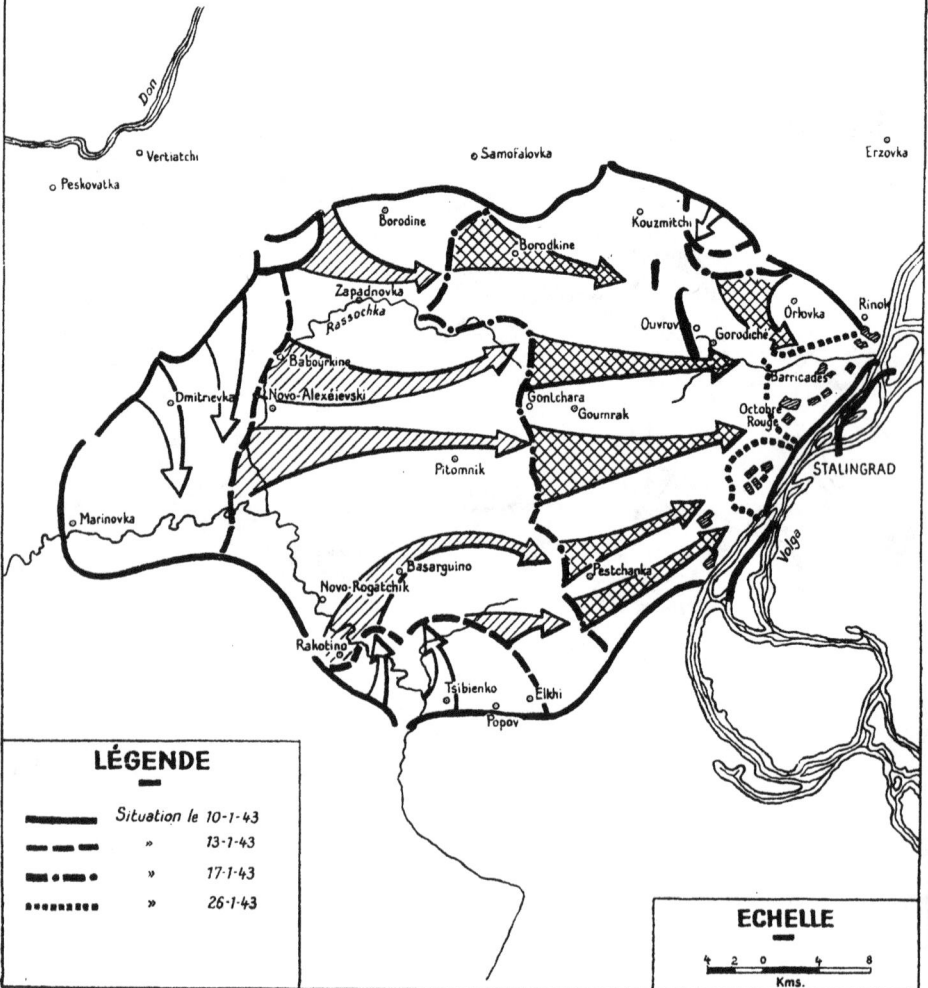

Don

Vertiatchi

Peskovatka

Samofalovka

Erzovka

Borodine

Kouzmitchi

Borodkine

Zapadnovka

Rassochka

Ouvrov

Gorodiché

Orlovka

Rinok

Baboufkine

Novo-Alexéievski

Dmitnevka

Barricades

Gontchara

Gournrak

Octobre Rouge

Pitomnik

STALINGRAD

Marinovka

Basarguino

Novo-Rogatchik

Pestchanka

Volga

Rakotino

Tsibienko

Elkhi

Popov

LÉGENDE

	Situation le 10-1-43
	» 13-1-43
	» 17-1-43
	» 26-1-43

ECHELLE

4 2 0   4   8
Kms.

CROQUIS N°17

SAILLANT DE KOURSK
TRACÉ DU FRONT FIN MARS 1943

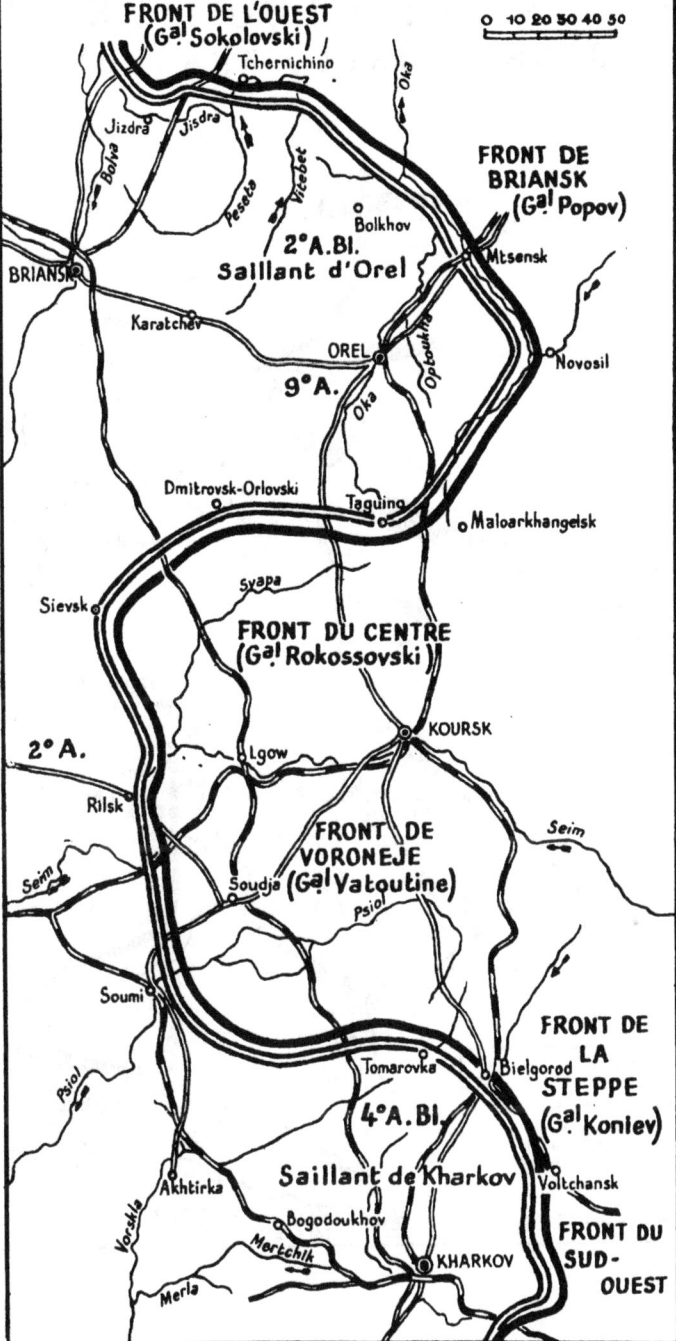

FRONT DE L'OUEST
(G.al Sokolovski)

Tchernichino

0 10 20 30 40 50

Jizdra   Jisdra

Bolva   Pesota   Vitebet   Oka

Bolkhov

FRONT DE
BRIANSK
(G.al Popov)

2°A.Bl.
Saillant d'Orel

Mtsensk

BRIANSK

Karatchev

OREL   Opboukna   Novosil

9°A.   Oka

Dmitrovsk-Orlovski

Taguino

Maloarkhangelsk

Svapa

Sievsk

FRONT DU CENTRE
(G.al Rokossovski)

KOURSK

2°A.   Lgow

Rilsk

Seim

FRONT DE
VORONEJE
(G.al Vatoutine)

Soudja   Psiol

Seim

Soumi

FRONT DE
LA
STEPPE
(G.al Koniev)

Tomarovka   Bielgorod

4°A.Bl.

Akhtirka   Saillant de Kharkov   Voltchansk

Vorskla   Bogodoukhov

Mertchik   FRONT DU
SUD-
OUEST

Merla   KHARKOV

Psiol

CROQUIS N°18

LA RUPTURE DE L'ÉQUILIBRE 1943
(KOURSK · OREL · KHARKOV)

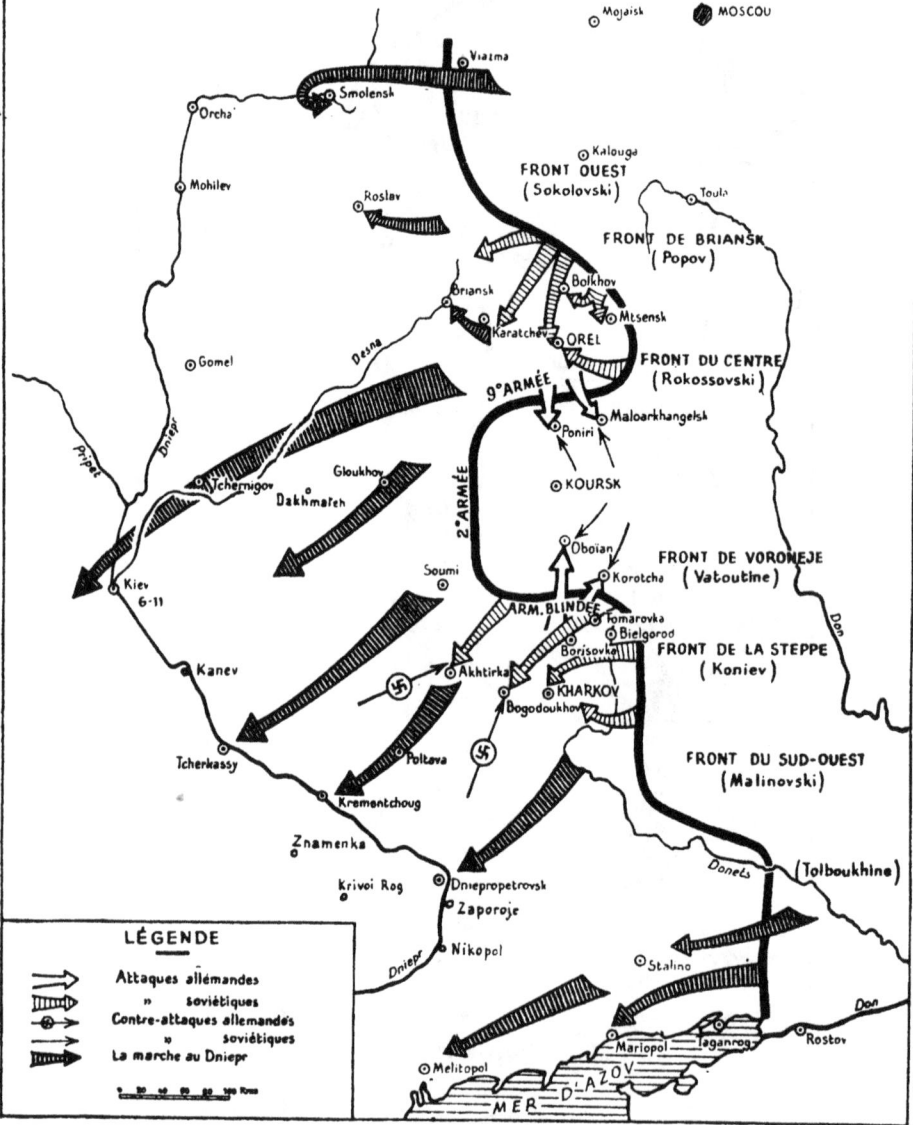

Mojaisk   ⬡ MOSCOU

Viazma

Orcha   Smolensk

Mohilev   Roslav   Kalouga

FRONT OUEST
(Sokolovski)   Toula

FRONT DE BRIANSK
(Popov)

Briansk   Bolkhov

Gomel   Karatchev   Mtsensk

Desna   OREL

FRONT DU CENTRE
(Rokossovski)

9° ARMÉE   Maloarkhangelsk

Pripet   Dniepr   Poniri

Tchernigov   Gloukhov

Dakhmaîeh   ⊙ KOURSK

2° ARMÉE

Soumi   Oboian   **FRONT DE VORONEJE**
(Vatoutine)

Kiev
6-11   Korotcha

ARM. BLINDÉE   Tomarovka

Kanev   Bielgorod

Akhtirka   Borisovka   **FRONT DE LA STEPPE**
(Koniev)

KHARKOV

Bogodoukhov

Tcherkassy   Poltava

FRONT DU SUD-OUEST
(Malinovski)

Krementchoug

Znamenka

Krivoi Rog   Dniepropetrovsk   Donets   (Tolboukhine)

Zaporoje

Dniepr   Nikopol   Stalino   Don

LÉGENDE

→ Attaques allemandes
⇛ " soviétiques
⊕→ Contre-attaques allemandes
" " soviétiques
⬛ La marche au Dniepr

0 20 40 60 80 100 Kms

Mariopol   Taganrog   Rostov

Melitopol   MER D'AZOV

CROQUIS N°19

PLAN ALLEMAND EN VUE DE LA RÉDUCTION DU SAILLANT DE KOURSK

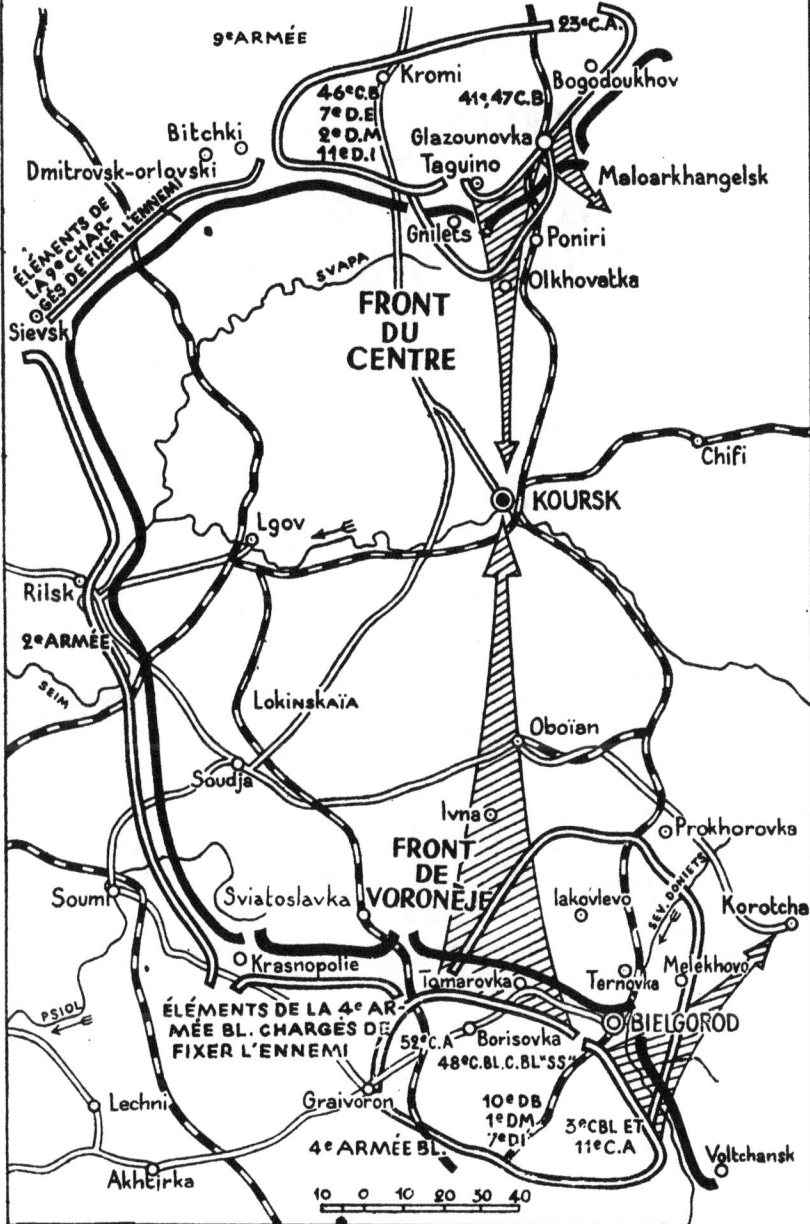

9ᵉ ARMÉE

23ᵉ C.A.

Kromi

46ᵉ C.B.
7ᵉ D.E
2ᵉ D.M
11ᵉ D.I

41ᵉ,47 C.B.

Bogodoukhov

Bitchki

Glazounovka

Dmitrovsk-orlovski

Taguino

Maloarkhangelsk

ÉLÉMENTS DE
LA 9ᵉ CHAR-
GÉS DE FIXER L'ENNEMI

Gnilets

Poniri

SVAPA

Olkhovatka

Sievsk

FRONT
DU
CENTRE

Chifi

Lgov

KOURSK

Rilsk

2ᵉ ARMÉE

SEIM

Lokinskaïa

Oboïan

Soudja

Ivna

Prokhorovka

FRONT
DE
VORONÈJE

Iakovlevo

SEV.DONIETS

Korotcha

Soumi

Sviatoslavka

Melekhovo

Krasnopolie

Tomarovka

Ternovka

BIELGOROD

PSIOL

ÉLÉMENTS DE LA 4ᵉ AR-
MÉE BL. CHARGÉS DE
FIXER L'ENNEMI

52ᵉ C.A

Borisovka

48ᵉ C.BL.C.BL"SS"

Lechni

Graivoron

10ᵉ DB
1ᵉ DM
7ᵉ DI

3ᵉ CBL ET
11ᵉ C.A

Voltchansk

Akhtirka

4ᵉ ARMÉE BL.

10   0   10   20   30   40

CROQUIS N°20

ATTAQUE ALLEMANDE AU NORD DE KOURSK
FRONT DU CENTRE : 5-8 JUILLET 1943

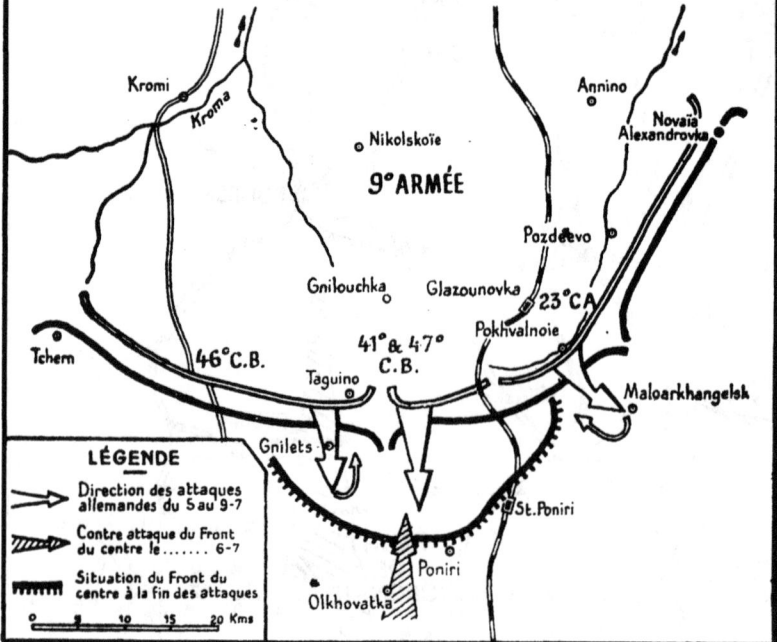

Kromi

Kroma

Annino

Novaïa
Alexandrovka

Nikolskoïe

9° ARMÉE

Pozdéevo

Gnilouchka   Glazounovka   23° CA

Pokhvalnoie

Tchern   46° C.B.   41° & 47°
C.B.   Maloarkhangelsk

Taguino

Gnilets

St. Poniri

Poniri

Olkhovatka

LÉGENDE

Direction des attaques
allemandes du 5 au 9-7

Contre attaque du Front
du centre le 6-7

Situation du Front du
centre à la fin des attaques

0   5   10   15   20 Kms

CROQUIS N°21

L'ATTAQUE ALLEMANDE AU SUD DE KOURSK
5-15 JUILLET 1943

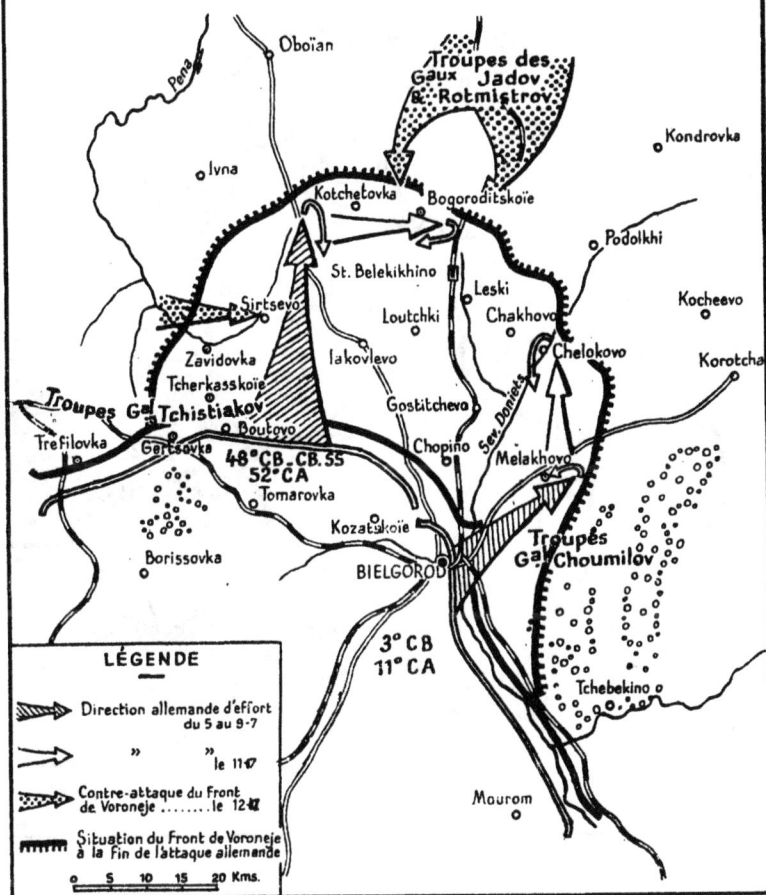

Oboïan

Troupes des
Gaux Jadov
& Rotmistrov

Kondrovka

Ivna

Kotchetovka

Bogoroditskoïe

Podolkhi

St. Belekikhino

Leski

Kocheavo

Sirtsevo

Loutchki

Chakhovo

Zavidovka

Iakovlevo

Chelokovo

Korotcha

Tcherkasskoïe

Troupes Gal Tchistiakov

Gostitchevo

Sev. Donietz

Trefilovka

Boutovo

Chopino

Melakhovo

Gertsovka

48° CB - CB. 55
52° CA

Tomarovka

Kozatskoïe

Troupes
Gal Choumilov

Borissovka

BIELGOROD

3° CB
11° CA

Tchebekino

LÉGENDE

→ Direction allemande d'effort
du 5 au 9-7

→ " " le 11-7

→ Contre-attaque du Front
de Voroneje .... le 12-7

Situation du Front de Voroneje
à la fin de l'attaque allemande

0   5   10   15   20 Kms.

Maurom

CROQUIS N°22

SITUATION LE 12 JUILLET 1943 et PLAN SOVIÉTIQUE

AILE GAUCHE DU FRONT DE L'OUEST

Troupes du Gal Boldine
Troupes du Gal Bagramian
338 D.I.
110 D.I.
55 CA.
296 D.I.
5° D.B. & 1 D.I.
707° D.I.
INF.
INF.
BRIANSK
1 D.I. 1 DB.
INF.
9 A
8° Corps Hongrois
72 D.I.
45 D.I.
137 D.I.
251 D.I.
Troupes du Gal Galanine
Troupes du Gal Batov
102 D.I.
256 D.I.
FRONT DU CENTRE

FRONT DE BRIANSK
Troupes du Gal Belov
Plavsk
25° D.M.
112° D.I.
Groupement d'Attaque
208 D.I.
Troupes du Gal Gorbatov
34 D.I.
56 D.I.
55 CA.
ORE
2 AC
8 DB.
283 D.I.
Troupes du Gal Kolpaktchie Verkhovie
Troupes du Gal Romanenko
20° D.B. 10° D.M.
292 D.I.
238° D.M.
216 D.I.
Troupes du Gal Poukhov

LÉGENDE
Objectif principal
secondaire

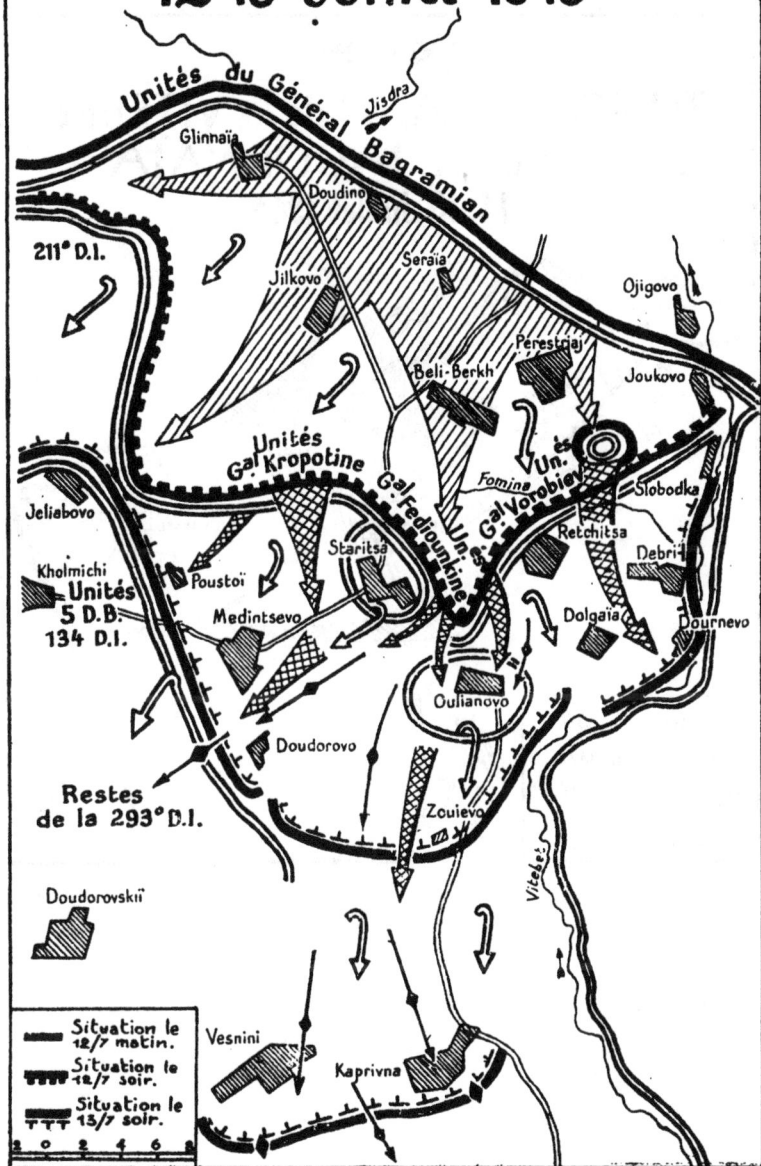

CROQUIS N°23

PERCÉE DU FRONT ALLEMAND PAR LES TROUPES DU Gᵃˡ BAGRAMIAN 12-13 Juillet 1943

Unités du Général Bagramian

Jisdra

Glinnaïa

Doudino

211° D.I.

Jilkovo

Seraïa

Ojigovo

Perestiaj

Beli-Berkh

Joukovo

Unités Gal Kropotine

Gal Fediounine

Un. Gal Vorobiev

Fomina

Slobodka

Jeliabovo

Staritsa

Retchitsa

Debri

Kholmichi

Poustoï

Unités 5 D.B 134 D.I.

Medintsevo

Dolgaïa

Dournevo

Oulianovo

Doudorovo

Restes de la 293° D.I.

Zouieva

Vitebes

Doudorovskiï

Vesnini

Kaprivna

Situation le 12/7 matin.
Situation le 12/7 soir.
Situation le 13/7 soir.

2 0 2 4 6 8

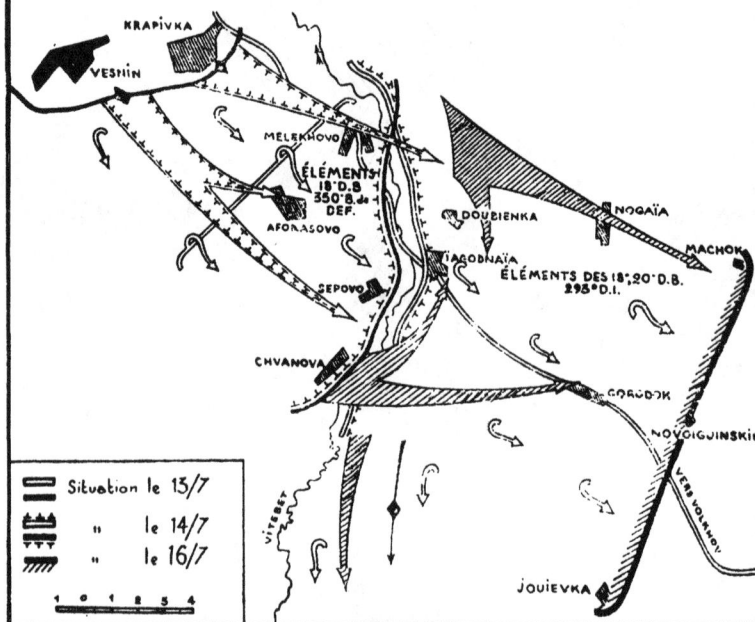

CROQUIS N°24

FRANCHISSEMENT de la VITEBET
ET PRISE DE IAGODNAÏA
14-16 Juillet 1943

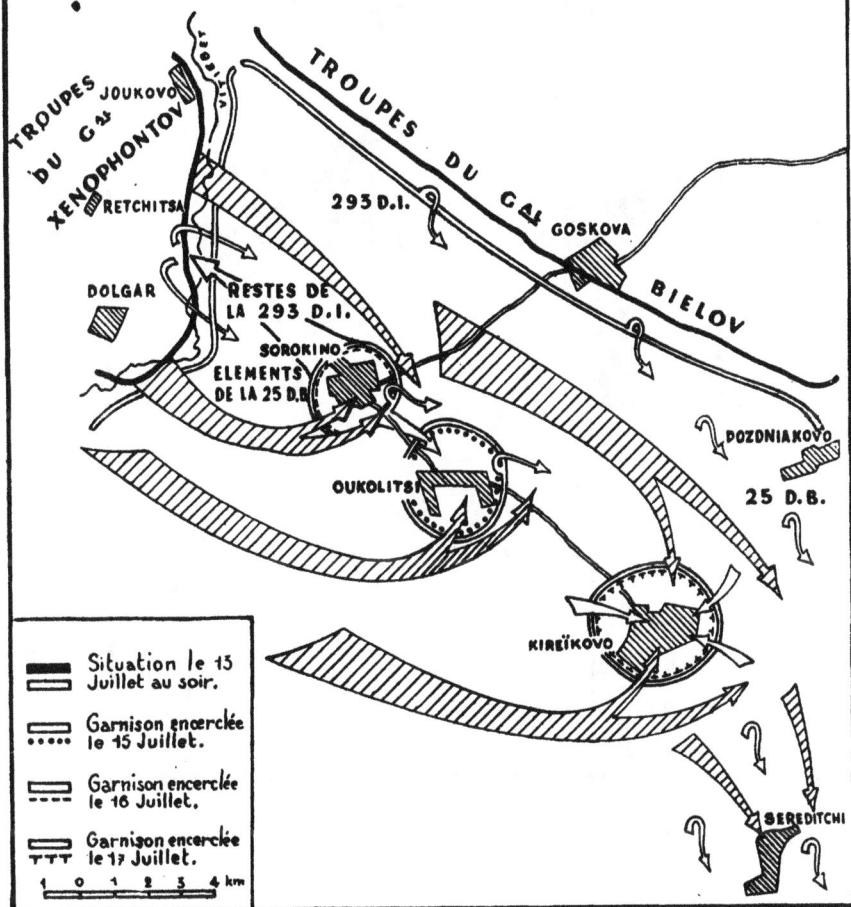

CROQUIS N°25

DESTRUCTION DES FORCES ALLEMANDES DES POINTS D'APPUI DE SOROKINO · OUKOLITSI · KIREIKOVO

CROQUIS N°26

PERCÉE DU FRONT ALLEMAND
EN DIRECTION DE BOLKHOV

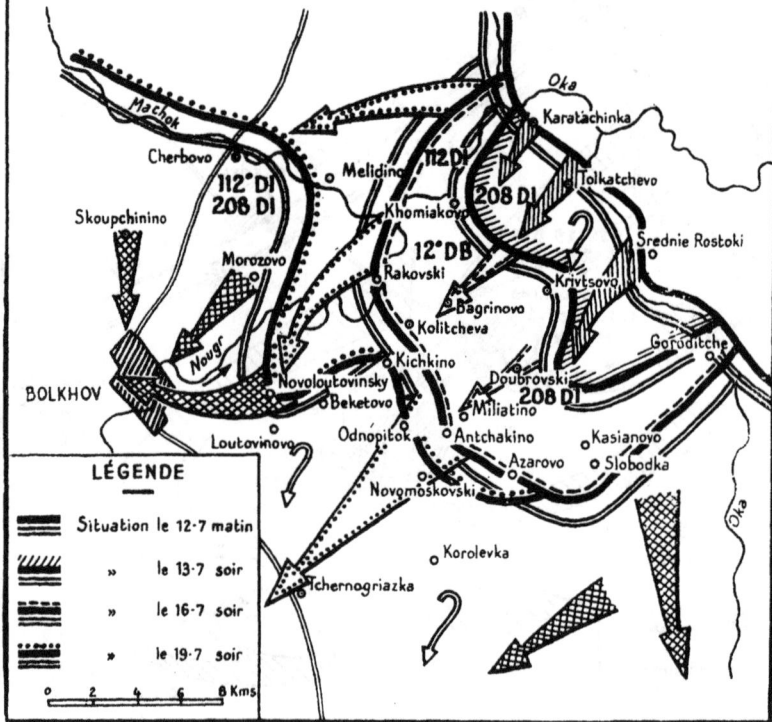

LÉGENDE

Situation le 12-7 matin		
» le 13-7 soir		
» le 16-7 soir		
» le 19-7 soir		

0 2 4 6 8 Kms

Mordok
Oka
Karatachinka
Cherbovo
Melidino
112 DI
Tolkatchevo
112° DI
208 DI
Khomiakovo
208 DI
Skoupchinino
Srednie Rostoki
Morozovo
12° DB
Rakovski
Krivtsovo
Nougr
Bagrinovo
Kolitcheva
Gorûditche
Kichkino
BOLKHOV
Novoloutovinsky
Doubrovski
208 DI
Beketovo
Miliatino
Kasianovo
Loutovinovo
Odnopitok
Antchakino
Slobodka
Azarovo
Novomoskovski
Oka
Korolevka
Tchernogriazka

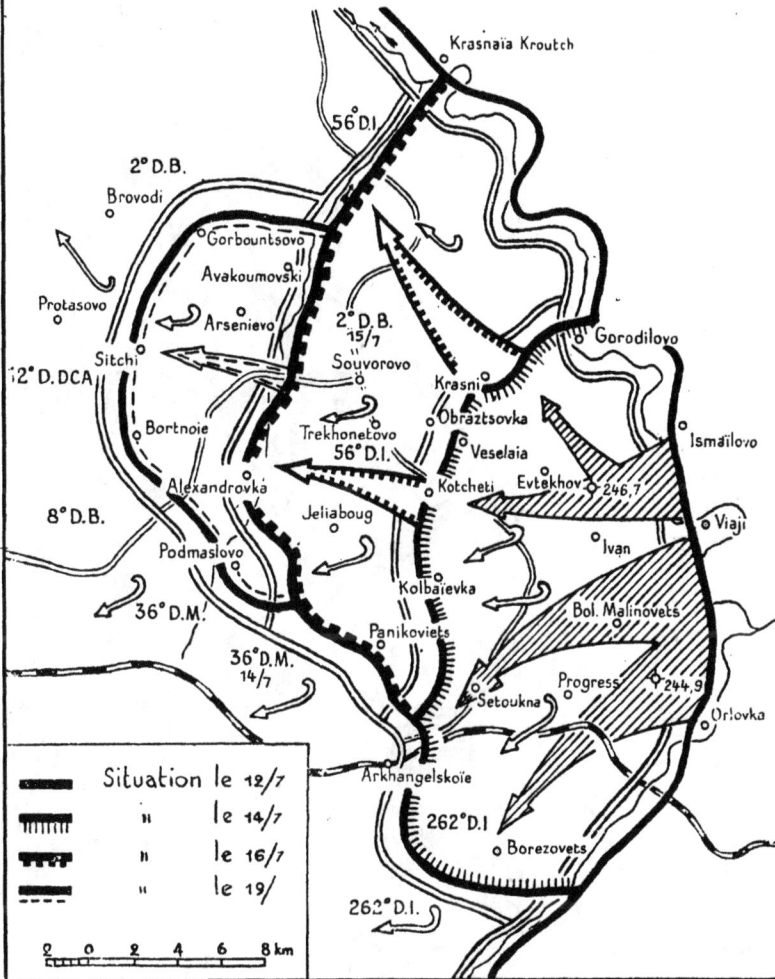

CROQUIS N° 27

PERCÉE du FRONT ALLEMAND dans le SECTEUR des G⁻ᵃᵘˣ GORBATOV et KOLPAKTCHA

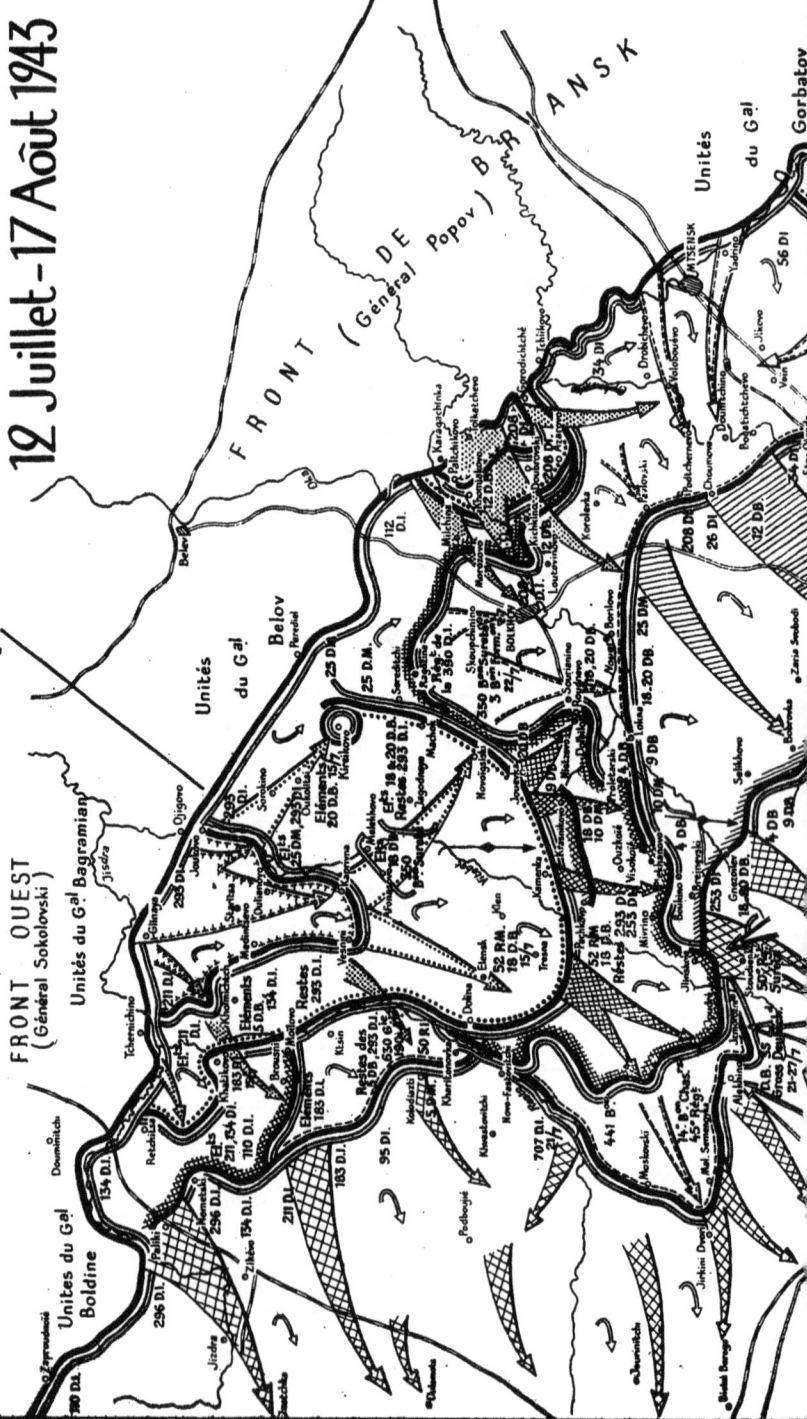

CROQUIS N°28

L'OFFENSIVE SOVIÉTIQUE SUR OREL
12 Juillet-17 Août 1943

Unités du Général Kolpatchke

Unités du Général Romanenko

Unités du Général Poukhov

Unités du Gal Galanine

Unités du Gal Batov

FRONT DU CENTRE
(Général Rokossovski)

Aksi Ilmaievo
Vitzi
Jovka
262 DI
Bolcheretz
Olkhovetz
299 DI
Vogodoukhovka
Alexisovka
343 DI
36 DM
216 DI
Karssaa
78 DI
Arkhangelskoe
262 DI
Nicolakoit
86 DI
Korpovo
36 DM
78 DI
8 DB
Aleksandrowa
Ermolino
56 DM
8 DB
8 DB
78 DI
78 DI
36 DM
262 DI
Krouloe Gora
Gremiatchi
Protassovo
290 RI (95 DI)
216 RI (68 DI)
383 DI
195 RI (78 DI)
292 DI
216 DI
6 DI
Mikoulino
Jouravka
Oriel
2 DB
Marishkino
8 DB
12 DB
36 DM
299 DI
6 Bd Blindé
6 DI
31 DI
258 DI
Bitritza
Nicolaevo
Novo Kolodez
Olennitkovo
Gnonii
Glazounovka
18 DB
8 DB
2 DI
6 DI
7 DI
31 DI
Tsagaye Poliane
Olkhovatka
Malonarkhangelsk
Maloarkhangelsk
Poon
258 DI
Monastirchtchine
Malakhovo Slobode
Khotkovo
7 DI
6 DI
31 DI
258 DI
7 D.I.
102 DI
Krasnikovo
Tchern
Oliakhovtsi
Dmitrovsk-Orlovski
Braniszevo
Leski
Reni

Échelle

Situation le 11 Juillet (matin)
Situation le 13 Juillet (soir)
Situation le 18 Juillet (soir)
Situation le 19 Juillet (soir)
Situation le 30 Juillet (soir)
Situation le 5 août

L'OFFENSIVE SOVIETIQUE sur BIÉ

Snagost

Obodi

88 D.I.

Basovka

Bélopolé

Retchki

325 D.I.

Andrevka   Aleksevka

Khoten

Troupes du Gal Vatoutin

Miropolié

Kondratovka

75 D.I.

Bilitsa

Vel. Ribitsa

FRONT

Unités du Gal Tchibissov

Troupes du Gal Kourzoun

Bol. Tcheriotchina

Soumi

Zatserni

Tokari

Osoievka

Strelki

Repakhovka

Besi   Bezdrik

Loutsikovka

Jelezniak

Krasna Jarou

68 D.I.

Eléments 88, 68 D.I.

Bol. Bobrik

Krasnopolé

Visoki

Tchernetchina

Mejiritch

Grebennikovka

57 D.I.
Staroselé

Vel. Istoro

Bichkine

Jigailovka
Eléments du Gal
Korzoung
Beremlia

Lebedine

Eléments
57, 332 D.I.
11 D.B.

Slavgorod

Noboselovka

Grouzskoié

Eléments
75,332,255,57
D.I.
11,19 D.B. D.B. Gross Deutchl.

Patchini

Fedorovka

Kostev

Pojnia

Eléments du Gal
Bourkov   Nitsakha

Veprik

Olechnia

Trostiane
7
D.B.

B. Piserovka

Petrovski

Kirikovka

Staraia Riabina
Spasnoié

Zenkov

Groun

D.B.
Gross Deut.
7, 11 D.B.
10 D.M.

Eléments du Gal
Poloubotkov
Iablotchnoié

Akhtirka

Visokoié

Novo-Sofievka

Vesioli Gai

Eléments
57, 255 D.I.

Bogodoukhov

Koupievakha

Kaplounovka

Eléments
du Gal
Tchistiakov

El 19
D.B.

Parkhomovka

Krasnokoutsk   Merla

Eléments du Gal
Katoukov.

Eléments du
Gal
Kravtchenko

Kotelva

Kolontaev

Khrouchtchovaia
Akhtovka
Mourafe
Sotnia
Tcherovka
Aleks

Tchervom
Prapor
Marino

Bol. Roubliovka

D.B.
Totenkopf le
11/8

Konstantinovka
Alekseievka

Visokopolié

D.B. Totenkopf
le 13/8

Kolomak

Echelle.

Situation le 3 août au matin.
Direction des attaques et situation des forces soviétiques le 6 août.
Direction le 7 août au soir.
Direction le 11 août au soir.
Direction des attaques soviétiques du 13 au 23
Contre attaques allemandes

29

ROD-KHARKOV 3-23 AOUT 1943

CROQUIS N°30

POSITIONS ALLEMANDES
SUR LA DIRECTION BIELGOROD-KHARKOV

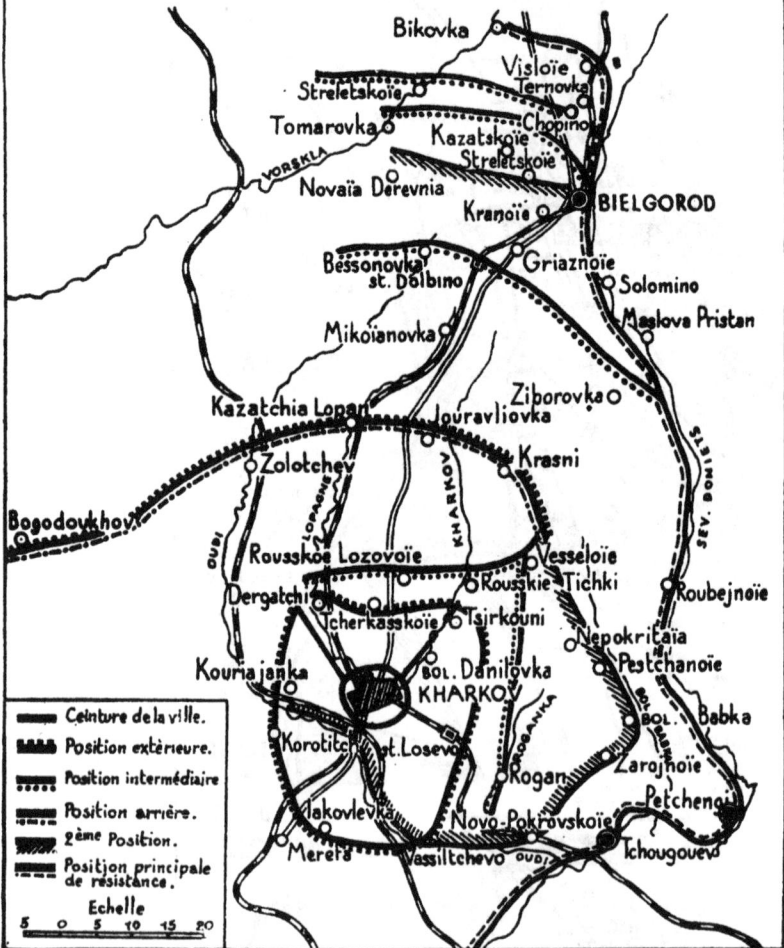

Bikovka

Visloïe
Ternovka
Streletskoïe
Chopino
Tomarovka
Kazatskoïe
Streletskoïe
VORSKLA
Novaïa Derevnia
Kranoïe
BIELGOROD

Bessonovka
st. Dolbino
Griaznoïe
Solomino
Maslova Pristan

Mikoïanovka

Ziborovka
Kazatchia Lopan
Jouravliovka
Krasni
Zolotchev
SEV. DONIETS
Bogodoukhov

KHARKOV
Rousskoïe Lozovoïe
LOPAGNE
Vesseloïe
Rousskie Tichki
Roubejnoïe
Dergatchi
OUDI
Tcherkasskoïe
Tsirkouni
Nepokritaïa
Pestchanoïe
Kouriajanka
BOL. Danilovka
BOL. Babka
KHARKOV
RODANIA
Korotitch
st. Losevo
Zarojnoïe
Rogan
Petchenoi
Iakovlevka
Novo-Pokrovskoïe
Tchougouev
Merefa
Vassiltchevo
OUDI

Légende

Ceinture de la ville.
Position extérieure.
Position intermédiaire.
Position arrière.
2ème Position.
Position principale de résistance.

Echelle
5 0 5 10 15 20

CROQUIS N°31

PLAN DE L'OFFENSIVE SOVIÉTIQUE SUR KHARKOV

CROQUIS N°32
—
DESTRUCTION DU GROUPEMENT ALLEMAND DE BIELGOROD

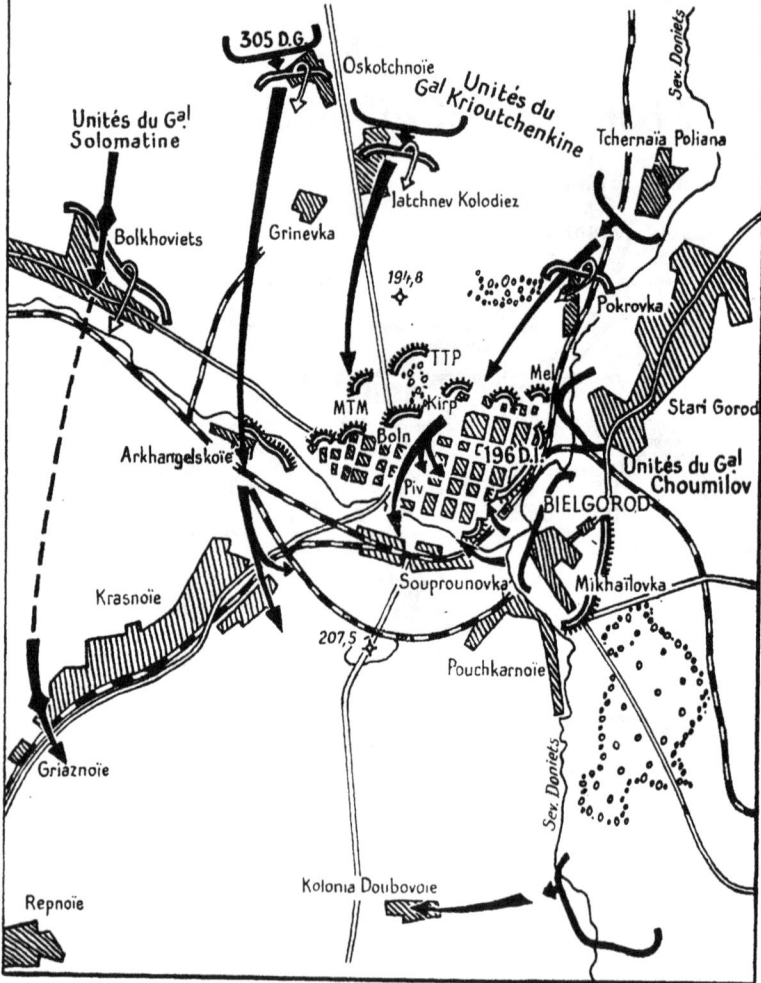

305 D.G.

Oskotchnoïe

Unités du
Gal Krioutchenkine

Sev. Doniets

Tchernaïa Poliana

Unités du Gal
Solomatine

Iatchnev Kolodiez

Grinevka

194,8

Pokrovka

Bolkhoviets

TTP

Mel

Stari Gorod

MTM

Kirp

Arkhangelskoïe

Boln

C196 D.I

Unités du Gal
Choumilov

Piv

BIELGOROD

Krasnoïe

Souprounovka

Mikhaïlovka

207,5

Pouchkarnoïe

Sev. Doniets

Griaznoïe

Repnoïe

Kolonia Doubovoïe

CROQUIS N°33

DESTRUCTION du GROUPEMENT ALLEMAND DE BORISOVKA (5-7 AOUT 1943)

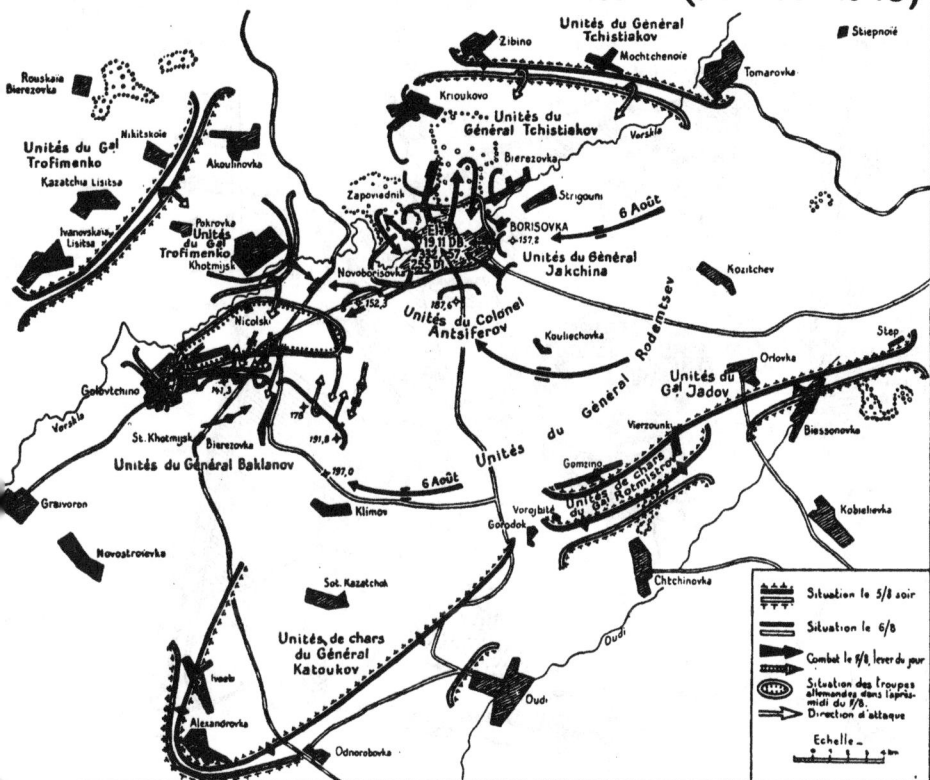

Unités du Général Tchistiakov

Zibino

Mochtchenoie

Tomarovka

Stiepnoié

Rouskaia Bierezovka

Nikitskoie

Krioukovo

Unités du Général Tchistiakov

Unités du Gal Trofimenko

Akoulinovka

Bierezovka

Vorskla

Kazatchia Lisitsa

Zapoviednik

Strigouni

Ivanovskaia Lisitsa

Pokrovka

Unités du Gal Trofimenko

BORISOVKA

157.2

6 Août

Kozitchev

Khotmijsk

Novoborisovka

Unités du Général Jakchina

152.3

187.6

Nicolski

Unités du Colonel Antsiferov

Kouliechovka

Step

Orlovka

Unités du Gal Jadov

Golovtchino

191.3

du Général Rodomtsev

Vierzounki

Biessonovka

Vorskla

179

191.8.4

St. Khotmijsk

Bierezovka

Gomzino

Unités de chars du 5th Kotmistrov

Unités du Général Baklanov

157.0

6 Août

Unités

Kobielievka

Graivoron

Klimov

Vorojbité

Novostroievka

Gorodok

Chtchinovka

Sot. Kazatchak

Oudi

Unités de chars du Général Katoukov

Ivaets

Oudi

Alexandrovka

Odnorobovka

Oudi

Echelle —

Situation le 5/8 soir

Situation le 6/8

Combat le 6/8, lever du jour

Situation des troupes allemandes dans l'après-midi du 5/8.

Direction d'attaque

DESTRUCTION DU GROUPEMENT ALLEMAND DE KHARKOV

LÉGENDE
Situation des Troupes
Soviétiques le 11-8 soir

Attaques Soviétiques le 13-8
—"— 20-8
—"— 22-8
—"— 23-8

ÉCHELLE: 2 0 2 4 6

Éléments 3 D.B.
Michenkov
Cheptouchine
Zamirta
Troupes du Général Managarov
167 D.I.
Alekscievka
Troupes du Général Krioutchenkine
Rouskiié Tickki
Tcherkaskié Tickki
198 D.I.
DERGATCHE
TCHERKASKOIS LOZOVOIA
Polevoie
Semionovka
Zaïtchik
168 D.I.
6 D.B.
Tsirkouni
Troupes du Génél Choumilov
Klioutchkine
106 D.I.
320 D.I.
Bolchaia Danilovka
Koutouzovka
Severni Post
Sokolnoki
Chevtchenki
Prieliestni
Tchervona Roganka
Kouriajanka
167 D.I.
320 D.I.
Gavrilovka
Savtchenko
282 D.I.
Bol Babko
Éléments 167 D.I. et 3 D.B.
168 D.I.
Zalioulino
KHARKOV
Kievpichlia
Radtoichi
Troupes du Général Hajen
Korotitch
Éléments 198 D.I.
Gorbotchou
Taiki
Gossevo
282 D.I.
Tietliega
Osnova
Tchoulikbine
39 D.I.
Jikhor
282 D.I.
Fedortsi
39 D.I.
Lialiouki
Kamennaia Jarouga
Jayni
355 D.I.
39 D.I.
Biezlioudovka
Tchougouiev
Jakovlauka
Merefa
Vasichevo
Vedanskoié
Ternovoie
Lizogoubovka
Konstantinovka
19-8
355 D.I.

CROQUIS N°35

TRACÉ DU FRONT ET DISPOSITIF ALLEMAND LE 1er JANVIER 1944

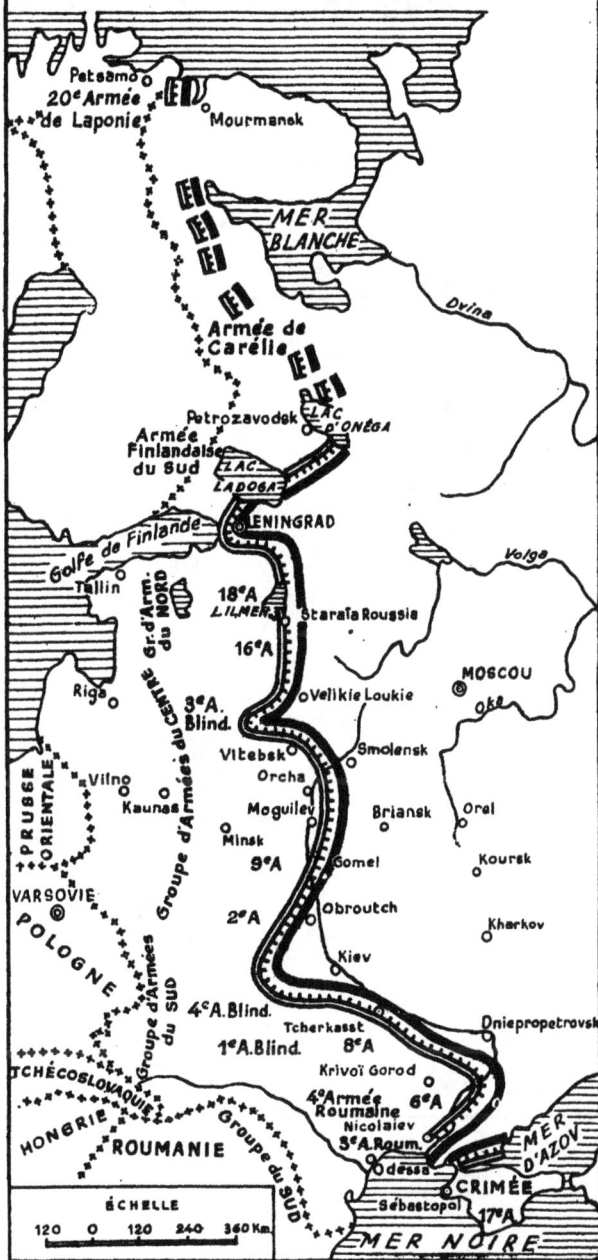

Petsamo
20e Armée
de Laponie
Mourmansk

MER BLANCHE

Dvina

Armée de Carélie

Petrozavodsk
LAC D'ONÉGA

Armée Finlandaise du Sud

LAC LADOGA

LÉNINGRAD

Golfe de Finlande

Tallin

Volga

18e A
L.II.MER

Starata Roussia

16e A

MOSCOU

Oka

Riga

3e A. Blind.

oVelikie Loukie

Smolensk

PRUSSE ORIENTALE

Vilno

Vitebsk

Orcha

Kaunas

Moguilev

Briansk

Orel

Minsk

9e A

Gomel

Koursk

Gr. d'Arm. du NORD

Groupe d'Armées du CENTRE

VARSOVIE

POLOGNE

2e A

Obroutch

Kharkov

Kiev

Groupe d'Armées du SUD

4e A. Blind.

Dniepropetrovsk

Tcherkasst

1e A. Blind.

8e A

TCHÉCOSLOVAQUIE

Krivoï Gorod

4e Armée Roumaine

6e A

HONGRIE

Nicolaiev

Groupe du SUD

ROUMANIE

3e A. Roum.

MER D'AZOV

Odessa

CRIMÉE

ÉCHELLE

Sébastopol

17e A

120   0   120   240   360 Km.

MER NOIRE

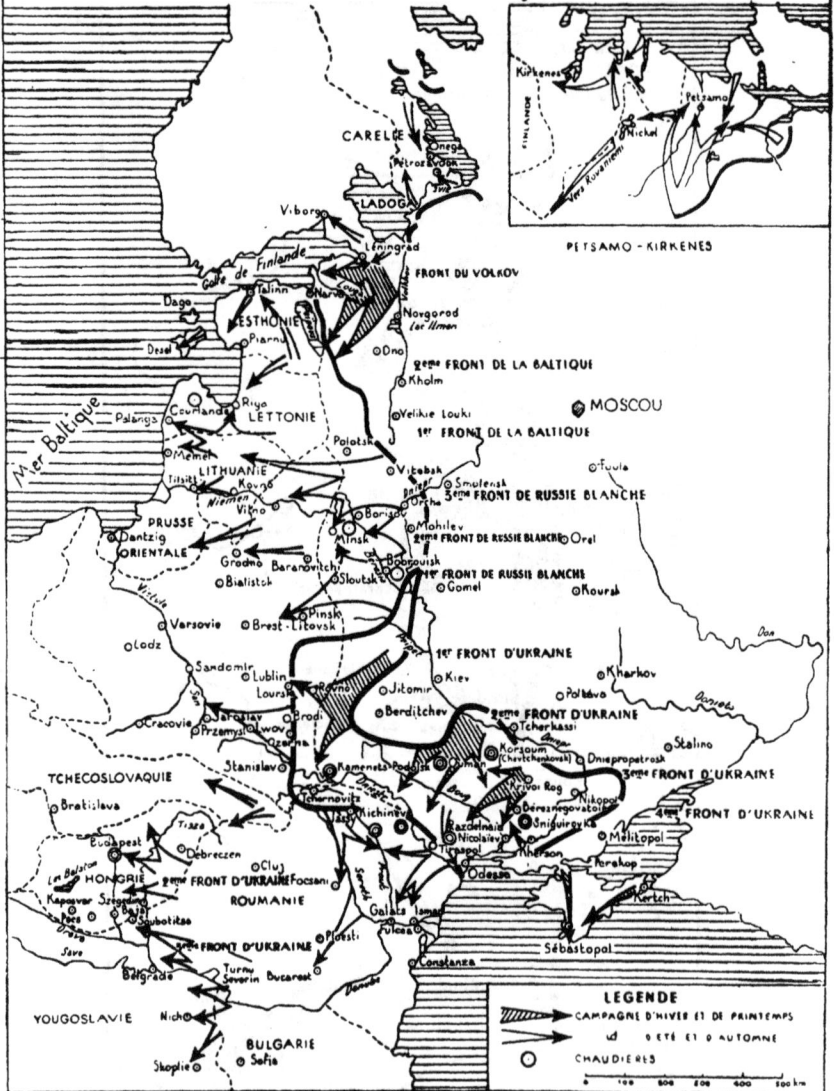

CROQUIS N°36

LES DIX OFFENSIVES DE L'ARMÉE ROUGE

CROQUIS N° 37

LA DÉFAITE ALLEMANDE DEVANT LENINGRAD
Janvier-Février 1944

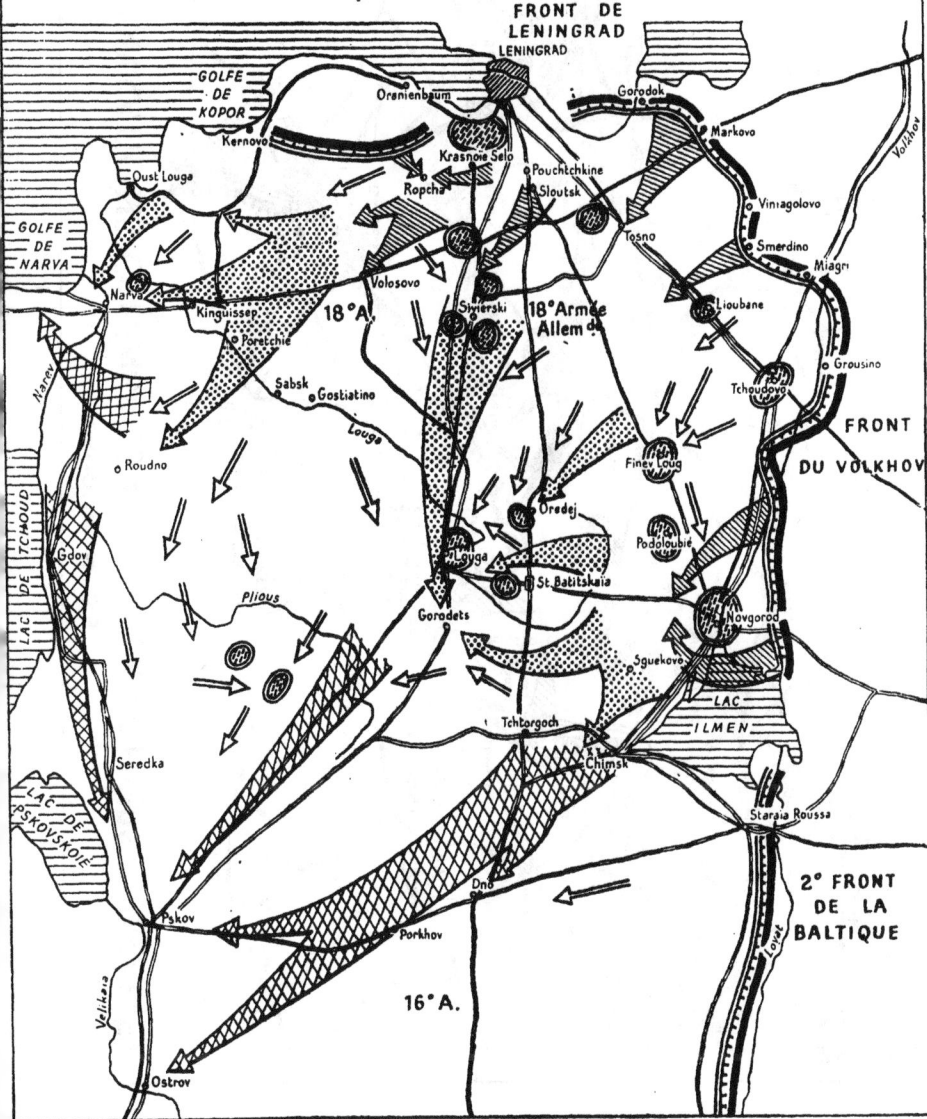

FRONT DE LENINGRAD
LENINGRAD

GOLFE DE KOPOR

Oranienbaum

Gorodok

Markovo

Kernovo

Krasnoie Selo

Pouchtchkine

Oust Louga

Ropcha

Sloutsk

Viniagolovo

GOLFE DE NARVA

Volosovo

Tosno

Smerdino

Miagri

Narva

Sivierski

18° Armée Allem.

Lioubane

Grousino

Kinguissep

18° A.

Poretchie

Tchoudovo

Sabsk

Gostiatino

FRONT DU VOLKHOV

Louga

Roudno

Finev Loug

Gdov

Oredej

Plious

Louga

Podoloubié

St Batitskaia

Goradets

Novgorod

Seredka

Sguekovo

LAC ILMEN

LAC DE PSKOVSKOIE

Tchtorgoch

Chimsk

Staraia Roussa

2° FRONT DE LA BALTIQUE

Dno

Pskov

Porkhov

16° A.

Velikaia

Ostrov

LAC DE TCHOUD

Narva

Volkhov

Situation au début des opérations   Troupes allemandes encerclées   1° phase   2° phase   3° phase

10 0 10 20 30 40 50 60

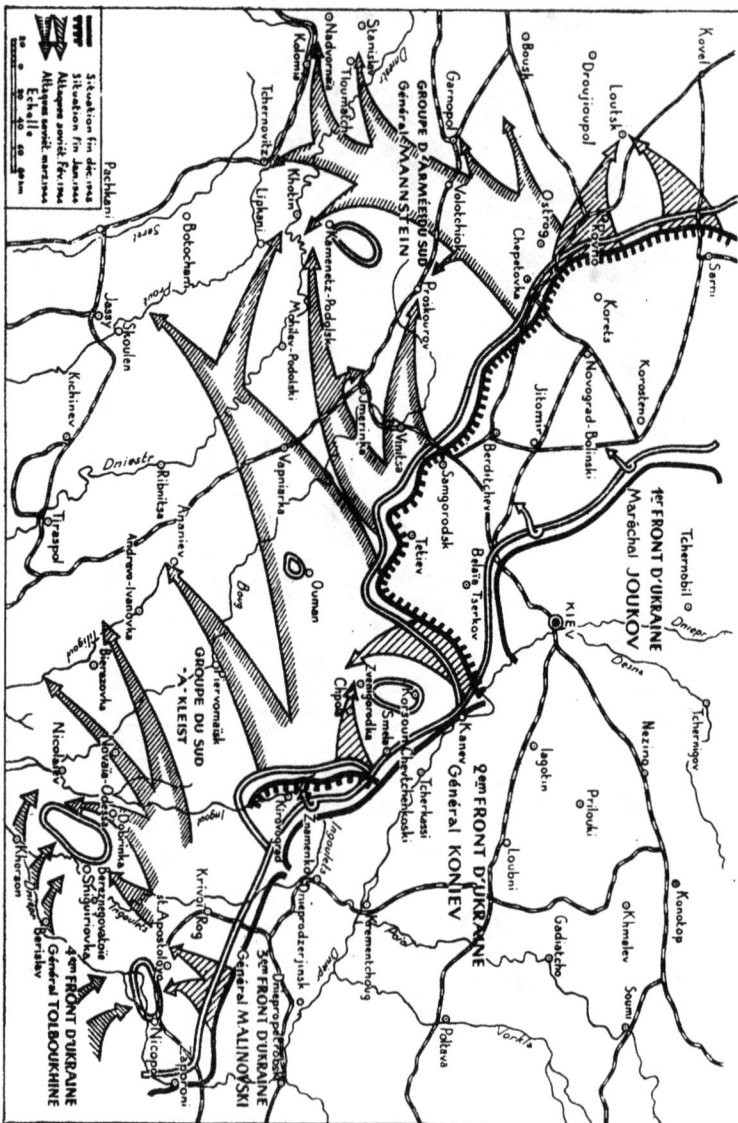

CROQUIS N° 38

OPERATIONS OFFENSIVES DES 1er, 2, 3 et 4em FRONTS D'UKRAINE

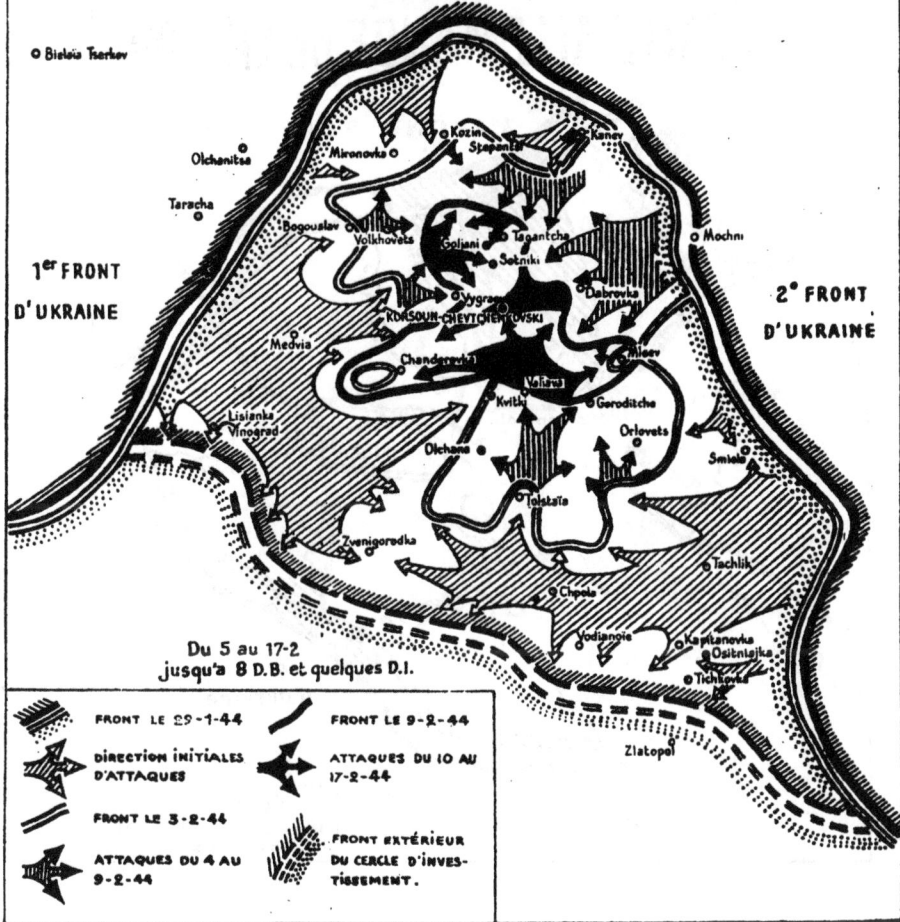

CROQUIS N°39
LE DÉSASTRE de KORSOUN~CHEVTCHENKOVSKI

Bielaia Tserkov

Olchanitsa

Taracha

Mironovka   Kozin
            Stepantsi   Kanev

1er FRONT
D'UKRAINE

Bogouslav
Volkhovets   Goliani   Tagantcha   Mochni
              Sotniki
         Vygrav   Dabrovka
    KORSOUN-CHEVTCHENKOVSKI
Medvia   Chilaev
         Chandarenki   Valava
                Kvitki   Goroditche
Lisianka   Orlovets
Vinograd   Smiela
         Olchana
                  Tolstaia   Tachlik

2° FRONT
D'UKRAINE

    Zvenigorodka
                  Cherca
                    Podianoie   Kapitanovka
                         Ositnlejka
Du 5 au 17-2   Tichkovka
jusqu'à 8 D.B. et quelques D.I.
                              Zlatopol

FRONT LE 29-1-44	FRONT LE 9-2-44
DIRECTION INITIALES D'ATTAQUES	ATTAQUES DU 10 AU 17-2-44
FRONT LE 3-2-44	
ATTAQUES DU 4 AU 9-2-44	FRONT EXTÉRIEUR DU CERCLE D'INVESTISSEMENT.

CROQUIS N°40

LA DÉFAITE ALLEMANDE DE NIKOPOL

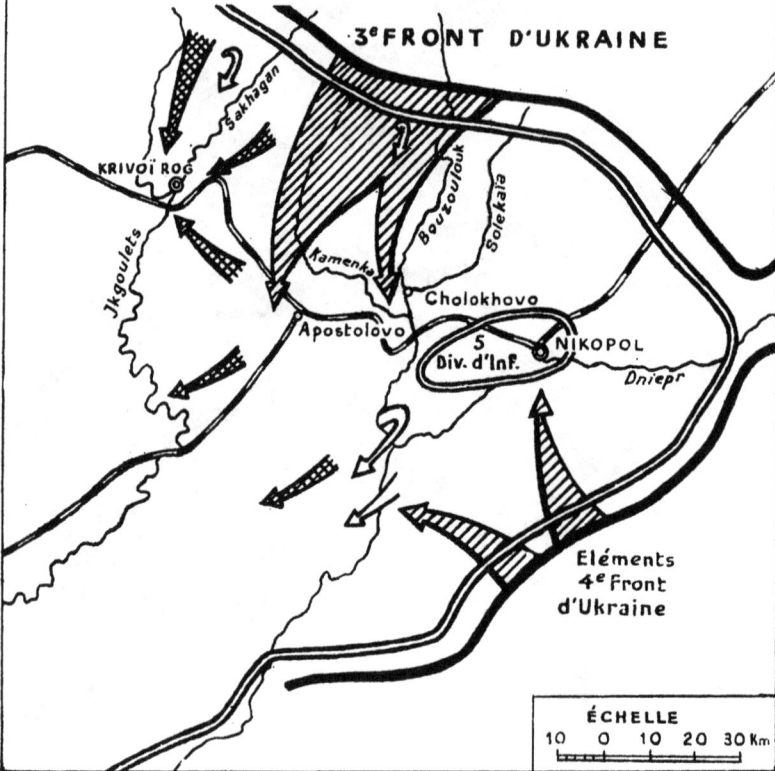

3ᵉ FRONT D'UKRAINE

Saksagan

KRIVOÏ ROG

Ikgoulets

Kamenka

Boutoulouk

Solekaïa

Cholokhovo

Apostolovo

5 Div. d'Inf.

NIKOPOL

Dniepr

Eléments
4ᵉ Front
d'Ukraine

ÉCHELLE

10   0   10   20   30 Km

CROQUIS N° 41

L'OFFENSIVE SOVIÉTIQUE de TCHERNOVITS

CROQUIS Nº 42

DÉFAITE DES FORCES ALLEMANDES D'OUMAN

1er FRONT D'UKRAINE

2e FRONT D'UKRAINE

Jmerinka

Zvenigorodka

Chpola

Ouman

Mohilev-Podolski

Vaniarka

Kirovograd

Jampol

Boug

Piervomaïsk

Dniester

Vers Odessa

Ananiev

Skoulieni

Situation au début de mars
Attaques soviétiques jusqu'au 10-3
»   »   31-3

ÉCHELLE : 10 0 10 20 30 Km.

CROQUIS N° 43

DESTRUCTION de la 6ᵉ ARMÉE ALLEMANDE A BEREZNEGOVATOÏÉ

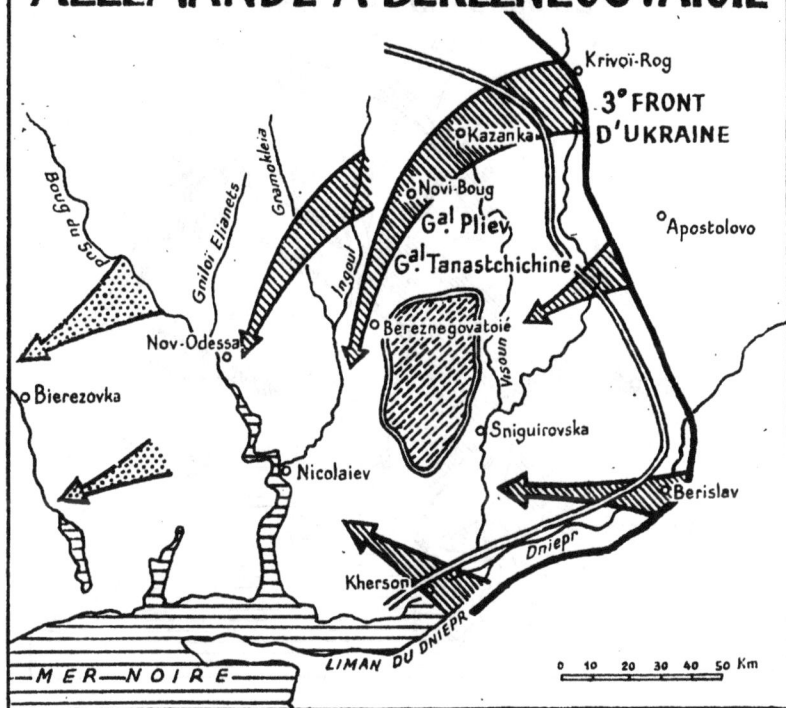

Krivoï-Rog

3ᵉ FRONT D'UKRAINE

Kazanka

Novi-Boug

Gᵃˡ Pliev

Gᵃˡ Tanastchichine

Apostolovo

Gramokleia

Gniloï Elianets

Boug du Sud

Ingoul

Nov-Odessa

Bereznegovatoïé

Visoun

Bierezovka

Sniguirovska

Nicolaiev

Berislav

Dniepr

Kherson

LIMAN DU DNIEPR

MER NOIRE

0 10 20 30 40 50 Km

CROQUIS N°44

DÉFAITE DES TROUPES ALLEMANDES
DEVANT ODESSA
28 Mars - 16 Avril 1944

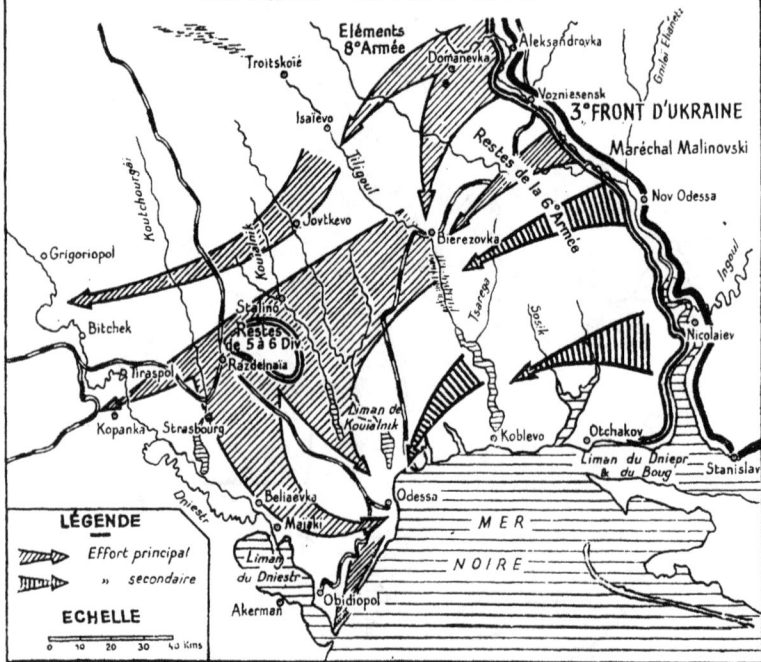

Eléments
8°Armée

Troitskoïe

Domanevka

Aleksandrovka

Voznesensk

3°FRONT D'UKRAINE

Maréchal Malinovski

Isaïevo

Nov Odessa

Jovtkevo

Bierezovka

o Grigoriopol

Bitchek

Stalino
Restes
de 5 à 6 Div.

Razdelnaia

Nicolaiev

o Tiraspol

Restes de la 6° Armée

Liman de
Kouïalnik

Kopanka   Strasbourg

Koblevo

Otchakov

Liman du Dniepr
& du Boug

Stanislav

Beliaevka

Maïaki

Odessa

MER

NOIRE

LÉGENDE

Effort principal

»   secondaire

Liman
du Dniestr

Obidiopol

Akerman

ECHELLE

0   10   20   30   40 Kms

CROQUIS N°45

OPÉRATIONS DE CRIMÉE MAI 1944

4ᵉ FRONT D'UKRAINE (G.ᵃˡ Tolboukhine)

Mer d'Azov

Mer Noire

Troupes du G.ᵃˡ Zakharov

Troupes du G.ᵃˡ Kreiser

ARMÉE AUTONOME DU LITTORAL (G.ᵃˡ Eremenko)

Détroit de Kertch

17° A.

Échelle
1ᵉʳ Phase.
2ᵉᵐ Phase.

Port Khorli
Perekop
Tchigary
Tarkhan
Boï Kazak
Jchoun
Baïssari
Voronitsovka
Tganach
St. Tchongar
Guenitchesk
Kerleout
Ak Netchet
Karadja
Aïbari
Fraïdorf
Topalovka
Evpatoria
Saki
Temech
Andrevki
Bironkonlar
Koratcha-Kanguil
Kontouga
SIMFÉROPOL
Boulganakh
Katcha
Lioubimovka
SEBASTOPOL
Bakda
Baïokleva
Tchoul
Zalankoï
Namout Soultan
Ouskout
Alouchta
Demerdji
Iouak
Iälta
Soudak
St. Krim
Feodosia
Kachikh
Opouk
Mama Rouskaïa
Kertch
Soultanovka
Rouski
Kitén
Adjibaï
Ak-Mokaï
Seitler
Biouk Karassou
Djankoï

CROQUIS N°46
—
ATTAQUE de SÉBASTOPOL
7-8 Mai 1944

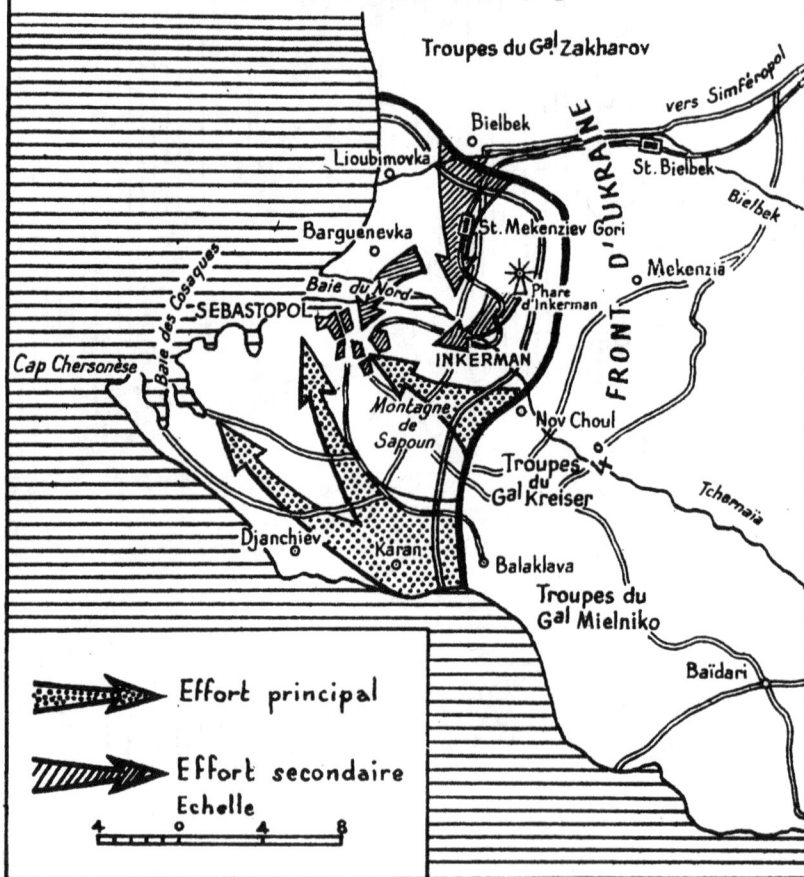

Troupes du Gal Zakharov

vers Simféropol

Bielbek

St. Bielbek

Lioubimovka

Bielbek

St. Mekenziev Gori

Barguenevka

Mekenzia

Baie du Nord

Phare d'Inkerman

Baie des Cosaques

SEBASTOPOL

FRONT D'UKRAINE

Cap Chersonèse

INKERMAN

Montagne de Sapoun

Nov Choul

Troupes du Gal Kreiser

Tchernaïa

Djanchiev

Karan

Balaklava

Troupes du Gal Mielniko

Baïdari

➤ Effort principal

➤ Effort secondaire

Echelle

CROQUIS N° 47

DISPOSITIF ALLEMAND au DÉBUT des OPÉRATIONS de L'ÉTÉ 1944

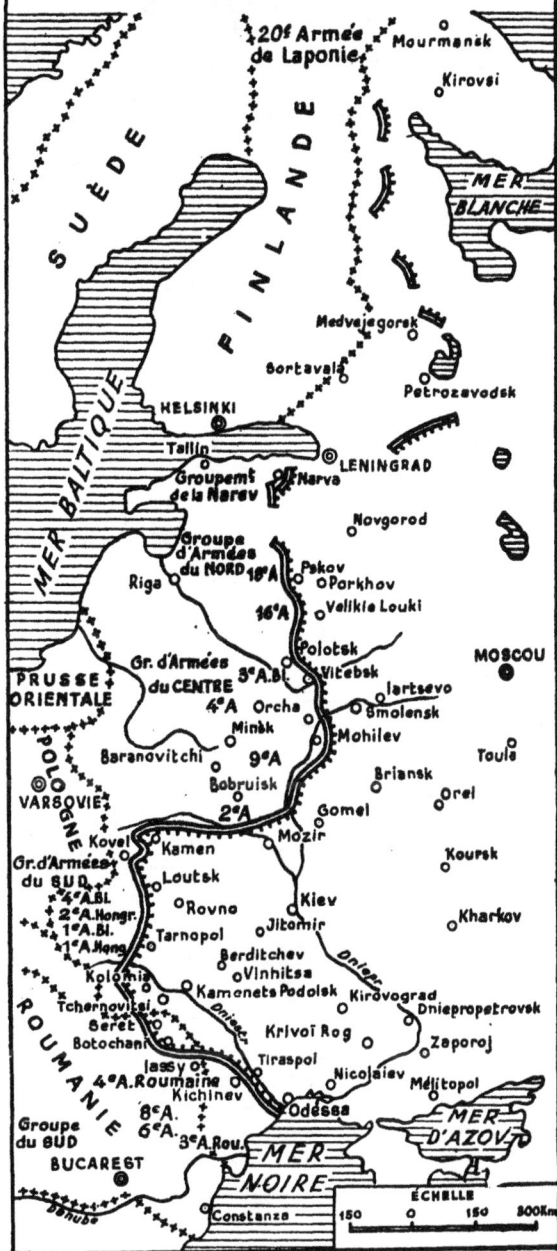

SUÈDE

FINLANDE

20e Armée de Laponie

Mourmansk

Kirovsi

MER BLANCHE

Medvajagorsk

Sortavala

Petrozavodsk

MER BALTIQUE

HELSINKI

Tallin

Groupemt de la Narev

Narva

LENINGRAD

Novgorod

Groupe d'Armées du NORD

18eA

Riga

Pskov

Porkhov

Velikie Louki

16eA

Polotsk

Gr. d'Armées du CENTRE

3eA.Bl.

Vitebsk

MOSCOU

PRUSSE ORIENTALE

4eA

Orcha

Iartsevo

Smolensk

Mohilev

Minsk

Baranovitchi

9eA

Touls

POLOGNE

VARSOVIE

Bobruisk

Brlansk

Orel

2eA

Gomel

Kovel

Kamen

Mozir

Koursk

Gr. d'Armées du SUD

4eA.Bl.

Loutsk

Rovno

Kiev

2eA.Hongr.

Jitomir

Kharkov

1eA.Bl.

1eA.Hong.

Tarnopol

Berditchev

Vinhitsa

Kolomia

Kamenets Podolsk

Kirovograd

Tchernovitsi

Dniepropetrovsk

Seret

Krivoï Rog

Zaporoj

Botochani

Tiraspol

Iassy

Nicolaïev

Mélitopol

ROUMANIE

4eA.Roumaine

Kichinev

8eA.

Odessa

MER D'AZOV

6eA.

3eA.Rou.

Groupe du SUD

BUCAREST

MER NOIRE

Danube

Constanza

ÉCHELLE

150   0   150   300Km

CROQUIS N°48

DÉFAITE DES TROUPES FINLANDAISES DE CARÉLIE
Juin-Juillet 1944

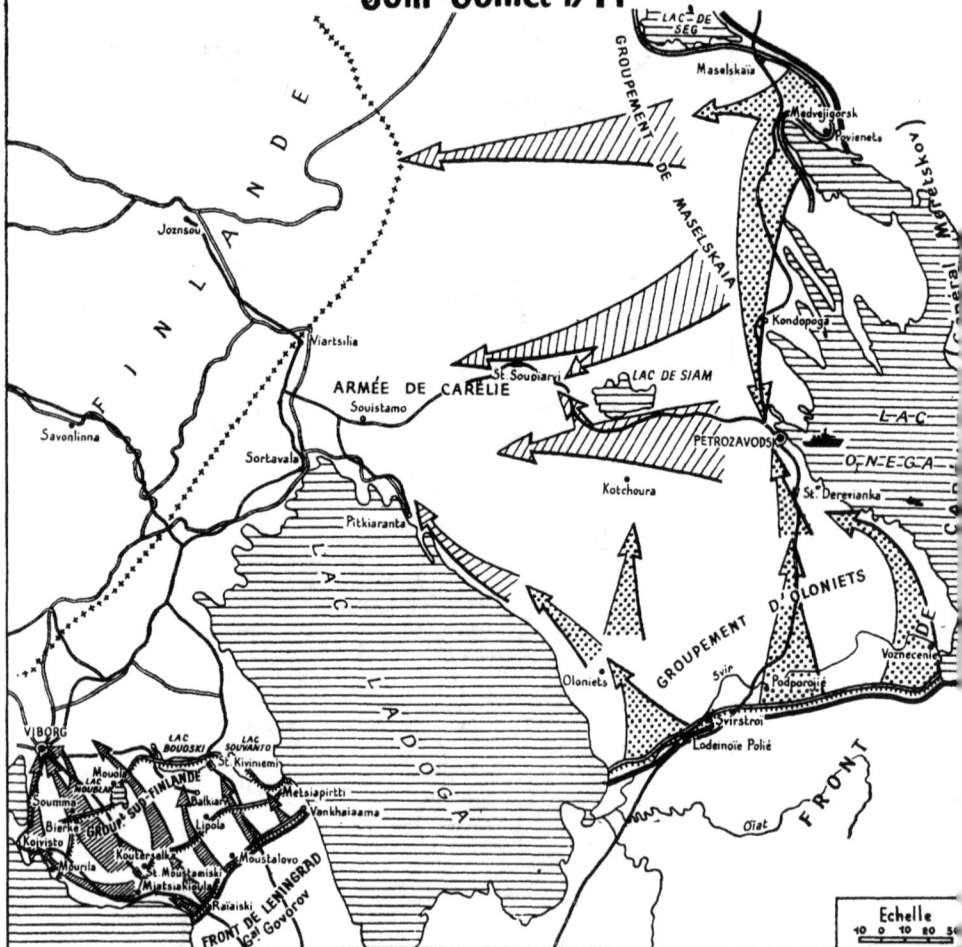

LAC DE SEG

GROUPEMENT DE MASELSKAIA

Maselskaia

Medvejigorsk

Povienets

(Général Méretskov)

Joznsou

FINLANDE

Miartsilia

St Soupiarri

ARMÉE DE CARÉLIE

Souistamo

LAC DE SIAM

Kondopoga

Savonlinna

Sortavala

PETROZAVODSK

Kotchoura

LAC ONEGA

St. Derevianka

Pitkiaranta

GROUPEMENT D'OLONIETS

Voznecenie

LAC LADOGA

Oloniets

Svir

Podporojié

VIBORG

LAC BOUDSKI

LAC SOUVANTO

St Kiviniemi

Svirstroi

Lodeinoie Polié

Mouolb LAC MOUOLAR

GROUPE SUD FINLANDE

Balkian

Metsiapirtti

Oiat

FRONT

Soumma

Lipola

Vankhaiaama

Bierke

Kojvisto

Koutarselka

Moustalovo

Pourla

St Moustamiski

Miatsiakioula

Raiaiski

FRONT DE LENINGRAD
G.al Govorow

Echelle
10 0 10 20 30

CROQUIS N°49

LA DÉFAITE ALLEMANDE EN RUSSIE BLANCHE JUIN-JUILLET 1944

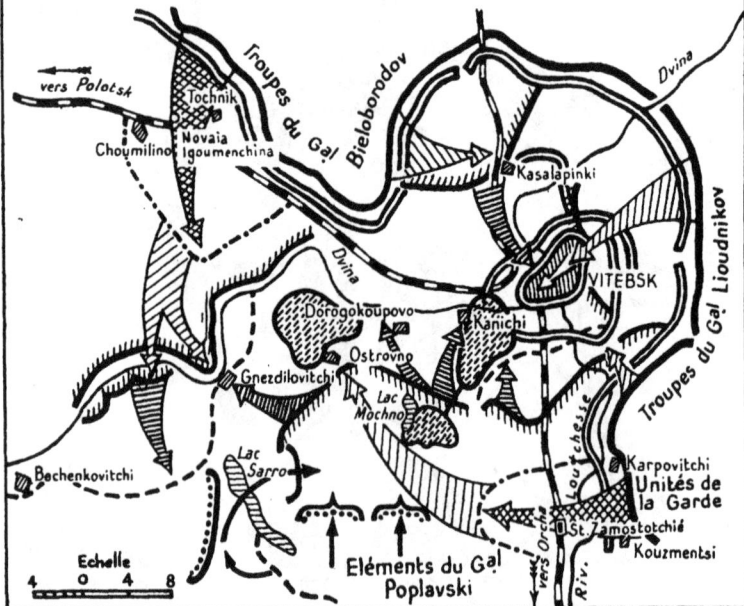

CROQUIS N°50

OPÉRATION de VITEBSK

vers Polotsk

Troupes du Gal Bieloborodov

Dvina

Tochnik
Novaia
Choumilino Igoumenchina

Kasalapinki

Dvina

VITEBSK

Dorogokoupovo

Kanichi

Ostrovno

Troupes du Gal Lioudnikov

Gnezdilovitchi

Lac
Mochno

Lac
Sarro

Bechenkovitchi

Koutchesse

Karpovitchi
Unités de
la Garde

St Zamostotchié

vers Orcha

Riv.

Kouzmentsi

Echelle
4   0   4   8

Eléments du Gal
Poplavski

Situation initiale.		Situation le 25-6.	
Situation le 23-6 (soir).		Situation le 26-6.	
Situation le 24-6.		Forces allemandes encerclées.	

CROQUIS Nº 51

OPÉRATIONS DE BOBRUISK
SITUATION LE 23 JUIN 1944 ET PLAN D'OPÉRATIONS
DU 1er FRONT DE RUSSIE BLANCHE

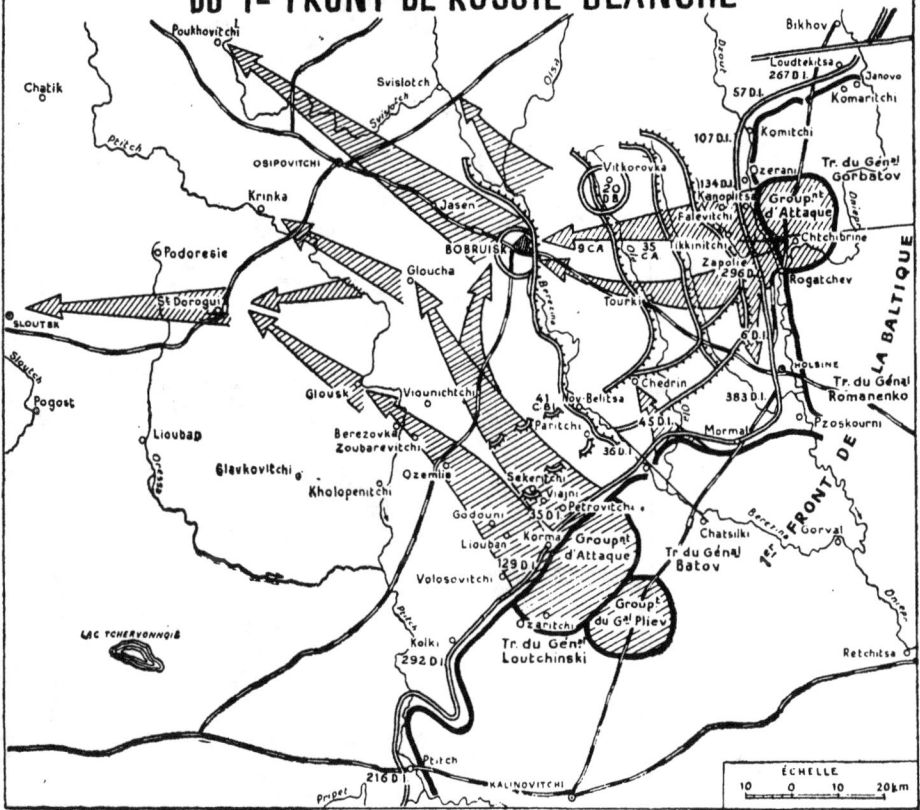

Poukhovitchi
Chatik
Svislotch
Bikhov
Loudtekitsa
267 D.I.
Janovo
Komaritchi
57 D.I.
107 D.I.
Komitchi
OSIPOVITCHI
Vitkorovka
Dzerani
Tr. du Génl Gorbatov
Krinka
134 D.I.
Kanoplitsa
Falevitchi
Groupnt d'Attaque
Jasen
Chtchibrine
Podoresie
BOBRUISK
9 CA
35
Tikkinitchi
Zapolié
Rogatchev
Gloucha
Berezina
296 D.
Tourki
St Daroqui
SLOUTSK
50 D.I.
Pogost
Glousk
Viaunichtchi
Chedrin
POLSINE
Tr. du Génl Romanenko
Liouban
41 C.A.
Nov-Belitsa
383 D.I.
Pzoskourni
Glavkovitchi
Berezovka
Zoubarevitchi
Paritchi
45 D.I.
Mormal
Kholopenitchi
Ozemlie
Sekeritchi
36 D.I.
Godouni
Viajni
Petrovitchi
Gorval
Liouban
Korma
Groupnt d'Attaque
Chatsilki
Tr. du Génl Batov
129 D.
Volosovitchi
Groupt du Gl Pliev
Ozaritchi
Koiki
292 D.I.
Tr. du Génl Loutchinski
Retchitsa
LAC TCHERVONNOÏE
Ptitch
216 D.I.
Pripet
KALINOVITCHI

ÉCHELLE
10   0   10   20 km

1er FRONT DE LA BALTIQUE

OPÉRATIONS
PERCÉE du FRONT et DESTRUCTION

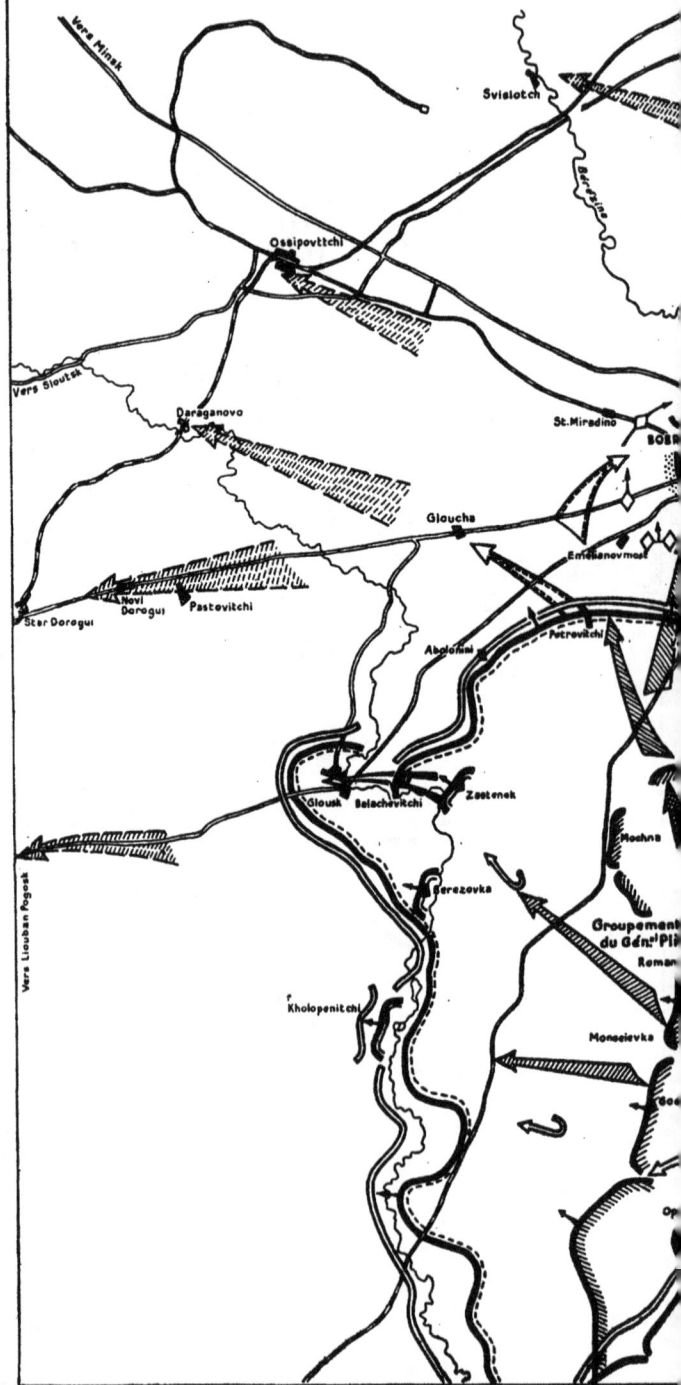

Vers Minsk

Svislotch

Bérésina

Ossipovttchi

Vers Slouisk

Daraganovo

St. Miradino

SOBR

Glaucha

Emelianovmost

Novi
Doragui

Pastovitchi

Star Doragui

Abalaini

Petrovitchi

Gloush

Selschevitchi

Zastenek

Mochna

Groupement
du Génl Pi

Berezovka

Roman

Vers Liouban Pogosk

Kholopenitchi

Manseievka

Op

BOBRUISK
RCES ALLEMANDES DE BOBRUISK

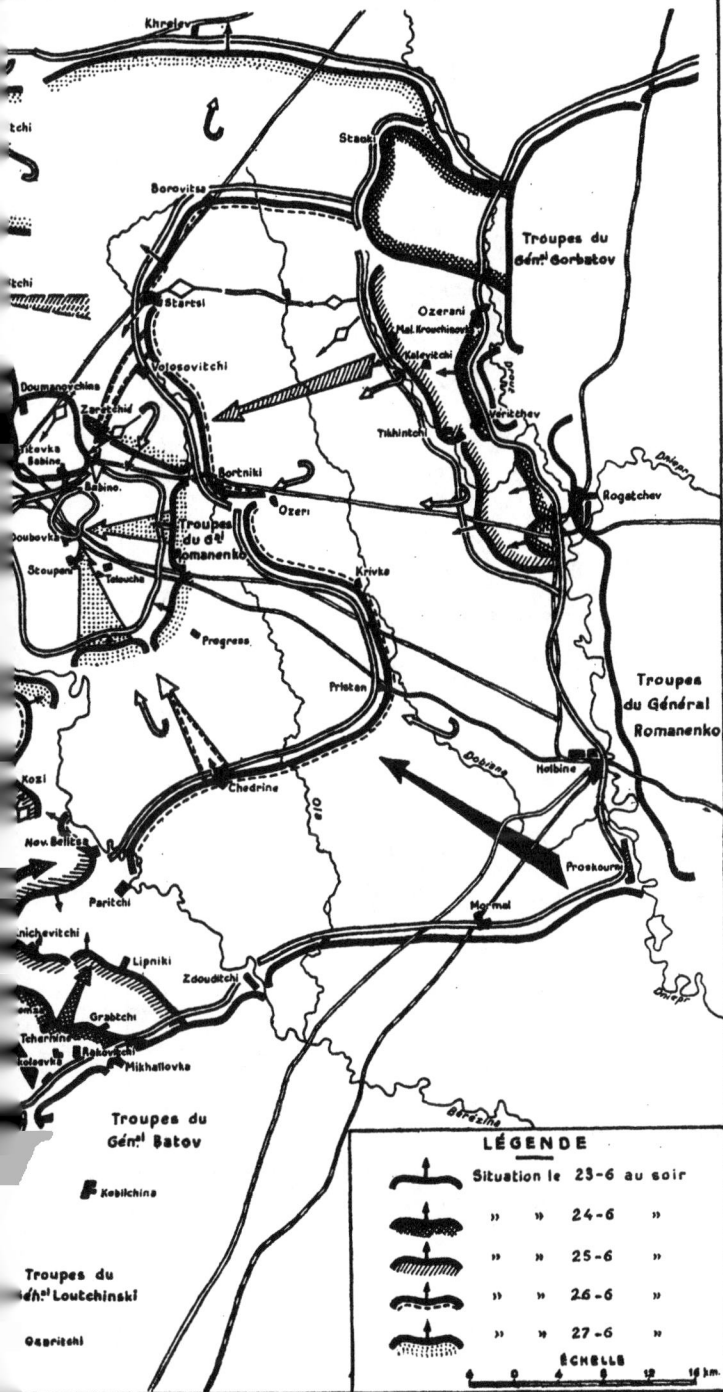

Khrelsv

Staak

Borovitza

Startsi

Troupes du
Gén.¹ Gorbatov

Ozerani

Mal.Krouchinovka

Volosovitchi

Kalevitchi

Doumanovchina

Zaretchié

Tikhintchi

Veritchev

Titevka

Sabine

Bortniki

Sabine

Ozeri

Rogatchev

Doubovka

Troupes
du d.¹
Romanenko

Stoupeni

Telouchi

Krivka

Progress

Prieton

Troupes
du Général
Romanenko

Chedrine

Holbine

Now. Belitza

Proskourn

Paritchi

Mormal

nichevitchi

Lipniki

Zdouditchi

Grabtchi

Tcherhino

Rohovitchi

kolsovka

Mikhaïlovka

Kozi

Troupes du
Gén.¹ Batov

Kobilchina

Troupes du
dh.¹ Loutchinski

Gaaritchi

Dniepr

Bérésina

Olz

Dobroa

LÉGENDE

	Situation le 23-6 au soir	
	» » 24-6 »
	» » 25-6 »
	» » 26-6 »
	» » 27-6 »

ÉCHELLE

0   5   10   15 km.

CROQUIS N°53

OPÉRATION DE MINSK

Dvinsk

Dvina

Drissa

Opsa

Disna

Charkovchizna

Polotsk

Koziani

1er FRONT DE LA BALTIQUE

Gloubokoie

Ouchatchi

Vitebsk

Postavi

Lepel

Lac de Narotch

Begomel

Dolginovo

3e FRONT DE RUSSIE BLANCHE

Smorgon

Vileika

Kholopenitchi

Krasnoie

Kroulki

Molodetchno

Logoisk

2e FRONT DE RUSSIE BLANCHE

Borissov

Rakov

Smolevitchi

Tcherniavka

Pekalin

MINSK

Volma

Pogost

Djerjinsk

Berezino

Svislotch

Tcherven

Stolbtsi

Ouzda

Poukhovitchi

Gorodeia

Chatsk

Svislotch

Ossipovitchi

Nesvitch

Bobruisk

Baranovitchi

Sloutsk

1er FRONT DE RUSSIE BLANCHE

Jlobin

Liouban

Berezina

Situation le 29/6	Tracé du front le 4-7
Situation le 3o/6	Directions d'effort des troupes soviétiques.
Situation le 2/7	Directions de repli des troupes allemandes.

50   0   30   60

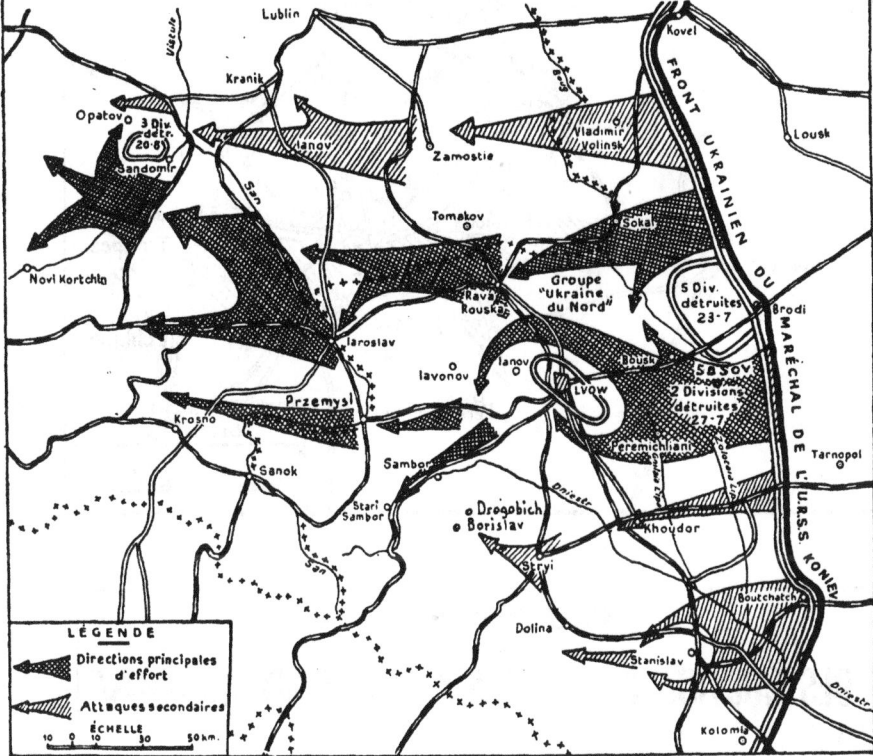

CROQUIS Nº 54

DÉFAITE ALLEMANDE EN UKRAINE OCCIDENTALE
(JUILLET-AOÛT 1944)

Lublin
Kranik
Opatov
3 Div.
détr.
20-8
Sandomir
San
Novi Kortchla
Janov
Zamostie
Tomakov
Ravā
Rouskaē
Groupe
"Ukraine
du Nord"
Vladimir
Volinsk
Kovel
Lousk
Sokal
5 Div.
détruites
23-7
Brodi
Iaroslav
Iavonov
Ianov
Lousk
Lvow
Sasov
2 Divisions
détruites
27-7
Tarnopol
Przemysl
Krosno
Sanok
Sambor
Stari
Sambor
Drogobich
Borislav
Stryi
Peremichliani
Khoudor
Boutchatch
FRONT UKRAINIEN DU MARÉCHAL DE L'URSS KONIEV
Dolina
Stanislav
Kolomia

LÉGENDE
Directions principales
d'effort
Attaques secondaires
ÉCHELLE
10 0 10   30   50 km.

CROQUIS N° 55

DESTRUCTION des FORCES ALLEMANDES de BRODI

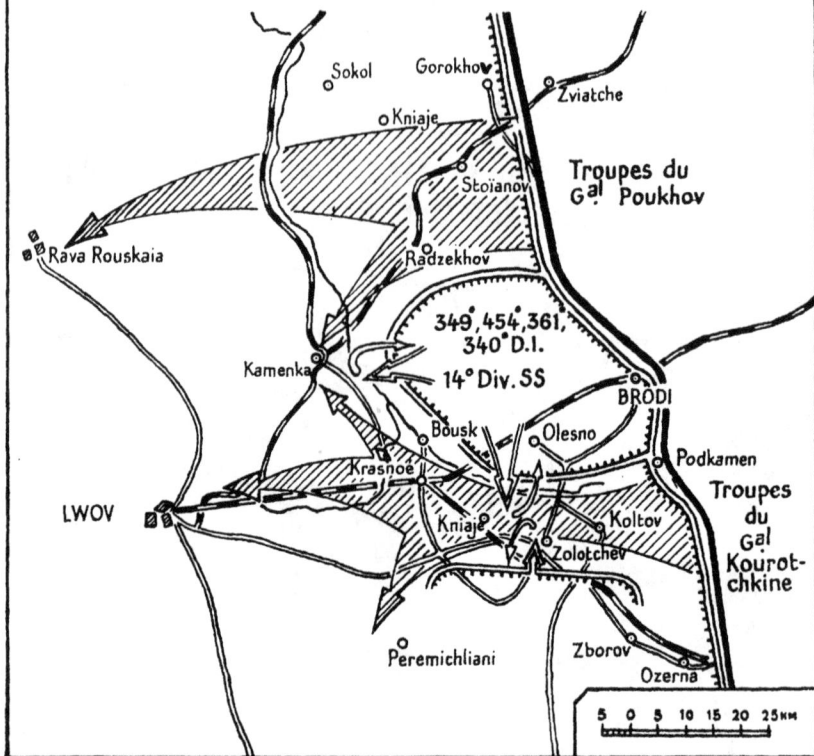

Sokol
Gorokhov
Zviatche
Kniaje
Stoïanov
Troupes du Gal Poukhov
Rava Rouskaia
Radzekhov
349, 454, 361, 340° D.I.
14° Div. SS
Kamenka
BRODI
Bousk
Olesno
Podkamen
Krasnoé
Troupes du Gal Kourotchkine
LWOV
Kniaje
Koltov
Zolotchev
Peremichliani
Zborov
Ozerna

5 0 5 10 15 20 25 км

CROQUIS N° 56

DESTRUCTION DES FORCES ALLEMANDES de LWOV

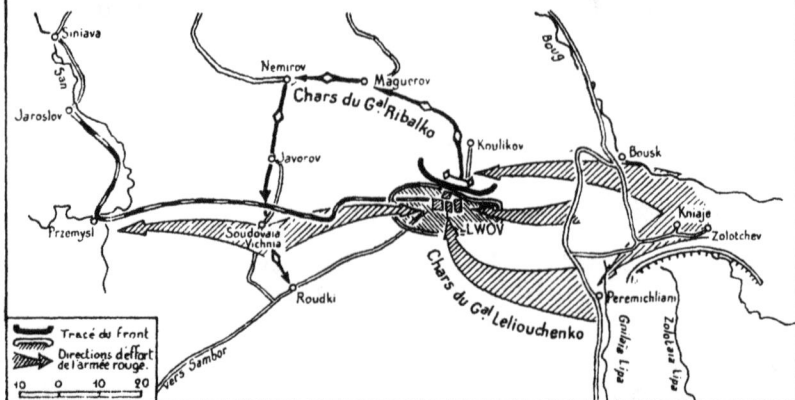

Siniava
Nemirov
Magurov
Boug
Chars du Gal Ribalko
Jaroslov
Knulikov
Bousk
Javorov
Kniaje
Zolotchev
Przemysl
Soudovaia Vichnia
LWOV
Peremichliani
Chars du Gal Leliouchenko
Roudki
vers Sambor

Tracé du front
Directions d'effort de l'armée rouge.
10 0 10 20

CROQUIS N°57
BATAILLE de SANDOMIR

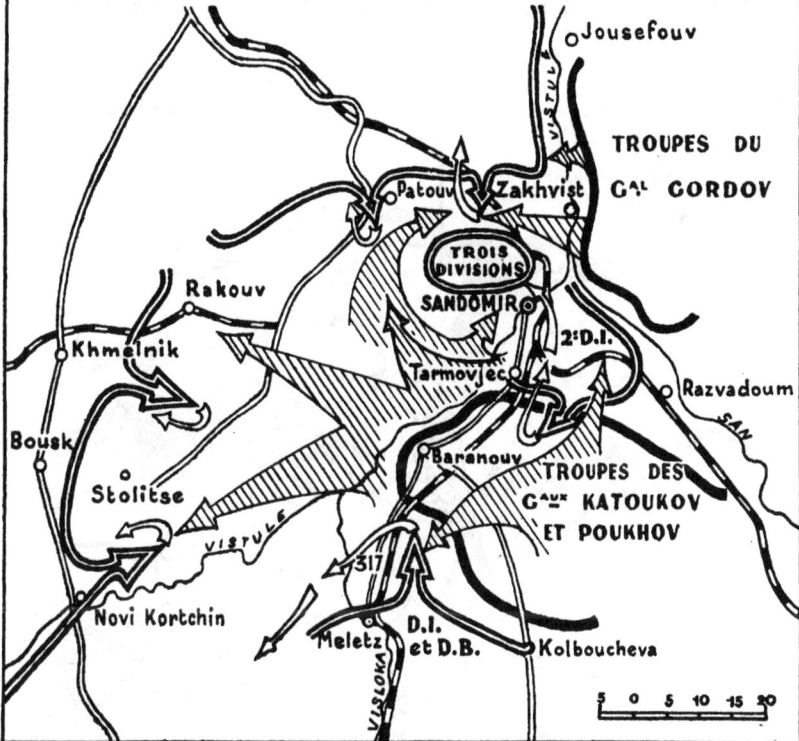

Jousefouv

VISTULE

TROUPES DU
G^{AL} GORDOV

Patouv   Zakhvist

TROIS
DIVISIONS
SANDOMIR

Rakouv

2°D.I.

Khmelnik

Tarmovjec

Razvadoum

SAN

Bousk

Baranouy

TROUPES DES
G^{AUX} KATOUKOV
ET POUKHOV

Stolitse

VISTULE

Novi Kortchin

317

Meletz   D.I.
et D.B.   Kolboucheva

VISLOKA

5 0 5 10 15 20

| Tracé du front | Directions d'effort soviètique | Directions d'effort allemand |

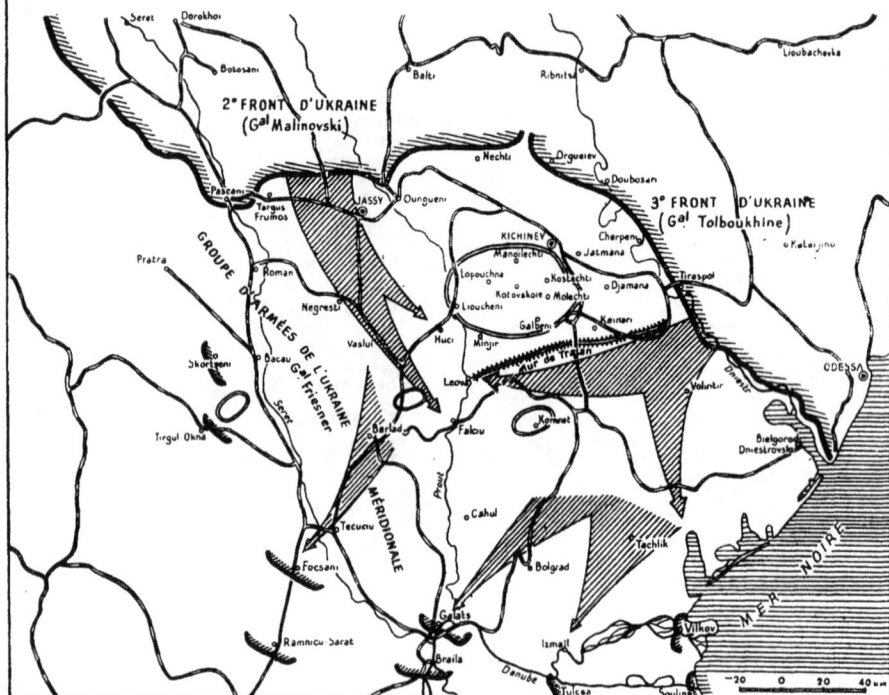

CROQUIS N°58

OPÉRATION DE JASSY-KICHINEV
AOUT 1944

CROQUIS Nº 59

DÉFAITE ALLEMANDE DANS LES PAYS BALTES
SEPTEMBRE - OCTOBRE 1944

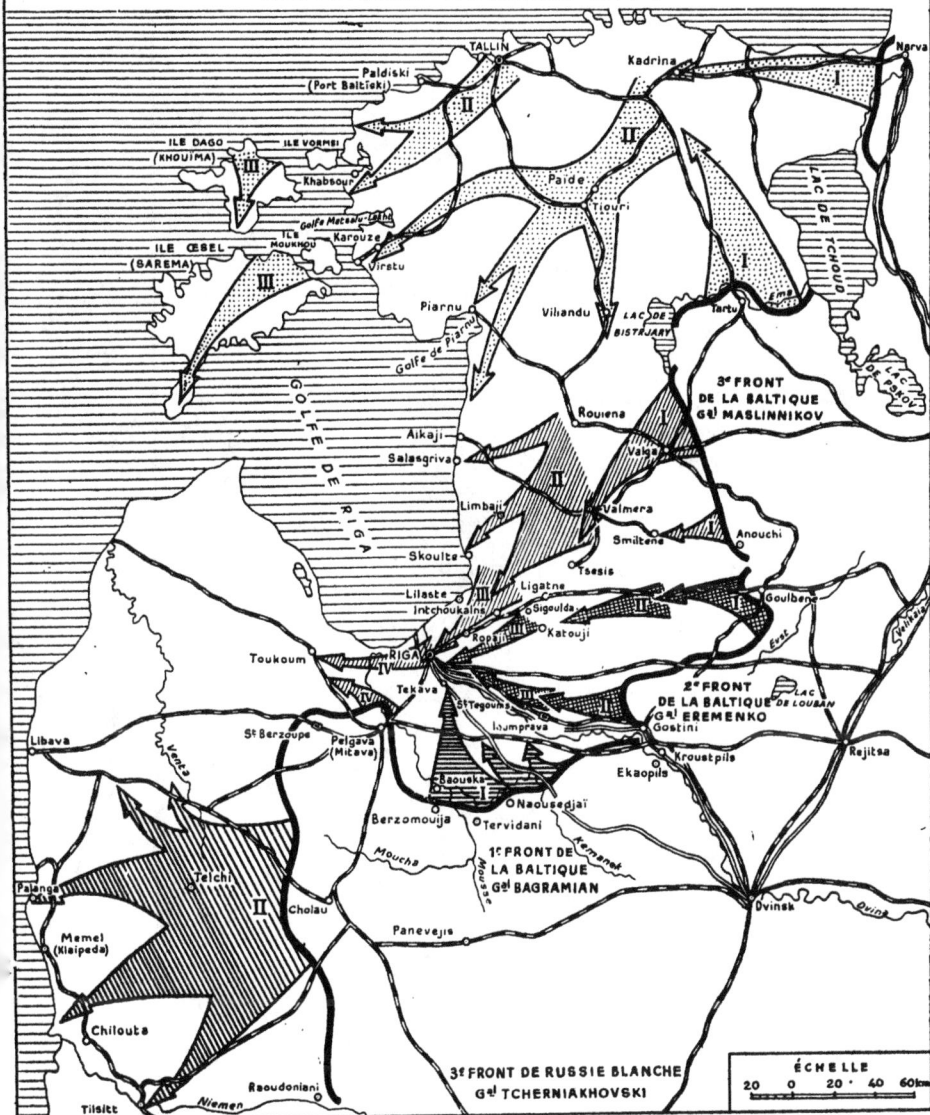

TALLIN
Paldiski
(Port Baltiski)
Kadrina
Narva

ILE DAGO
(KHOUIMA)
ILE VORMSI
Khabsour
Paide
LAC DE TCHOUD
Tiouri

Golfe Metcalu-Lakht
Karouze
ILE MOUKHOU
Virstu

ILE ŒSEL
(SAREMA)
Piarnu
Vihandu
LAC DE
BISTRIJARY
Tartu
LAC DE PSKOV

Golfe de Piarnu

GOLFE DE RIGA

Aïkaji
Salasgriva
Rouena
3e FRONT
DE LA BALTIQUE
Gal MASLINNIKOV

Limbaji
Valmera
Vaka

Skoulte
Smiltene
Anouchi
Tsesis

Lilaste
Ligatne
Intchoukalns
Sigoulda
Goulbene
Evst
Katouji

Toukoum
RIGA
Rop
LAC
DE LOUBAN
2e FRONT
DE LA BALTIQUE
Gal EREMENKO

Libava
Tekava
St Tegoums
Gostini
Rajitsa

St Berzoupe
Pelgava
(Mitava)
Inumprava
Kroustpils

Venta
Baoueka
Ekaopils
Naousedjaï

Palanga
Berzomouija
Tervidani
Kemenet
Dvinsk
Quink

Telchi
Moucha
Mousse
1e FRONT DE
LA BALTIQUE
Gal BAGRAMIAN

Memel
(Klaipeda)
Cholau
Panevejis

Chilouta

Raoudoniani
3e FRONT DE RUSSIE BLANCHE
Gal TCHERNIAKHOVSKI
ÉCHELLE
20   0   20 · 40   60km

Tilsitt
Niemen

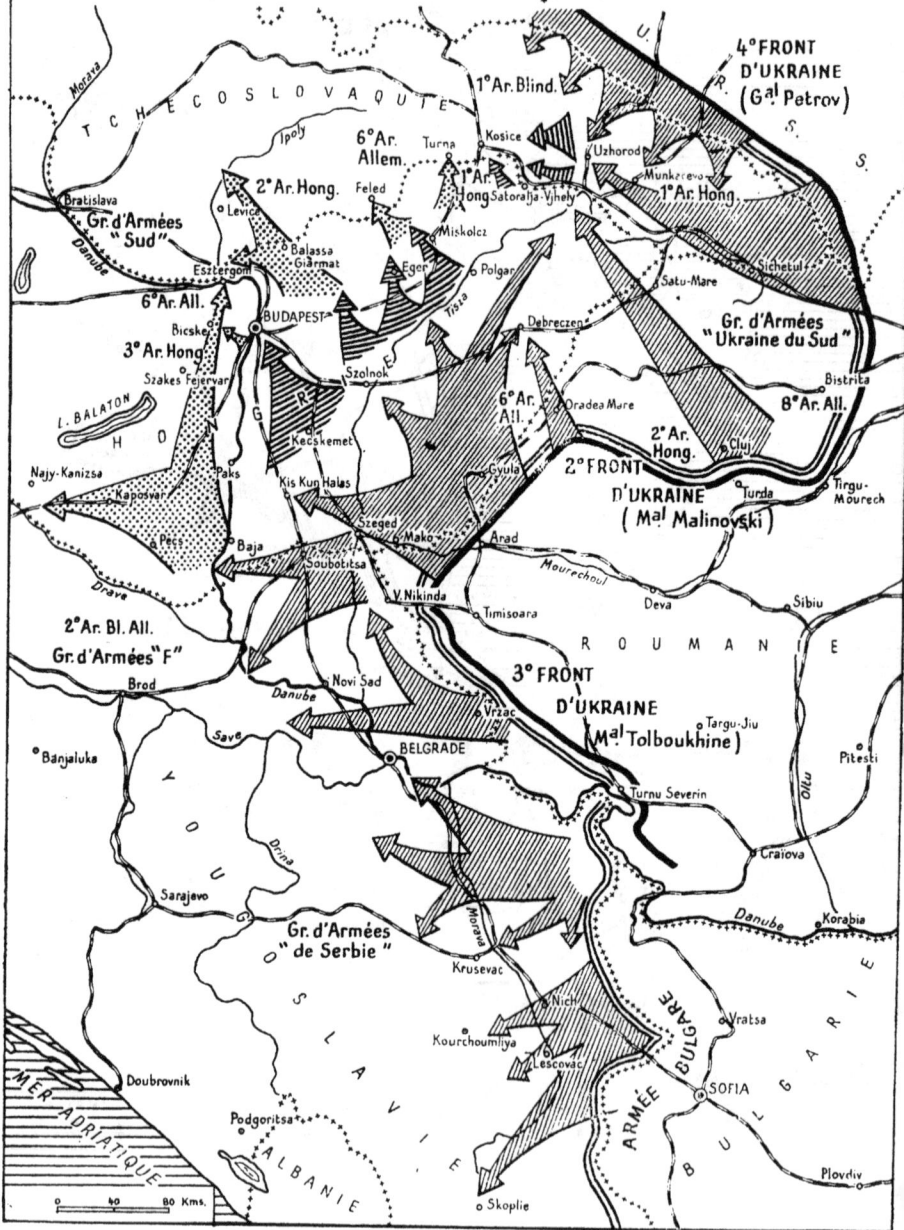

CROQUIS N°60

DÉFAITE DES ARMÉES GERMANO-HONGROISES EN HONGRIE

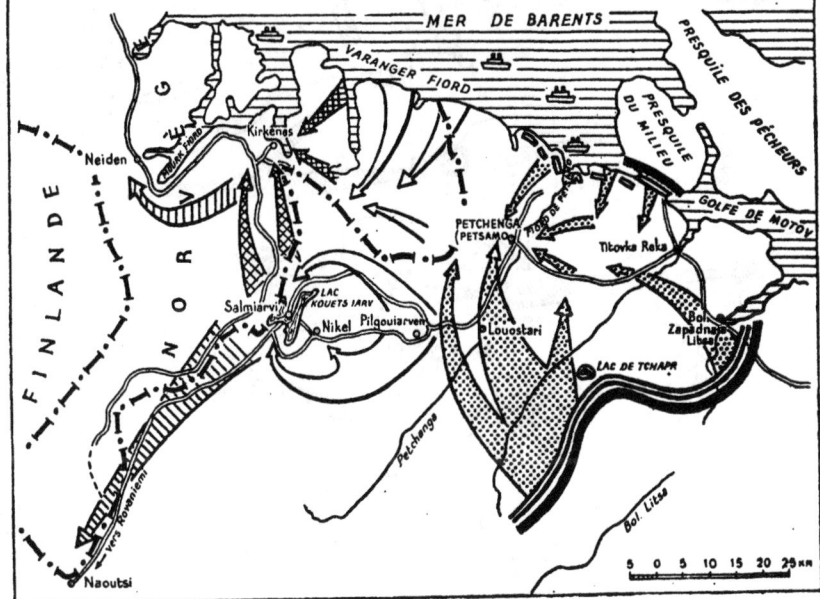

CROQUIS N°61

DÉFAITE DE LA 20° ARMÉE ALLEMANDE DE LAPONIE DANS LA RÉGION DE PETSAMO (PETCHENGA)

CROQUIS N°62
L'EFFONDREMENT : 1945

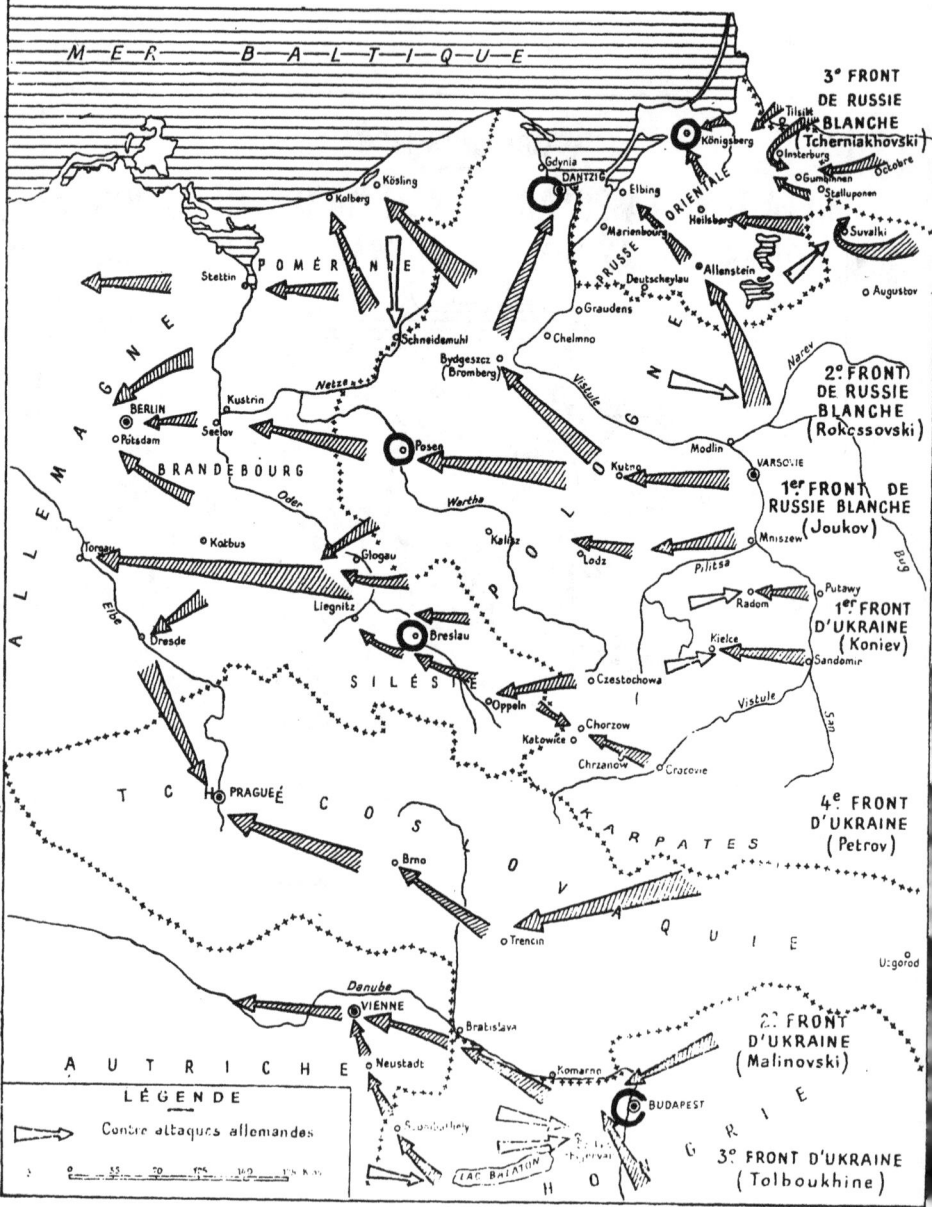

MER BALTIQUE

3ᵉ FRONT
DE RUSSIE
BLANCHE
(Tcherniakhovski)

Tilsitt
Interburg
Cobre
Königsberg
Gumbinnen
Stalluponen

Gdynia
DANTZIG
Elbing
Suvalki

Kösling
Marienbourg
Heilsberg

Kolberg
PRUSSE ORIENTALE
Allenstein
Augustov

Stettin
POMÉRANIE
Deutscheylau
Graudens

Schneidemuhl
Chelmno
Narev

Netze
Bydgoszcz (Bromberg)
2ᵉ FRONT
DE RUSSIE
BLANCHE
(Rokossovski)

Kustrin
Vistule
COULOIR
Modlin
VARSOVIE

BERLIN
Seelov
1ᵉʳ FRONT DE
RUSSIE BLANCHE
(Joukov)

Potsdam
BRANDEBOURG
Oder
Wartha
POLOGNE
Mniszew
Bug

Torgau
Katbus
Kalisz
Pilitsa

Elbe
Glogau
Lodz
Putawy
1ᵉʳ FRONT
D'UKRAINE
(Koniev)

Liegnitz
Radom
Dresde
Breslau
Kielce
Sandomir

SILÉSIE
Oppeln
Czestochowa
Vistule

Chorzow
San
Katowice
Chrzanow
Cracovie

PRAGUE
TCHÉCOSLOVAQUIE
4ᵉ FRONT
D'UKRAINE
(Petrov)

KARPATES
Brno

Trencin
U:gorod

Danube
VIENNE
2ᵉ FRONT
D'UKRAINE
(Malinovski)

AUTRICHE
Neustadt
Bratislava
Komarno

LÉGENDE
Contre attaques allemandes
HONGRIE

BUDAPEST
LAC BALATON
3ᵉ FRONT D'UKRAINE
(Tolboukhine)

CROQUIS N°63

LA LIBÉRATION DE PRAGUE
(6-9 MAI 1945)

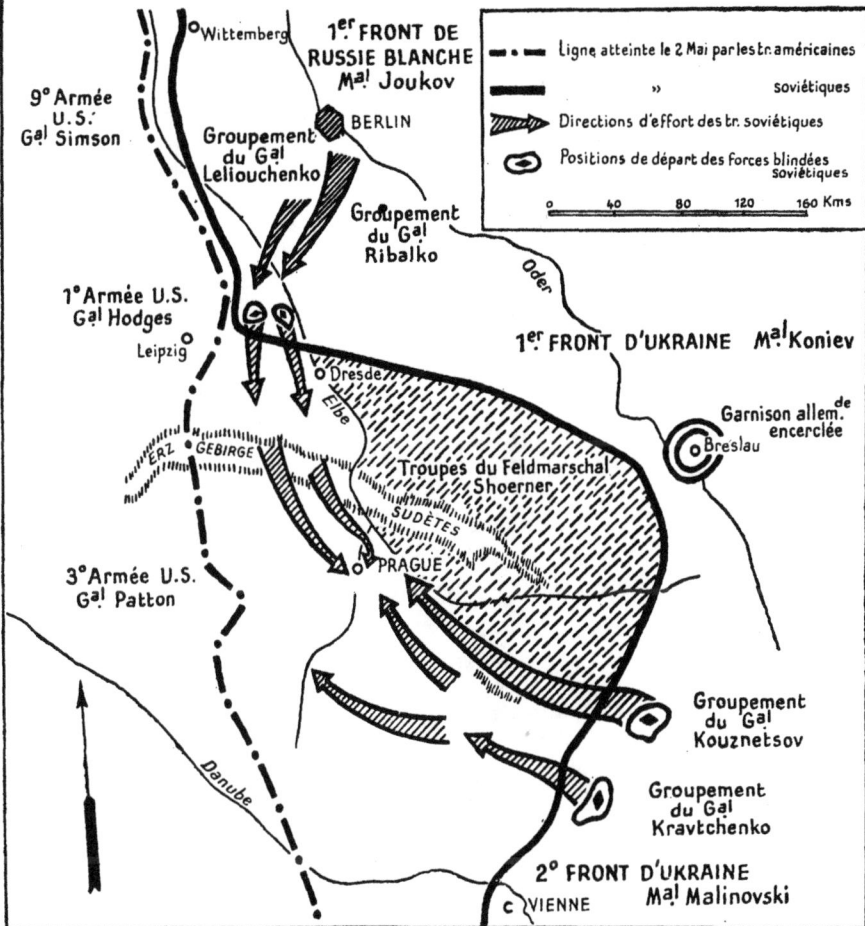

Wittemberg

9° Armée
U.S.
Gal Simson

1er FRONT DE
RUSSIE BLANCHE
Mal Joukov

BERLIN

Groupement
du Gal
Leliouchenko

Groupement
du Gal
Ribalko

Ligne atteinte le 2 Mai par les tr. américaines

»   soviétiques

Directions d'effort des tr. soviétiques

Positions de départ des forces blindées
soviètiques

0   40   80   120   160 Kms

Oder

1° Armée U.S.
Gal Hodges

Leipzig

1er FRONT D'UKRAINE   Mal Koniev

Dresde

Elbe

ERZ GEBIRGE

Garnison allem. de
encerclée

Breslau

Troupes du Feldmarschal
Shoerner

SUDÈTES

3° Armée U.S.
Gal Patton

PRAGUE

Groupement
du Gal
Kouznetsov

Danube

Groupement
du Gal
Kravtchenko

2° FRONT D'UKRAINE
Mal Malinovski

VIENNE

www.ingramcontent.com/pod-product-compliance
Lightning Source LLC
Chambersburg PA
CBHW060422100426
42812CB00030B/3269/J